Implementing European Environmental Policy

NEW HORIZONS IN ENVIRONMENTAL ECONOMICS

Series Editors: Wallace E. Oates, *Professor of Economics, University of Maryland, USA* and Henk Folmer, *Professor of General Economics, Wageningen University and Professor of Environmental Economics, Tilburg University, The Netherlands*

This important series is designed to make a significant contribution to the development of the principles and practices of environmental economics. It includes both theoretical and empirical work. International in scope, it addresses issues of current and future concern in both East and West and in developed and developing countries.

The main purpose of the series is to create a forum for the publication of high quality work and to show how economic analysis can make a contribution to understanding and resolving the environmental problems confronting the world in the twenty-first century.

Recent titles in the series include:

Implementing European Environmental Policy

The Impacts of Directives in the Member States

Edited by

Matthieu Glachant

Research Fellow at CERNA, Ecole des Mines de Paris, France and Jean Monnet Fellow, Robert Schuman Centre, European University Institute, Italy

NEW HORIZONS IN ENVIRONMENTAL ECONOMICS

Edward Elgar
Cheltenham, UK • Northampton, MA, USA .

Published by
Edward Elgar Publishing Limited
Glensanda House
Montpellier Parade
Cheltenham
Glos GL50 1UA
UK

Edward Elgar Publishing, Inc.
136 West Street
Suite 202
Northampton
Massachusetts 01060
USA

A catalogue record for this book
is available from the British Library

Library of Congress Cataloguing in Publication Data
Implementing European environmental policy : the impacts of directives in the member states / edited by Matthieu Glachant.
    p. cm. — (New horizons in environmental economics)
  Includes bibliographical references and index.
  1. Environmental policy—European Union countries. 2. Environmental protection—European Union countries. I. Glachant, Matthieu, 1966–
  II. Series.

  GE190.E85 I46 2001
  363.7'056'094—dc21   2001033073

ISBN 1 84064 659 4

Printed and bound in Great Britain by MPG Books Ltd, Bodmin, Cornwall

Contents

List of figures

List of tables

List of boxes

List of contributors

Matthieu Glachant is Research Fellow at CERNA, Ecole des Mines de Paris and Jean Monnet Fellow, Robert Schuman Centre, European University Institute. Address for correspondence: 60, boulevard Saint Michel, 75272 Paris cedex 06, France. Tel: +33 (0)1 40 51 91 91, Fax: +33 (0)1 44 07 10 46, glachant@cerna.ensmp.fr.

Simone Schucht is a Junior Researcher and PhD Candidate at CERNA, Centre of Industrial Economics, Ecole des Mines de Paris, 60, boulevard Saint Michel, 75272 Paris cedex 06, France. Tel: +33 (0)1 40 51 92 98, Fax: +33 (0)1 44 07 10 46, schucht@cerna.ensmp.fr.

Dr Malcolm Eames is Research Fellow, Environment and Energy Programme, SPRU – Science and Technology Policy Research, University of Sussex, Brighton, BN1 9RF, United Kingdom. Tel: +44 (0)1273 678467, Fax: +44 (0)1273 685865, m.eames@sussex.ac.uk.

Kris R.D. Lulofs is senior research associate, Center for Clean Technology and Environmental Policy, University of Twente, PO box 217, 7500 AE Enschede, The Netherlands. Tel: +31 534 894539, Fax: +31 534 894850, k.r.d.lulofs@cstm.utwente.nl.

Frank Wätzold is senior researcher at the UFZ-Centre for Environmental Research, Leipzig-Halle, Department of Economics, Sociology and Law, PO box 500136, 04301 Leipzig, Germany. Tel: +49 341 2352670, Fax: +49 341 2352511, waetzold@alok.ufz.de.

Alexandra Bültmann is junior research associate at UFZ-Centre for Environmental Research Leipzig-Halle, Department of Economics, Sociology and Law, PO box 500136, 04301 Leipzig, Germany. Tel: +49 341 235-2670, Fax: +49 341 235-2511, buelt@alok.ufz.de.

Acknowledgements

This book is an outcome of The Implementation of EU Environmental Policies: Efficiency Issues (IMPOL) project. The IMPOL project involved four research institutes (CERNA, Ecole des Mines de Paris; SPRU – Science and Technology Policy Research, University of Sussex; CSTM, University of Twente; UFZ Leipzig-Halle). It was financially supported by the European Commission's DG RTD under its Environment and Climate RTD Programme, 'Human Dimensions of Environmental Change' and by national institutions (including ADEME, the French environmental agency). The editor also thanks Frans Berkhout, Olivier Godard and François Lévêque for their scientific advice, Simone Schucht for her continuous commitment in the project, Katri Kosonen for helping in the relations with the Commission, and Véronique Dubarry for preparing the manuscript.

1. Introduction: a policy perspective on the implementation of the Community environmental legislation

Matthieu Glachant

The environment is one of the most developed policy fields of the European Union (EU). Since the 1960s and despite fragile initial legal foundations – the protection of the environment is not even mentioned in the Treaty of Rome – more than 200 Directives and Regulations have been adopted. The legislation now deals with the '*quasi complete*' range of environmental concerns: waste management, material recycling, atmospheric pollution, noise, and water quality problems, etc. While the European Union has proved to be very efficient and motivated in policy formulation, the implementation of this impressive body of legislation was a neglected issue for a long time. This changed around the end of the 1980s and the idea of an 'implementation deficit' in EU environmental policy is now a recurrent theme in the policy debate.

There are very strong reasons for paying attention to implementation. Implementation is the *raison d'être* of any policy. It is the moment where intentions, which any policy text is made of, become reality, or don't. In fact, implementation is policy viewed from the perspective of its practical consequences for implementation bodies and policy targets. This perspective is crucial, since the success of a policy can only be judged on the impacts it has on the ground. Jordan (1999) recently cited a formula by Joseph Stalin, going straight to the heart of the matter: 'to govern is not to write resolutions and distribute directives; to govern is to control the implementation of the directives'.

How wide is the implementation gap in EU environmental policy? Evidence for answering the question is simply lacking. Since 1984, comprehensive data are seemingly available in the annual reports published by the Commission on the application of EU law in the Member States. These reports however mainly deal with *formal compliance*, that is the legal transposition of EU law into national legislation. They show that only 91% of the Directives were fully transposed in 1995 and that the number of

1

infringement proceedings against Member States has grown almost continuously for twenty years. But commentators have intensively criticised both the reliability and the usefulness of this data for judging implementation effectiveness. For instance, the evolution in the number of infringement proceedings tells us nothing about genuine implementation failures on the field. The increase may just as likely be the result of a change in the enforcement behaviour of the Commission. As a matter of fact, many elements allude to the increasing attention paid by the Commission to the application of Directives. The lack of evidence is even more acute regarding *practical compliance*, i.e. whether the objectives of the Directives are actually met in practice. Studies measuring and explaining the degree of attainment of policy goals are too scarce to form even a general impression.

Even though the existence of an implementation gap might prove difficult to establish formally, there are several theoretical arguments supporting the thesis that the implementation of EU policy might prove more difficult than the implementation of conventional national policies. A first line of argument refers to the heterogeneity of the space in which implementation takes place. Directives are constructed in Brussels and subsequently put into practice in locations as diverse as Malmö and Porto or London and Athens. Of peculiar importance is the heterogeneity in the national administrative structures in charge of implementing the Directives. EU policy should accommodate very different administrative traditions. Other analysts point out that poor implementation is related to institutional features of the EU political system possibly causing an in-built 'pathology of non-compliance' (Mendrinou, 1996). In particular, the institutional architecture establishes a very clear-cut separation between policy making and implementation activities. This may provide incentives to the supra-national institutions that are heavily involved in policy formulation (most noticeably the Commission and the European Parliament) to push for very ambitious regulations that impose costs and efforts on others, namely the Member States in charge of implementing them. In relation with this argument, the international character of EU policy is also emphasised. Unlike conventional implementation of national policies, implementation is a two-stage process. The European regulation is firstly transposed in the Member States' legislation[1] and then put into practice by national administrations through activities of permitting, enforcement, monitoring and so forth. This threatens effective implementation by way of a double risk. In addition to the classical risk of non-compliance by the polluters, the States may fail to transpose the Directives or to apply correctly its provisions. And State compliance is not always viewed as less problematic than polluters' compliance, given the balance of power between the EU institutions involved (the Commission and the European Court of Justice) and powerful countries established for a much longer time. This is somehow reflected in the weakness of the legal enforcement instruments available against Member States. An amazing illustration is that a ruling by the European Court of Justice against a non-complying State did not entail any sanctions or formal punishments for a long time. It only had a declaratory effect! This has changed recently under a provision of the Maastricht Treaty which made it legally possible to fine States. Until now, this provision has only been used once, against Greece in July 2000.

These themes – the genuine impacts of EU environmental policy in the Member States, the causes for a possible implementation deficit – are explored in this volume. The core of the book is concerned with a careful ex post evaluation of the implementation of three pieces of EU environmental legislation in France, Germany, the Netherlands and the United Kingdom. A first focus of the evaluation is environmental effectiveness – do implementation outcomes meet the environmental goals set out in the Directives? Also investigated is the cost effectiveness of implementation, that is the impacts of implementation on the costs borne by the policy targets so as to comply with the policy's goals. There are strong justifications for this interest in cost issues. One important lesson of economic analysis is that cost effectiveness arises by properly taking into account local circumstances. Within the overall policy process, adjustments to local conditions typically take place at the implementation stage.

The legislation studied is the Directive 89/429 regulating atmospheric emissions from domestic waste incinerators, the Directive 88/609 dealing with SO_2 and NO_x emissions from large combustion plants (LCP) and the Council Regulation 1836/93 concerning the voluntary participation of industrial companies in an EU Eco-Management and Audit scheme (EMAS). They are policies implemented in the 1990s and as such are expected to have already produced their impacts, a precondition for measuring them. They cover a wide spectrum of policy approaches from traditional pollution source regulation in the case of the Directive 89/429, to an innovative voluntary instrument in the case of EMAS.

The number of implementation processes considered (3 policies x 4 countries) provides a significant empirical basis to explore the problem of effective implementation. However, the sample of countries considered is not representative of the diversity of the European Union. In particular, there is no evaluation made here of Mediterranean countries like Italy, Spain, Greece or Portugal, where implementation is said to be more problematic. Rather, the sample provides good coverage of the central states of the European Union, very influential in EU environmental policy, and in an average position in terms of the less and the more environmentally advanced Member States. The results below could probably best be construed as delivering some kind of 'average' picture of the Member States' response to EU environmental policy.

1.   EVIDENCE OF EX POST EVALUATION

What do the evaluation's results suggest about the implementation deficit and its causes? They clearly challenge the 'implementation deficit' view as highlighted by the points listed below.

Over-compliance is possible. As shown by Table 1.1, the policy goals were exceeded in seven out of the eight cases for which the notion is meaningful.[2] This clearly suggests that the Directives were only one of many drivers of change. However, in many cases, the explanatory factors are simply pre-existing domestic policies that cover the same environmental problem but which are more ambitious than the Directive. This simply reflects the 'leader–laggard' dynamic of certain European Member States and illustrates the role that the EU plays in the diffusion of policy. Other factors are the impacts of non-environmental policies such as energy and competition policy (for instance, the privatisation of the British electricity supply industry in the case of the Large Combustion Plant Directive), the anticipation of future regulatory requirements, or strong public pressure because an environmental problem is perceived as severe (e.g., the 'Waldsterben' in Germany in the 1980s and SO_2 emissions from combustion plants).

Table 1.1 Environmental outcomes as percentage of the policy goal

	France	Germany	Netherlands	United Kingdom
Large Combustion Plant Directive Aggregate emissions as percentage of the SO_2 national ceiling (1993 target)	37%	67%	50%	75%
Municipal Waste Incineration Directive Average emissions as percentage of EU limits (1995 target)	> 150 % (estimated)	3.2%	15.4%	< 100% (estimated)

The environmental response to Community legislation is strongly affected by policy interactions. The main causes of the over-compliance outlined above are the impacts of other policy processes (domestic policies, other non-environmental policies, etc.). But in fact policy interactions were not just restricted to cases of over-compliance. In other cases such interactions were observed to have negative impacts on environmental goal attainment. The influence of policy interactions on implementation outcomes, being both positive and negative, is thus pervasive. Table 1.2 summarises these interactions in the cases studied. This should lead to a change in the way the implementation of EU policy is viewed. The implementation of environmental Directives is not a top-down process, but a piece in a patchwork of policy processes arising at different governance levels (international, European, national, local) and in different policy arenas (environmental and non-environmental).

Table 1.2 Policy interactions in implementation

	Interactions with:
Large Combustion Plant Directive no 88/809/EEC	- Privatisation and liberalisation of energy markets (UK, NL)
	- Nuclear energy policy (F)
	- Regulatory reform (UK)
	- UNECE agreements (all countries)
	- Pre-existing national legislation (G, NL)
Municipal Waste Incineration Directive no 89/429/EEC (1995 deadline)	- Waste recycling policy (all countries)
	- Landfill policy (almost all countries)
	- Energy policy (UK)
	- Pre-existing national legislation (G, NL)
EMAS Council regulation no 1863/93/EEC	- ISO 14001 (all countries)
	- Regulatory reform (NL)

Surprises at the implementation stage are the rule rather than the exception. This is related to the preceding point: many policy interactions remain difficult for the environmental regulator to anticipate, especially those arising from non-environmental policy areas. The implementation of the Large Combustion Plant Directive in the United Kingdom provides a good illustration. The United Kingdom was very reluctant with this Directive when it was formulated because it expected to bear very high costs in order to comply with the national targets set by the Directive. But when implementation kicked in, the context had changed drastically making compliance very easy. At the end of the 1980s the British government decided to privatise the British energy sector to liberalise energy markets launched. One consequence was the massive closure of coal-fired plants, in deficit for years but kept open for social reasons. It provoked a very drastic and fast substitution of coal – by gas-fired electricity. Since gas turbines emit far less sulphur dioxide, a side effect was the compliance without effort with the Large Combustion Plant Directive's targets.

Poor enforcement does not appear to be the crucial issue. There is a tendency to consider that policy implementation is above all a problem of enforcement. According to this view, implementation basically consists of monitoring the individual behaviour of the policy targets and applying sanctions where necessary. This assumption is certainly made by economists for whom enforcement and implementation are basically synonymous. It is also present in many policy makers' minds. The recent Council resolution on 'the drafting, implementation and enforcement of Community environmental law' (CEC, 1997) chiefly put the emphasis on enforcement, reporting provisions, sanctions and inspections. In fact in the case studies presented here, compliance problems resulting from poor enforcement were observed in just one case: the implementation of the Municipal Waste Incineration Directive in France.

Administrative compliance differs from environmental compliance. Albeit anecdotal, it is worthwhile to remark that legal compliance with the Directives' requirements may diverge from compliance with the Directives' environmental goal. For example, with respect to the Large Combustion Plant Directive, legal difficulties were encountered in the Netherlands, France and the United Kingdom. These problems were of absolutely no consequence to the environmental compliance of these countries. In a further case, the Netherlands failed to transpose the Waste Incineration Directive in time, thereby technically breaching EU requirements. However, a more stringent domestic policy was in fact already in place in the Netherlands, in the form of a Ministerial Guideline, which was directly binding on the permitting authorities but not on incinerator operators. The transformation of the Guideline into a material Law took longer than expected but was of no environmental consequence.

National contexts strongly influence cost effectiveness. The evaluation of cost effectiveness stressed the importance of contextual variables. Cost effectiveness appears largely to depend upon an appropriate fit between particular implementation procedures or instruments and these variables. Among contextual variables, it is worthwhile underlining national differences in terms of initial levels of pollution. Given differences in the pre-existing policies, initial levels of emissions and thus compliance costs were very different in the cases studied. Another crucial aspect was the degree of heterogeneity of the national parks of polluting sources. The comparison of the domestic waste incinerators in France and Germany is a good illustration. The French park of about 300 incinerators was extremely heterogeneous with a few 'giant' incinerators and hundreds of very small incinerators burning less than one ton of waste per hour whereas there was a much more homogeneous park of about 50 big incinerators in Germany. Flexibility and cost effective implementation procedures were thus more of an imperative in France than in Germany where a 'one size for all' policy approach based on undifferentiated uniform emission standards was less cost damaging. As a matter of fact cost effectiveness has been more intensively sought in France at the implementation stage. This is a general result: the countries' relative responses appear rational in the sense that the search for more cost effective implementation routes was more intense in countries where both the expected overall compliance cost and the heterogeneity among polluting sources were comparatively high.

All in all, the evaluation does not support the 'implementation deficit' view. While policy outcomes are rarely found to be in line with expectations, both non- and over-compliance appear possible. The general result is thus not about a general pattern of either over-compliance or non-compliance, as environmental responses are dramatically affected by parallel policy processes. These processes have different origins: other EU Directives, national policies or even international policy schemes (for instance, the impact of the ISO14001 standard on the implementation of EMAS). In this way, the ubiquity of policy interactions is the inevitable by-product of a complex EU policy system highly differentiated both vertically (territorial differentiation) and horizontally (functional differentiation). Implementation is not a top-down process initiated by a policy decision at the EU level, which progressively reaches the policy targets in a hierarchical mode. Instead implementation of a particular European text should rather be viewed as part of a complex patchwork of dynamic interactions across a multi-level and multi-centred policy system.

2. THE POLICY LESSON: PROMOTING ADAPTIVE POLICY DESIGN AND IMPLEMENTATION

The shift of perspective pointed out above has immediate consequences for the way one might look at solutions to the implementation problem. The 'implementation deficit' view is a diagnosis about the overall compliance with EU Directives but it also suggests a certain type of solution to the problem. It pleads for 'managerial' solutions consisting of an increase in the legal, human, or financial resources dedicated to implementation. The underlying rationale is to enable implementation bodies to get closer to the policy's goals. Alternatively, stressing the importance of policy interactions and of ex post surprises implies that the central challenge of implementation is cognitive – the poor predictability of policy impacts. Given that policy interactions are difficult to predict at the policy formulation stage, adjustments necessarily occur at the implementation stage. In this context, implementing EU environmental policy requires policy systems that have the ability to adjust at low costs. We call this property *adaptability*. This means, both in policy design and implementation, promoting the following.

Flexible policy solutions in the face of unanticipated exogenous changes, in particular those entailed by non-environmental policy measures, by avoiding over-specifying the means by which regulated agents shall attain policy goals. This militates for the use of economic instruments and 'bubble' approaches (e.g. voluntary agreements), where polluters are given maximal freedom regarding abatement choices.

Integration with parallel environmental measures. Here the message is to link together different environmental policy components in order to exploit synergies or avoid inconsistencies. This stems from the fact that ex post surprises are the by-product of policy fragmentation. At the EU level, this militates for broadening the scope of individual pieces of legislation.

Improved horizontal co-ordination between different policy branches. The basic point is that unanticipated policy interactions are a negative side effect of differentiated political structures.

Decentralisation and subsidiarity. The rationale is two-fold. Firstly decentralised political systems are more likely to adjust easily when unanticipated changes occur, especially because they do not occur in all Member States at the same time and in the same way. Secondly, given the heterogeneity in cost-relevant variables amongst countries, the national level is usually better informed, and therefore better able to select the appropriate policy instrument to allocate abatement efforts between polluting sources. This means that Directives should focus on specifying environmental objectives rather than the means through which these should be achieved.

Policy learning and ex post evaluation. The existence of ex post surprises leads us to stress the importance of: 1) incorporating reporting requirements in Directives; 2) the necessity of developing ex post evaluation within the Commission and at the Member State level. The Commission has recently been very active in promoting ex ante cost benefit analysis of proposed Directives. Albeit undoubtedly very useful, the results of these studies need to be linked to ex post analyses in order to gain experience in this exercise and to verify whether the outcomes predicted by ex ante analysis are actually obtained.

3.   STRUCTURE OF THE BOOK

The volume is structured into seven chapters. In Chapter 2, Matthieu Glachant introduces the issue of implementation in the European environmental policy context. He examines how the implementation of EU policy differs from the implementation of a conventional national policy. Based on a discussion of some basic legal principles of EU law it is shown how implementation is at the core of the allocation of roles between the EU level and the national level. Member States are in charge of implementing policies devised in Brussels. Given their central responsibility in implementation, the enforcement tools available against Member States are of prime importance. Their characteristics and their possible deterrent effect are then discussed. The chapter also reviews the available evidence about the existence of an implementation deficit in environmental policy, and its possible causes.

In Chapter 3 Simone Schucht presents a review of the academic literature on policy implementation focusing on the two disciplines which have most significantly explored the issue: economics and political sciences. It is striking how the perspective can be different however. Economic analysis has dealt in depth with one peculiar dimension of the whole problem: the enforcement aspect. A central economic insight is that the implementation gap is not a bad thing per se. Enforcement being costly, the search for an overall social efficiency necessarily entails a trade-off between administrative enforcement costs and environmental benefits attached to improved compliance. It follows that the level of administrative cost entailed by maximal compliance (defined as 100% compliance) has a strong likelihood of being socially inefficient. Policy implementation is also a traditional subject of research for political science. Its focus is more on explaining the processes rather than on evaluating implementation outcomes. Political scientists are very much aware of the necessity of 'framing' implementation. They rightly claim that appropriate analysis of implementation requires a wide view involving the whole policy process of which implementation is a step identified by somewhat arbitrary limits.

The following three chapters constitute the core of the book. Each one is dedicated to a comparative evaluation of one Directive or Regulation in France, Germany, The Netherlands and the United Kingdom. Chapter 4 by Malcolm Eames deals with the implementation of the Large Combustion Plant Directive 88/609 in the electricity supply industry. This Directive adopted in 1988 was aimed at important reductions of sulphur dioxide and NO_x by the Large Combustion Plants (electricity generating plants, refineries, etc.). The evaluation focuses on the targets for sulphur dioxide in existing plants. The main conclusion is that the policy outcome has been dramatically affected by factors not related to the Directive itself. In particular, other parallel policy processes leading to major changes in the energy market have had a crucial impact (for example, the privatisation in the UK outlined above). As a result, over-compliance has been pervasive. An interesting feature of the Directive was that it only fixed aggregate national abatement targets for existing plants, leaving maximal discretion to the Member States as to the means to reach them. These flexible requirements proved very useful in accommodating the unanticipated drivers that affected the environmental outcomes.

In way of contrast with the flexible Large Combustion Plant Directive, Kris Lulofs studies in Chapter 5 the implementation of a very classical Command and Control policy, consisting of a set of detailed air emission standards for domestic waste incinerators – the Directive 89/429. The implementation outcomes appear very contrasted given the gap between highly differentiated national contexts and the uniform character of the policy to be implemented. The case interestingly shows how certain countries bearing the highest compliance costs such as France found ways to erode the stringency of the requirements at the implementation stage through imperfect enforcement and compliance.

Chapter 6 deals with the certification of environmental management systems promoted by the Council Regulation 1836/93 concerning the participation of industrial companies in an EU Eco-Management and Audit scheme (EMAS). EMAS is a totally new policy approach based on the voluntary participation of industry. It has been viewed as emblematic of a new way of making environmental policies in the EU. In comparison with the two previous cases, the focus of the evaluation by Alexandra Bültmann and Frank Wätzold is different. The analysis mainly deals with the level of industry participation and relates it to the way the scheme has been implemented in the different countries. The most striking story relates to the competition between the EMAS standard and the alternative ISO14001 standard that has deeply marked the implementation process and its outcome. Further, the chapter includes a qualitative discussion of whether the costs entailed by the scheme exceed its benefits. Bültmann and Wätzold's conclusions are favourable for EMAS. While modest benefits tend to be obtained in the long run, the cost of running the system is sufficiently low for EMAS to be judged a successful policy approach.

A more theoretical chapter by Matthieu Glachant concludes the book. Taking as a starting point the pervasive and often tremendous impacts of non-anticipated parallel policy measures outlined above, it gives a precise content to the notion of adaptive policy design and implementation summarised above.

NOTES

1. Rigorously, this is not legally true for one class of legal instruments – the Regulations – that are said to be 'directly applicable' in the Member States. But in practice, environmental Regulations generally need additional measures at the national level to be fully effective. This is developed in detail in Chapter 2.

2. EMAS's outcome is not included in this table since the notion of the goal's attainment itself is difficult to handle with this policy: no measurable goals are set in the Regulation 1836/93.

REFERENCES

CEC (1997), Council Resolution of 7 October 1997 on the drafting, implementation and enforcement of Community environmental law, OJ C 321/1 of 22.10.97.

Jordan, A. (1999), 'The implementation of the Environmental policy: a policy problem without a political solution?', *Environment and Planning C: Government and Policy*, 17, pp. 69–90.

Mendrinou, M. (1996), 'Non compliance and the European Commission's role in integration', *Journal of European Public Policy*, 3(1), pp. 1–22.

2. The implementation of environmental policy in the European Union context

Matthieu Glachant

1. INTRODUCTION

Implementing an EU policy presents distinct features from conventional implementation of domestic policy in a national context. A first obvious factor lies in the heterogeneity of the EU space with respect to ecological, economic, administrative and political variables. It led the inventors of the European Union to imagine a flexible political system which produces policies that are, on average, less detailed and less constraining as to the means open to reach policy goals than national equivalents. By leaving large discretion to Member States to accommodate domestic peculiarities, it de facto leads to implementation processes 'richer' in terms of decision making. Further implementation of environmental policy is the prime responsibility of the Member States. The supranational bodies (the Commission, the European Court of Justice, and the European Parliament) do not enjoy any powers of control or sanction in the field. This engenders a sharp demarcation between the policy formulation and the implementation stages. Many commentators have viewed this as threatening the effectiveness of implementation. Based on a review of the literature, the goal of this chapter is to identify some of the peculiarities of implementation in the EU context and their potential impacts on the effectiveness of implementation of EU environmental policy. Special attention is dedicated to legal issues since these are the basic constraints determining the nature of implementation in the European Union.

I provide a definition and a description of policy implementation in the first section. I go on to discuss the legal machinery available to enforce EU law against Member States in those cases where they fail to correctly implement the Directives, and discuss its weaknesses. The final section asks whether there is a significant 'implementation deficit' of EU environmental policy and investigates its possible causes.

2.   WHAT DOES IMPLEMENTATION OF EU ENVIRONMENTAL LEGISLATION CONSIST OF?

2.1   The Legal Foundations of the EU Environmental Policy

Before entering into the subject of implementation, a brief reminder of a few basic legal principles of the European Union is useful to clarify the allocation of the role between the EU and the national levels of government. Of particular relevance to the subject of implementation is the so-called Subsidiarity Principle that is discussed below.

The environment is one of the most developed policy fields of the European Union. The more than 200 Council regulations and Directives in force constitute a very significant *acquis communautaire*. One paradox is that a non-ambiguous legal basis for an environmental policy at the EU level is only available since the Single Act of 1986 in which Article 130R states that a high level of environmental protection shall be an objective for the European Union. Prior to this, environmental Directives or Council Regulations were either based on Article 100 of the Treaty of Rome which permits actions to promote the 'establishment or the functioning of the common market' or on the 'catch all' article 235. This applies if 'action by the Community should prove necessary (...) and this treaty has not provided the necessary power'. Since then, this initial legal ambiguity has largely disappeared. In 1993, the Maastricht Treaty reinforced the legitimacy of an EU environmental policy, giving in particular a heavy emphasis to the necessity of promoting sustainable growth. But the Maastricht Treaty also introduced a novelty, the Subsidiarity Principle, which might prove to have important impacts on the way environmental policy is made. This Principle that applies to all kinds of policies clearly pushes towards more decentralisation. As stated in Article 3b, it requires that the Community shall take action 'only if and in so far as the objectives of that action cannot be sufficiently achieved by the Member States and can therefore by reason of scale or effects of the proposed action, be better achieved by the Community'.

Some commentators have viewed this Principle as potentially weakening the ambition of EU environmental policy. The fear is that the Subsidiarity Principle could act to restrict the scope of environmental issues that can be potentially regulated at the EU level. In particular, looking at existing environmental Directives and Regulations suggests that local pollution concerns were given at least as much attention as transfrontier problems like SO_2 emissions or ozone layer depletion by the European Union before Maastricht. Taking some recent examples, the Directive 91/271/EEC on urban wastewater treatment or the Directive 91/676/EEC on the protection of waters against nitrates were two very important pieces of EU legislation dealing with very local concerns. Based on the Subsidiarity Principle, one may wonder 'how it comes about that a supranational body, which might be thought best tailored to the protection of international public goods has spent a great deal of time and effort on matters concerned with local public goods including urban air quality, drinking water or bathing water?' (Weale, 1999). Of course, Article 100 could have provided an alternative legal basis for making law on local environmental issues on the grounds of the necessity imposed by the single market. This has been extensively used for Directives on waste, for instance. The underlying rationale here is that enacting policies at the EU level helps to maintain a 'level playing field' by controlling the dispersion of the regulatory costs incurred by the economic competitors in the different Member States. However, this rationale is predicated on the existence of an EU-wide market concerned with the policy at stake. In many cases (e.g. urban wastewater, bathing water), the mere existence of economic competitors concerned by the issue at stake cannot be taken for granted.

Clearly one possible interpretation of the Subsidiarity Principle could thus have been that local environmental concerns no longer belong to the European agenda, and are the sole responsibility of the Member States. In fact the Commission did not interpret the Subsidiarity Principle in this way. Instead it has been viewed as the catalyst to the transition to more 'framework' Directives, as illustrated by the recent Directive 96/61/EEC on the integrated pollution and prevention control (Flynn, 1997) and on 'soft laws' (like voluntary agreements). Hence the choice made has been to move away from the 'Command and Control' type of Directive including a comprehensive set of quantitative standards very widespread in the early EU legislation. This is one key orientation of the Fifth Programme of Action and Policy in relation to the environment (1993–2000). This was reinforced in 1996 by paragraph 6 of the Amsterdam Treaty according to which 'other things being equal, directives should be preferred to regulations and framework directives to detailed measures'.

This interpretation of the Subsidiarity Principle has in fact confirmed the historical allocation of roles between the EU and the national level. Through a comparison of German and American federalism, Weale (1999) develops a very interesting view on this issue. To the extent that the EU is federal in its form, it is closer to German federalism rather than US federalism in the sense that division is not one of responsibility for policy sector (i.e. fiscal issue, security, agriculture, etc.). Instead, each level is responsible for different stages of the policy process. The Member State implements measures adopted at the EU level. The primacy of the EU level is balanced by the decisive influence of the Member States in the policy-making process through the European Council, which could be compared to the German

Bundesrat. Whilst the recent orientations initiated by the Subsidiarity Principle tend to push the hardly clear-cut frontier between the different stages of the policy process towards more decentralisation, it is far from being an institutional revolution.

2.2   A Definition

The communication of the Commission on the implementation of EU environmental policy issued in 1996 contains in its appendix a reference definition of implementation (CEC, 1996). Implementation comprises 'the following three components:

- Transposition means any legislative, regulatory or administrative measure taken by any competent authority of a Member State in order to incorporate into the national legal order the obligations rights and duties enshrined in Community environmental directives (...).
- Practical application is defined as the incorporation of Community law by the competent authorities into individual decisions, for instance when issuing a permit executing a plan or a programme (...). It also includes providing the infrastructure and provisions needed in order to enable competent authorities to perform their obligations under Community law and to take the appropriate decisions.
- Enforcement is defined broadly as all approaches of the competent authorities to encourage or compel others to comply with existing regulation (e.g. monitoring, on-the-spot controls, sanctions and compulsory corrective measures) in order to improve the performance of environmental policy with the final goal of improving the overall quality of the environment.'

A crucial point is that, in the case of environmental policy,[1] implementation is primarily a task for competent authorities at the national level. No supranational bodies (the Commission, the Parliament, the Council, or the European Court of Justice) are directly involved in implementation. This is the responsibility of the Member States. However, the EU level is *indirectly* involved in enforcement: in case the States fail to implement correctly the legislation, article 211 of the EU Treaty confers on the Commission the task of ensuring 'that the provisions of this Treaty and the measures taken by the institutions pursuant thereto are applied'. This provides the basis for enforcement actions against Member States that will be considered in detail in section 3 below. But this task only concerns the State level. The Commission has neither the legal authority nor the technical means to enforce EU law against individuals or private entities non-compliant with the Directive's requirements.

Strictly speaking the definition above is only valid for the most widespread legal instrument in EU environmental policy – the Directive. It needs to be slightly amended to be valid for the other main tool – the Regulation. Regulations are binding upon all Member States and 'directly applicable' within all such States. Direct applicability means that Regulations are automatically part of the Member States' legal systems without the need for separate legal measures to be made at the national level to incorporate them (Craig and de Burca, 1998, pp. 106–7). Hence, implementing Regulations does not entail the transposition step of the definition.[2] One consequence is that 'such norms have to be capable of being parachuted into the legal systems of all the Member States just as they are' (Craig and de Burca, 1998, p. 108). They are thus far less convenient to use.

By contrast, Directives are binding in terms of the end to be achieved but leave some choice open to the Member States in terms of the means to bring this end about. This is why they need to be transposed to the national legislation in order to be applicable. They offer a very valuable flexibility. They are able to easily accommodate the diversity of national legal systems. This is the theory on the distinction between Directives and Regulations and is broadly applicable as a rule-of-thumb. Albeit, in practice, the content of some Directives is simply more detailed and more directly applicable in Member States than certain Regulations (see for instance in Chapter 5 the case of the Directive dealing with emissions from municipal waste incinerators).

2.3　The Nature of Implementation is Strongly Affected by the Nature of the EU Legislation

The definition above does not give a precise idea of the range of activities involved in implementation. In practice, these activities vary greatly and, in particular, are very dependent on the type of policy problem tackled or the policy approach used in the Directive. One might consider the three pieces of EU legislation studied in this volume (the Directive regulating emissions from existing domestic waste incinerators no. 89/429; the Directive on emissions of SO_2 and NO_x from Large Combustion Plants no. 88/609, and the Council Regulation on the Eco-Management and Audit Scheme no. 1863/93 or EMAS) to illustrate this diversity:

1. The Large Combustion Plant Directive only sets a national aggregate target for NO_x and SO_2 emissions for existing plants. A major implementation issue has thus been the choice of the instrument to

allocate efforts among the different pollution sources. Certain countries considered using tradable permits then withdrew the idea (the United Kingdom). Three out of four countries (France, Germany, and the Netherlands) signed voluntary agreements with industry.

2. By contrast, the Municipal Waste Incineration Directives incorporate very precise rules, including emission standards, comprehensive monitoring and reporting requirements 'ready to use' by national implementation bodies. Very few decisions have then been left to the implementation stage. Consequently, the central challenge for implementation was basically restricted to enforcement, i.e. to monitor the emissions of individual incinerators and to apply sanctions where necessary.

3. The EMAS regulation is again a very different case because it was a totally new and original policy approach. As a consequence, the pre-existing implementation institutions were not adapted. Hence, one central task of implementation was to create the institutional bodies able to manage the scheme. Furthermore, due to the voluntary character of the policy scheme, there was a clear necessity to provide incentives for firms to participate in the programme. These requisites led some countries to delegate implementation of EMAS to private or hybrid public/private institutions (Germany). In the end, the institutional outcome of the implementation of EMAS has been very significant and original as compared to conventional implementation bodies.

To sort out this diversity, the degree of policy centralisation is a first useful discriminating variable. The contrast between the Large Combustion Plant (LCP) Directive and the Directive on domestic waste incineration illustrates this point. The problem they aimed to tackle is comparable – air emissions by fixed large emitters – but the approach taken was very different with respect to the degree of centralisation. In the first case, the Directive only fixed national targets and thus left the Member States to determine all the other aspects. In the second case, the discretion for Member States was minimal. The Directive was a self-sufficient comprehensive legal text 'ready to use' by the Member States, which only had to transpose it in full into the national legislation and to enforce it. In the two cases, similar decisions (e.g. the choice of the policy instrument to allocate abatement efforts among polluting sources) were made at different stages (the implementation stage in the LCP Directive and the formulation stage in the waste incineration case). A logical consequence is that, when speaking of implementation in general, there is no clear-cut theoretical frontier between implementation and policy formulation. The choice of what will be fixed at the formulation stage and what will be decided afterwards is made on a case by case basis for each

Directive or Regulation. And this choice varies substantially, even though more recently the Subsidiarity Principle clearly pushes towards more decentralisation.

Another useful distinction is between substantive versus procedural legislation. Substantive EU legislation contains clearly defined environmental targets. Targets may apply to environmental parameters of market goods (e.g. emission standards for motor vehicles), to certain industrial pollution sources (e.g. emission standards for waste incineration plants), to certain environmental media (e.g. bathing water quality standards) or less frequently to all the polluting sources of the Member States (e.g. aggregate national targets for SO_2 emissions). The Large Combustion Plant Directive and the Directive on domestic waste incineration are two examples of substantive legislation. By contrast, procedural legislation does not target pollution abatement directly but compels national administrations or (potential) polluters to follow procedures, which are expected *indirectly* to lead to the protection of the environment. The EMAS regulation is of this type. It defines procedures and institutions to be set up not only by Member States, but also by companies willing to have their environmental management system EMAS registered. Another prominent illustration is the Directive 96/61/EC on Integrated Pollution Prevention and Control (IPPC) which affects national regulatory systems, posing as a principle for the setting of emission standards at the plant level based on the BATNEEC concept (Best Available Technologies Not Entailing Excessive Cost). As regards implementation, the main difference between the two lies in their impact on existing administrative structures. In general, the former type is implemented along pre-existing administrative channels whereas the latter usually requires changing these national structures. As a result, Macrory and Purdy suggest that implementation of procedural legislation is a more difficult exercise (1997, pp. 32–33) since it requires adjustments by administrative bodies in addition to the adjustments made in both cases by polluters.

3.   THE ENFORCEMENT OF EU LAW AGAINST MEMBER STATES

Enforcement is a crucial aspect of implementation. Given that compliance necessarily entails costs and effort on the part of the groups affected by the policy, a form of coercion is essential to ensure that policies ultimately have an impact on the ground. In the case of EU policy, enforcement against polluters that would not comply is the responsibility of the Member States. Once transposition is achieved (a step which is only required for the

Directives) EU law becomes national, and as such is fully enforceable within the national enforcement apparatus. But EU law may either not be properly transposed by the State or, albeit transposed, not applied correctly due to poor enforcement or other implementation deficiencies. Member States are held liable in these cases and the Commission is in charge of ensuring the application of EU law by the Member States. What legal tools are available to the Commission for enforcing EU law against them? Efficient enforcement is a concern here. Brussels may face difficulties in counter-balancing the power of Member States concerned with their prerogatives, and whose political systems have been established for a much longer time and may be perceived as more democratically legitimate when set against the *'bureaucrates bruxellois'*.

3.1   The Article 169 (now 226) Proceeding

The basic tool for the Commission in enforcing EU law is provided by Article 169 (now 226) of the Treaty. The Article 169 proceeding includes three formal steps in the event of a State's failure to comply:

- The sending of an Article 169 letter to the Member State, which basically consists of a formal notification of the infringement. The State is usually given two months to respond. Then the Commission decides whether or not to proceed based on the answers provided.
- The issue of a reasoned opinion, which states very clearly the motives for infringement and formally marks the two-month period within which the State must comply.
- The referral of the matter to the European Court of Justice; 80% of cases do not reach this step (CEC, 1997, p. 8).

The average time span between the first step and the judgement by the European Court is 56 months for environmental legislation (Krämer, 1996 cited by Macrory and Purdy, 1997). This length of time does not take into account the fact that informal exchanges and negotiations between the Commission and the Member State systematically precede the formal procedure.

For a long time, a major weakness of the proceeding was that a judgement of the European Court of Justice carried no sanctions and merely had a declaratory effect. That meant that the sole impact of a ruling against a Member State was the political embarrassment it engendered and the cost to the State's reputation in the eyes of the public or among the other Member States. The Maastricht Treaty introduced the possibility through Article 171 (now 228) of financially sanctioning the Member State. So far this tool has only been used once, against Greece in July 2000. This country was condemned to pay a fine of 24,600 EURO per day of non-compliance commencing on the day of the judgement. This case gives an idea of how long such proceedings might take. Greece was condemned for not having properly implemented two waste directives (75/442/EC and 78/319/EC) issued in the 1970s! The infringement procedure started in 1988 when the Commission became aware of the existence in Crete of an illegal landfill according to the above Directives. Greece was initially condemned in April 1992 but failed to comply (Corone, 2000).

Sanctioning State violations is certainly a crucial aspect. A prerequisite for the Commission, however, is to detect the breaches. In his manual of environmental policy, Haigh (1992) has made a now widely adopted distinction between formal compliance (the legal process of transposing EU law into national legislation) and practical compliance (whether the objectives of the Directives are actually met in practice).[3] As pointed out by Jordan (1999), formal compliance may not be too difficult to monitor for the Commission. In particular, the notification procedure is helpful since it compels the Member States to communicate national laws and the other measures taken to ensure the implementation of each Directive. But monitoring practical compliance might prove to be much more problematic. The Commission has no powers of inspection in the field of environmental policy. It thus heavily depends on information provided by States, which may not have peculiar incentives to give reliable information that might ultimately be used against them. To counter-balance this, the Commission increasingly relies on the complaints procedure through which individuals or Non Governmental Organisations (NGOs) can signal to the Commission suspected cases of infringements (see Table 2.1).

Table 2.1 Suspected infringements, 1988–1994: origins

Origin	1988	1990	1994
Complaints	929	1274	1145
Parliamentary questions	82	32	5
Petitions	8	18	6
Cases detected by the Commission	752	268	277
Total	1771	1592	1433

Source: Adapted from Jordan (1999, p. 80).

Macrory and Purdy also refer to key figures that give a measure of the difficulty the Commission may encounter in ensuring the application of EU environmental legislation by the Member States. The legal unit of DG Environment, in charge of implementation, consists of about 20 individuals whose job is to monitor the compliance of the 15 Member States with the 70 major items found in the EU environmental legislation (1997, p. 37).

3.2 The Bottom-up Enforcement Channel: the Direct Effect Doctrine and the Francovich Case

Article 169 proceeding is a top-down process, being led by the Commission and the European Court of Justice. But individuals may also challenge State violations directly before national courts. This bottom-up channel allows enforcement to be driven by individuals directly affected by the damages non-compliance may have inflicted. Furthermore, it leads to the involvement of national judges in the enforcement of EU law. The existence of the bottom-up channel places the enforcement of EU law against States at two levels. This is the so-called notion of dual vigilance, in legal parlance (Weatherill, 1995, p. 98). The use of the bottom-up channel is nevertheless constrained by legal niceties that are worth considering.

First of all, the bottom-up route works well when applied to Regulations. This is one aspect of the notion of 'direct applicability': it confers rights onto individuals that can ipso facto be claimed before the relevant national court. It led some observers to advocate the extensive use of Regulations instead of Directives to solve the implementation deficit in EU law. Furthermore, it is also granted to Directives transposed into the national legal order. In this case, the Directive is a national law and, as such, confers rights onto individuals. The problem arises when the Directive is not transposed. Whilst contradicting some provisions of the Treaty, the European Court of Justice has progressively elaborated the so-called Direct Effect Doctrine since the 1960s. This doctrine extends the properties of transposed Directives to non-transposed Directives, under certain conditions. The main restricting condition is that the Directive must be sufficiently precise and unambiguous so that the granting of precise rights to individuals on its ground is possible. In reality, this is an important caveat, since many Directives are often of a programmatic nature leaving large discretion to the Member States.

A further step towards strengthening the bottom-up enforcement of non-transposed directives is the judgement of the European Court of Justice made in 1991 in the Francovich versus Italy case. The litigation was generated by the failure of the Italian government to implement the Directive 80/987 (Weatherill, 1995, p. 127). Among other things, this Directive requires Member States to create a guarantee fund to compensate workers in the event of employer insolvency. The Italian State did not create the fund, and several Italian workers (among whom was Andrea Francovich) put the matter before the European Court. In its judgement, the European Court ruled that the Italian State was financially liable for the damages to Francovich caused by non-implementation. The Francovich case thus created a precedent for financial reparation by the State.

The Direct Effect Doctrine and the Francovich case have generated a lot of speculation among lawyers and their legal basis is far from being assured. But, in the end, what are the real impacts of this possibility to invoke EU law before national courts in the Member States? Evidence is limited except in the UK where Chalmers (2000) has recently made a comprehensive review of the cases where EU law was invoked before British Courts. This study tends to be pessimistic regarding the genuine impacts of these legal possibilities. EU law was invoked in 1088 cases in the period 1973–1998. However only 39 cases concerned environmental law, with a recent acceleration since 31 cases have occurred since 1995. Finally, it was successfully invoked (that means that the judgement has at least partly been based on it) only 8 times!

4.   THE IMPLEMENTATION GAP IN ENVIRONMENTAL POLICY

The existence of an implementation gap or deficit in EU environmental policy is widely acknowledged among commentators (see for instance Jordan, 1999 or Macrory and Purdy, 1997). On the policy side, it is encapsulated in the basic statement of two major EU policy documents issued in the recent period: a communication to the Council entitled 'Implementing Community Environmental Law' (COM(96)500) and a Council Resolution of 7 October 1997 on the drafting, implementation and enforcement of community environmental law. On what evidence is the statement made? Further, what are the causes of the implementation gap?

4.1   How Wide is the Gap?

It is practically impossible to answer this question. Regarding formal compliance, the source that gives the most comprehensive view is the report on the monitoring of the application of community laws published every year since 1984 by the Commission. There are seemingly converging efforts by commentators to criticise the reliability of the information provided, its quality, and its usefulness to get a general and objective idea of the extent of the problem (see Jordan, 1999; Macrory and Purdy, 1997; Boerzel, 2000).

Based on these reports, it is clear that a problem of formal compliance exists. In 1995, the Member States had only notified 91% of the EU environmental directives, the two extreme countries being Denmark, having fully notified, and Italy, with a score of 75%. In Commission terminology, notification consists of the obligation for every Member State to communicate to the Commission the legal measures taken to transpose the Directives. This very formal indicator should be used with great caution since delays in notification may have very little relationship with practical compliance in some cases. As an illustration, in Chapter 5 of this volume, the Netherlands significantly delayed the notification of the Directive 89/809/EC on domestic waste incineration due to legal difficulties whereas meeting the pollution abatement limits set in the Directives did not pose them any problems.

It is also established by the Commission's annual reports that the number of infringement proceedings has been increasing almost continuously for twenty years. Again, it is difficult to draw conclusions from this since it is impossible to isolate the relative impact of the increasing attention paid to implementation by the Commission, from a potential increase in genuine implementation failures in the Member States. As argued by Jordan (1999), implementation has long been a neglected issue by the Commission.

Unsurprisingly, there is an even greater dearth of information concerning the level of practical compliance. In the annual report, the Commission relies on the number of complaints coming from individuals and NGOs as a rough indicator. The indicator is, however, extremely rough. As argued by Boerzel (2000), the bad score of Spain and the UK probably reflects to a significant extent the liveliness of local green groups.

In the same paper, Boerzel shows how the received wisdom that the Mediterranean Member States have particular difficulties implementing environmental Directives is difficult to base on sound evidence. If it is true that some of these countries performed badly in terms of notifying Directives for instance, it is no longer true for other indicators used in the Commission's report. For instance the number of referrals to the European Court of Justice might be a good indicator for genuine implementation problems since it is the ultimate step of the infringement proceedings (80% of proceedings are stopped before they get to this stage because the problem has already been solved). Based on statistics gathered by Boerzel (see Figure 2.1), the sharing out between countries places Germany with Belgium and Italy in the top three!

In a more qualitative way, Macrory and Purdy develop an interesting discussion on the fact that the ease of implementation has been strongly affected by the differing structural features of the legislation (1997, p. 33). They note that implementation problems are scarce in terms of those Directives dealing with environmental standards for market products (e.g. emissions from motor vehicles, lead content of paint). In these cases, monitoring is a structurally easy task and market forces push for compliance. By contrast, implementation is much more difficult when policies are dependent on national action taken within deep levels of the Member States. Examples would include directives dealing with groundwater, the protection of wild habitats, etc. Within this type of Directive, there are specific difficulties with those 'horizontal' directives which cut across conventional administrative boundaries; for example, the Directive 90/313/EEC concerning the access to environmental information, or the 1985 Environmental Impact Assessment Directive 85/337/EEC.

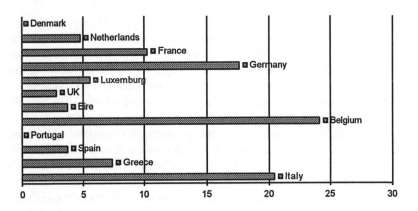

Source: Boerzel (2000, p. 8).

Figure 2.1 Average percentage of the referrals to the European Court of Justice and judgements (1988–1992)

4.2   Explaining the Implementation Deficit

If we admit the existence of an implementation gap in EU environmental policy, what factors may explain it? The political science and public policy literature has identified a wide set of generic factors that may apply to implementation in general. The most prominent of these is the structural impossibility for the policy makers to control the street-level bureaucrats in charge of practical implementation on the field (Sabatier, 1986) and the complexity of joint action (Pressman and Wildavsky, 1984), given that effective implementation requires the involvement of a set of different organisations and individuals, is often very badly co-ordinated due to a lack of consensus between them, etc. This literature is reviewed in Chapter 3 of this volume. Here are considered the specific factors rooted in the very nature of EU policy.

A key array of arguments refers to the substantive nature of the EU legislation (Jordan, 1999, p. 78). It includes the poor drafting of EU legislation (Macrory and Purdy, 1997, p. 46), the fact that Directives' aims are frequently vague or contradictory, and the neglect of implementation needs at the formulation stage.

Many legal arguments developed above on the weakness of the enforcement of EU law against Member States are other explanatory factors. In particular, the preferred tool in environmental policy, the Directives, suffer from legal weaknesses previously reviewed:

- The limited effectiveness of bottom-up enforcement by individuals before national courts, due to the fact that Directives do not have 'direct effect' when their content – as is frequent – is programmatic and general, and thus do not grant non-ambiguous rights to individuals.
- Limited monitoring and enforcement capacity of the Commission, especially when practical compliance is at stake, due to the absence of power of inspection in the Member States and the lack of human resources (the legal unit in the DG Environment constitutes about 20 individuals).
- The poor record of sanctions being levied against the non-complying Member States, though the very reinforcement of the principle of fining states under Article 171 of the Treaty might have improved the situation in recent times.

Beyond these aspects, one might ask whether there are structural institutional reasons which preclude effective implementation. On this question, a crucial argument refers to the institutional separation established for EU legislation between policy making and implementation activities. Jordan argues that this structure provides strong incentives for key EU level actors such as the Commission or the European Parliament (which is increasingly involved in environmental policy making since Maastricht) to propose ambitious Directives or Council Regulations that impose costs on other actors (i.e. the Member States) in charge of implementing them. This leads Mendrinou to speak of an 'in-built pathology of non-compliance' within the European Union (1996). Jordan invites us to push the argument one step further by considering the political game between the Member States and the supranational actors. In the perspective of the Member States, imperfect implementation allows them to fine-tune EU legislation to domestic exigencies. Under these terms, imperfect implementation is one of the tools available to Member States to control the speed and the scope of European integration. The implementation deficit is thus the inevitable consequence of a complex multi-level system. This raises a question, however (Jordan,

1999). Member States are closely involved at the formulation stage via the Council of the European Union. Why then do they not diminish the stringency of policies they consider to have domestic harmful impacts at this stage?

To explain the limited 'implementability' of Directives caused by ambiguity in the formulation or contradictory objectives, Collins and Earnshaw refer to the complexity of the EU policy-making process (1992). In particular, this process requires the consensus of many different actors. This leads to compromises, dispensations, and ambiguity in legislation that sow the seeds for subsequent difficulties in implementation.

Another explanation might focus on the challenge of implementing a policy text, adopted in Brussels, in local contexts as different as Sicilia, Sussex or Carelia. Of peculiar importance is the heterogeneity in national administrative structures. Based on case studies, Knill argues how the 'administrative fit' between the national administrative features and the Directive imperative affects the ease and likelihood of successful implementation (1998). He suggests focusing on two variables to predict the difficulty of implementation: the nature of the requirements set in the Directive, and the national administrative traditions. The latter designates the whole set of routines, habits, policy beliefs and procedures, both formal and informal, that characterise the way national administrations usually manage the issue at stake in the Directive. The greater the mismatch, the larger the adaptation of the administrative routines, and ceteris paribus, the more difficult the implementation. Criticising Knill's approach, Smith tells an interesting story of the implementation of the Urban Wastewater Treatment Directive in England and Wales, where implementation proved effective in spite of a wide initial degree of mismatch (Smith, 2000). His conclusion is that if the degree of mismatch determines the level of the adaptation pressure, it does not help to explain directly how the domestic actors ultimately adapt.

5.   CONCLUSION

In the end, what are the key differences between EU and national policy implementation? I think that two points are to be retained. First of all, EU policy leaves on average more discretion to the implementers (the Member States) than conventional national policies. This is primarily the result of the necessity to accommodate very different national contexts. It has been reinforced in recent times under the strictures imposed by the Subsidiarity Principle. The frontier between policy making and implementation is hence not located at the same place in both types of implementation: EU implementation is much richer in policy decisions. The second point is that there is a more clear-cut separation between implementation and policy making in the case of EU policy. More precisely, policy-making bodies (the Commission, the European Parliament, and the Council) do not enjoy a direct hierarchical control on the implementers (the environmental administration of the individual Member States). This will remain true in the future even though a trend to strengthen the enforcement tools against Member States through various legal means can be observed. One consequence is that implementation will have to rely mainly on the voluntary consent of the implementers rather than on coercive means that are simply too weak to commit them to comply with Directives' provisions. Having said that it should be immediately underlined that the incentives to comply with Directives for an individual Member State are not comparable with those faced by a self-interested polluter. Member States are political entities defending the general interest of their citizens, which a better environment is compatible with. As a matter of fact, the States have almost always agreed that a policy should be implemented once it has been adopted. It follows that the central challenge remains the implementation on the ground irrespective of whether the policy is European or national.

The EU environmental policy is evolving quickly, putting a greater emphasis on the Subsidiarity Principle, and increasing the use of voluntary approaches and economic instruments. This also entails a move away from command and control Directives including quantitative limits to 'framework' Directives, less clear-cut objectives and leaving more discretion to Member States. Will these Directives be more easily implemented? It is difficult to draw a clear-cut conclusion. On the one hand, using Knill's fit argument, this evolution gives Member States additional discretion that could facilitate the adjustments of national administrative structures to fit in with the legislation. On the other hand, precise quantitative objectives may in theory be more readily susceptible to monitoring and enforcement. Besides, one consequence of the Maastricht Treaty is that most Directives are now adopted by way of a qualified majority procedure. This clearly reinforces the chance that a Member State may find itself in a situation where it will be obliged to implement a text with which it disagrees.

NOTES

1. In other areas, most noticeably in EU competition law, the Commission enjoys powers to implement the law in the Member States (possibly to fine individuals and private entities, and make inspection in the field).

2. Another aspect of the 'direct applicability' is that Regulations give individuals rights that can be enforced through national courts. In this respect, Regulations are said to be directly effective. This second aspect has consequences for the legal enforcement of the Regulations that will be considered later in section 3. We will see that the European Court of Justice through the development of the so-called Direct Effect Doctrine has also partly given this latter property to Directives.

3. Another widespread terminology characterising the same idea is the distinction between policy output – 'the laws, regulations and institutions that governments employ in dealing with policy problems' – and policy outcome – 'the effects of those measures upon the state of the world' (Easton, 1965).

REFERENCES

Boerzel, Tanja A. (2000), 'Why there is no southern problem. On environmental leaders and laggards in the European Union', *Journal of European Public Policy*, 7(1) pp. 141–162.

CEC (1996), Implementing Community Environmental Law, Communication to the Council of the European Union and the European Parliament, 22 October 1996, COM(96)500.

CEC (1997), Council Resolution of 7 October 1997 on the drafting, implementation and enforcement of Community environmental law, OJ C 321/1 of 22.10.97.

Chalmers, Damian (2000), 'The much ado about judicial politics in the United Kingdom: a statistical analysis of reported decisions of United Kingdom Courts invoking EU Law 1973–1998', Jean Monnet Papers 1/00, Harvard Law School.

Collins, K. and D. Earnshaw (1992), 'The implementation and enforcement of EC environmental policy', *Environmental Politics*, 1 (4), pp. 213–249.

Corone, Stéphane (2000), 'Une condamnation historique', *Le Monde*, p. iv, 5 September.

Craig, Pail and Grainne de Burca (1998), *EU Law: Text, Cases and Materials*, Oxford, UK: Oxford University Press.

Easton, D. (1965), *A framework for policy analysis*, Englewood Cliffs, NJ: Prentice Hall.

Flynn, B. (1997), 'Subsidiarity and the rise of soft law', OP-40 Human Capital and Mobility Network University of Essex, Colchester, Essex.

Haigh, Nigel (1992), *Manual of Environmental Policy*, Harlow, UK: Longman.

Jordan, A. (1999), 'The implementation of EU environmental policy: a policy problem without a political solution?', Environmental and Planning C: *Government and Policy*, 17, pp. 69–90.

Knill, Christoph (1998), 'Implementing European policies: the impact of national administrative traditions', *Journal of Public Policy*, 18(1).

Krämer, Ludwig (1996), 'Public interest litigation in environmental matters before European courts', *Journal of Environmental Law*, 8(1), pp. 1–18.

Macrory, Richard and Ray Purdy (1997), 'The enforcement of EC environmental law against member states', in Jane Holder (ed.), *The Impact of EC Environmental Law in the UK*, Chichester, UK: John Wiley & Sons.

Mendrinou, M. (1996), 'Non compliance and the European Commission's role in integration', *Journal of European Public Policy*, 3(1), pp. 1–22.

Pressman, Jeffrey L. and Aaron Wildavsky, (eds) (1984), *Implementation: How Great Expectations in Washington are Dashed in Oakland*, third edition, Berkeley, Los Angeles and London: University of California Press.

Sabatier, P.A. (1986), 'What can we learn from implementation research?' in Franz X. Kaufmann, Giandomenico Majone and Vincent Ostrom (eds), *Guidance, Control, and Evaluation in the Public Sector*, Berlin and New York: Walter de Gruyter.

Smith, Adrian (2000), 'Fitting in with Brussels: implementing the Urban Waste Water Treatment Directive in England and Wales', *Journal of Environmental Policy and Planning*, forthcoming.

Weale, A. (1999), 'European environmental policy by stealth: the dysfunctionality of functionalism?' Environmental and Planning C: *Government and Policy*, 17, pp. 37–51.

Weatherill, Stephen (1995), *Law and Integration in the European Union*, Oxford, UK: Clarendon Press.

3. What can we learn from economics and political science analysis on the efficiency and effectiveness of policy implementation?

Simone Schucht

This chapter deals with the major areas of discussion relating to policy implementation. It focuses on literature from the two disciplines, Economics and Political Science, which have consistently dealt with this issue. In particular, the emphasis is on what the two disciplines have to say about effectiveness, efficiency and evaluation of policy implementation.

Policy implementation was for a long time a neglected issue in both disciplines. Early environmental economics focused on the question of the economic efficiency properties of policy instruments, but abstracted in the analysis the possible non-compliance of polluters. Hence, implementation was implicitly viewed as a self-fulfilling perfect process – perfect in the sense that it did not entail costs. And from the Political Sciences angle, the implementation of policy tended to be viewed as an unproblematic process so long as bureaucracies were obedient (Hill, 1997a and 1997b).

The view of a quasi-automatic implementation has been given up in both disciplines. They extended their assumptions by paying more attention to the behaviour of actors involved in implementation, their interests, incentives, information level, influence and restrictions. Implementation has become an important discourse in both disciplines although we find a striking contrast between their relative foci. Economics largely restricts its analysis to a sub-aspect of the whole implementation process: the monitoring and enforcement. By contrast, Political Science does not consider the issue of a regulation's enforcement in itself. The issue is merged in a general analysis of implementation. In addition, public policy analysis increasingly puts emphasis on the interactions between policy implementation and the (re-)formulation of policy objectives, thus extending its scope to the entire policy process instead of looking at implementation as a discrete policy step.

The chapter is organised as follows: in section 1 the economic view is presented; section 2 deals with the Political Science approaches. Section 3 summarises what can be learned from both disciplines for an analysis of implementation processes.

1. IMPLEMENTATION AS A QUESTION OF OPTIMALITY – THE ECONOMIST'S VIEW

Traditional economics concerned with environmental issues focused on policy instruments: in particular on a comparison of market based versus command-and-control instruments and their properties in terms of social welfare (Baumol and Oates, 1988). That polluters would comply was implicitly presupposed; implementation was thus assumed to be perfect and enforcement to be costless. The first coherent analysis of the role of enforcement was Gary Becker's (1968) seminal article 'Crime and Punishment: An Economic Approach' not specifically dealing with the environment but developing a more general economic model of crime. Following Becker, the economic literature has taken monitoring and enforcement into account.

1.1 The Becker Model

Becker's (1968) economic approach towards crime starts from the general recognition that obedience to legislation cannot be taken for granted. Instead, regulated agents will consider whether or not to comply with certain rules. Becker takes the economist's view by assuming regulated agents to be rational when making compliance decisions. This means that they decide whether to comply or not on the basis of a cost-benefit analysis: they compare expected compliance costs with non-compliance costs and choose the least cost option. For instance, in the case of environmental policy, compliance costs are the resources spent to meet a certain regulatory standard. Non-compliance costs are a bit more complex.

Monitoring is not complete in reality, either due to scarce administrative resources or efficiency reasons that will be considered below. Thus non-compliance will only be sanctioned within the terms of a certain probability and the cost of non-compliance is the statistical expectation of the sanction x, expressed in mathematical terms in the following way:

$$x = pf$$

where p is the probability of conviction, which can be influenced by the expenditure on police, courts, the monitoring frequency etc., and f the severity of the punishment, which may consist of financial sanctions or non-financial sanctions, such as imprisonment.

As indicated by the equation, offences only depend on the probability of detection and the penalty. These variables constitute the available political action variables from which a regulator, wanting to increase deterrence, can start. He can either raise the probability of detection and conviction – for example by increasing the monitoring probability via an increase in the monitoring frequency, by applying advanced monitoring technologies, or by changing legal rules to increase the probability of conviction – or the severity of the monetary or non-monetary sanction. In this regard, as a first result by Becker, a reduction in p could be compensated by an equal percentage increase in *f*, leaving the expected penalty *pf* unchanged. This means that p and *f* constitute perfect substitutes for deterring an individual from committing offences[1] (Becker, 1968).

However, these variables are not perfect substitutes from another point of view: that of society as a whole. As a matter of fact, administrative resources need to be spent in order to prevent offences, to apprehend offenders, etc. Given these costs, the socially efficient objective is to choose the optimal monitoring and enforcement scheme, i.e. the scheme that minimises overall costs borne by society. These costs include costs of apprehension, conviction and punishment (monitoring and enforcement) and costs in form of the harm[2] (damage) caused by an offence (non-compliance, pollution).

A key question addressed by Becker is thus how many resources and what level and measure of punishment should be used to enforce legislation. The optimal level is defined as the level where social costs related to offences are minimised. In order to keep social costs low Becker (1968) suggests that:

⇒ monetary sanctions (fines) – assumed to be a pure transfer and cost neutral – are preferable over non-monetary sanctions, as the latter are more costly, involving for example costs for prison guards.[3]
⇒ *f* should be increased relative to *p*, i.e. the fine should be set arbitrarily high and the probability of detection, depending on the monitoring effort, should be kept low, as by this costs for monitoring could be reduced.

One interesting result of the analysis is that the optimal level of enforcement differs from a maximal level defined as the level where the legislation is fully complied with by the regulated agents. In the economic literature, the so-called 'implementation gap' is not bad per se. Optimal enforcement schemes leave some polluters non-complying.

1.2 Further Developments in the Normative Theory of Enforcement

Becker's approach was soon applied to questions of environmental policy. Various strands of this literature can be distinguished – relaxing some of the assumptions and thus developing further Becker's base model in different directions – that bring the approach closer to reality. The main questions discussed in this literature are presented below.

1.2.1 What should be done if there is a limit to fines?

One issue, evoked by Becker (1968) and further elaborated in subsequent work, is the fact that there may be a limit to fines, and thus to the applicability or desirability of Becker's suggestion to arbitrarily increase fines while lowering the detection probability in order to keep costs low. Limits to high fines may call for an increase in the monitoring probability (and a corresponding reduction of the fine) and for non-monetary sanctions.

In reality, schemes where only few violators are monitored and detected but punished severely are rarely found (see for example Polinsky and Shavell, 1979). Limits to fines can have various origins. One is *insolvency*, which can arise in cases where the optimal fine exceeds the polluter's wealth and simply makes it impossible for him to pay the potential fine. In an extreme case, where the polluter can declare bankruptcy because of a penalty, the sanction may lose its deterrence effect (Cohen, 1998; Shavell, 1985; Heyes, 1998). *Risk aversion* of the regulated agents is another reason. The result of fines and monitoring probability being 'perfect substitutes', as in Becker's base model, was based on the assumption of polluters being indifferent to the level of risk related to their action. When introducing risk aversion, actors get a higher utility out of secure than out of insecure situations and payments. This means that their utility is higher if they are monitored more frequently and pay a lower fine if found non-compliant than if they are seldom monitored but have to pay a high penalty if found non-compliant (Cohen, 1998; Polinsky and Shavell, 1979). Finally, there may also be *exogenously imposed limits* to fines, be it due to legislation, social norms or just for reasons of perceived fairness (see for example Harrington, 1988; Polinsky and Shavell, 1979).

1.2.2 How can evasive behaviour of regulated agents be minimised?

An issue that is also partly linked to high penalties is the possibility that regulated agents may spend resources on trying to evade liability. If this is the case, monitoring probability and height of the penalty are no longer perfect substitutes for deterrence either.

Attempts to evade liability may take various forms: agents may falsify monitoring reports or try to hide pollution, for example emissions, in other ways. Once accused of non-compliance, they may evade punishment by challenging the enforcement agency's decision in court and contest enforcement, or try to bribe officials (Cohen, 1998).

Too high penalties or emission fees, or stricter regulation may constitute an incentive to evade liability and thus cause 'avoidance costs' to the firm and the enforcer. Instead of acting as a deterrent, the fines may then even have perverse effects. This may be the case if the costs of evading liability, such as the liability of paying an emission tax, are lower than the costs of reducing emissions (see for example Oh, 1995; Lee, 1984; Jost, 1997; Nowell and Shogren, 1994).

In the presence of evasive behaviour, the optimal monitoring effort is higher than without evasive behaviour and the fine or emission fees should be lower. Furthermore, command-and-control approaches may become desirable over emission fees (Oh, 1995; Lee, 1984).

1.2.3 How to save monitoring costs

Given these evolutions to the basic model and the finding that sanctions may be limited, it is worth coming back to the question of how, then, monitoring costs can be saved. Two classes of suggestions are made in this respect, one proposing to target non-compliant firms, the other to pass on monitoring costs to firms.

The first suggestion follows the idea that the intensity of monitoring a given polluter may be based on the firm's prior compliance history (Cohen, 1998). By introducing *state-dependent enforcement*, firms previously complying might be monitored less frequently than firms previously violating legislation. The threat of being placed in the more frequently monitored group serves as an incentive to comply. State-dependent enforcement schemes could – for a given level of compliance – save monitoring costs by decreasing the monitoring frequency of firms expected to comply[4] (Harrington, 1988; Harford, 1991).

The introduction of *self-reporting schemes* has been considered as a possible means of substituting government monitoring efforts by passing some of the monitoring responsibility and cost on to the firm without decreasing deterrence (Cohen, 1998). This may help save enforcement costs to the extent that the firm's self-monitoring and reports replace monitoring activity and detection by the government, and to the extent that related cost reductions would not be over-compensated by costs for processing the reports and by the potentially increased frequency of imposition of fines. This has, for example, been studied by Malik (1993).[5] As an additional incentive for firms to report correctly, it has been suggested that a combination of self-reporting schemes with differential penalties be implemented. The idea is to impose lower penalties on correctly reported violations or pollution than on unreported violations which have been detected by the authority (Kaplow and Shavell, 1994; Cohen, 1998; Heyes, 1996; Swierzbinski, 1994). In reality, environmental legislation frequently requires the regulated agents to report for example emissions, or violations of the regulations (as in cases of malfunction of abatement equipment).

1.2.4 What happens to efficiency properties of environmental policy instruments if monitoring and enforcement costs are taken into account?

A traditional issue of environmental economics literature has been the study of the efficiency and effectiveness properties of environmental policy instruments. The general conclusion drawn from this has been that market-based instruments (transferable discharge permits or emission taxes) show better cost efficiency properties – lower compliance costs for firms – than command-and-control type instruments (regulatory standards).

The question logically arising for the monitoring and enforcement literature was whether market-based incentives – which are assumed to yield lower compliance costs – might result in higher compliance as compared to command-and-control approaches and thus save costly monitoring expenditures. This literature, consequently, turned its interest to policy instruments, studying the impact of enforcement costs, introduced by possible non-compliance, on the instruments' cost efficiency properties. The only general result this literature has yielded so far is that economic instruments are no longer systematically preferable when enforcement costs are taken into consideration.

Variables that are indicative of the preferability of market-based over command-and-control instruments are, for example, the properties of the firms' cost curves, the polluter's risk attitude, his subjective monitoring probability expectation, the penalty or the number of firms in a transferable discharge permit market (Malik, 1990 and 1992).

1.2.5 Private litigation as an alternative enforcement channel?

The question of optimal enforcement was enlarged by asking not only how public enforcement schemes should be designed but also who should actually enforce legislation. In reality, there are generally two enforcement channels: the administrative enforcement channel and a legally based one (private litigation). The latter allows citizens to bring polluters before court for damage caused by them through non-compliance with regulation. A recent literature discusses the desirability of this so-called private enforcement route.

Advantages of a private involvement in enforcement are seen, amongst other things, in the direct affectedness of private agents, which may make them a better judge; in a potentially improved enforcement towards firm/industry types where public enforcers might lack the will to enforce, such as public polluters; and also in the possibility of saving government monitoring costs, as the limited public enforcement means can now be better targeted (Cohen, 1998; Naysnerski and Tietenberg, 1992). A disadvantage, however, is located in the possibility that private enforcement may lead to too much enforcement and thus to over-deterrence.[6] This may be the outcome when citizen suits are added to public enforcement and is particularly likely if a reward for private enforcement is available (Polinsky and Shavell, 2000).

1.2.6 Who should be punished? Individual versus corporate sanctions

Finally, a question arises when a regulated firm is no longer treated as a monolithic block and when it is instead acknowledged that pollution may often depend on the individual behaviour of employees. The question is how sanctions should be best allocated between the firm and the employee. It is argued that the actors in a position to affect risk (e.g. of pollution) should have sufficient incentives to reduce this risk. When the hierarchical control of the employees is limited or when specific allocations allow them to evade the burden, for example because the penalty is too high to be recovered from wage reductions, corporate and individual fines are not perfect substitutes. In these cases the allocation of penalties matters, i.e. the employee should be penalised rather than the firm and/or imprisonment rather than financial sanctions may be considered (Segerson and Tietenberg, 1992; Heyes, 2000; Gabel and Sinclair-Desgagné, 1993; Sinclair-Desgagné, 1994; Cohen, 1998).

1.3 What Are the General Lessons to be Derived from the Normative Literature?

A first interesting result, which distinguishes the normative literature's concern from that of many empirical studies is the implication that maximal compliance is not necessarily optimal. From an economics point of view, therefore, an implementation gap is not necessarily considered as a problem. Furthermore, this literature makes interesting suggestions on how to design a monitoring and enforcement scheme if the aim is to keep public control costs low. It shows that under certain circumstances it will be optimal to couple high penalties with a lower monitoring probability. This helps reduce monitoring costs, and thus costs borne by society, while regulated agents will be deterred from offences by the expected penalty.

However, not all situations permit an arbitrary increase in fines while lowering monitoring activity. Instead, such reductions in control costs of the monitoring and enforcement scheme and deterrence from offences, sometimes involve a trade-off. There are at least two reasons why high fines may be ineffective and inefficient or may even have detrimental effects on pollution. This will be the case when an offender's assets simply do not allow him to pay the sanction and he might thus get away without a penalty. Furthermore, too high penalties may induce regulated agents to invest in evasive behaviour instead of in a reduction of pollution. In both cases, perverse and counter-productive effects are possible, leading to an actual increase in pollution despite, or as a result of, high fines. A third reason why high fines are not always desirable is related to the agents' risk attitude. In the face of risk aversion, a combination of low monitoring and high penalties may reduce the actors' welfare.

In situations like this different ways to reduce control costs need to be found. Two approaches are suggested: to pass on monitoring costs to firms by actively involving them in monitoring and reporting activity via self-reporting schemes; or to apply differential schemes. The latter involves a targeting of enforcement resources on previously non-compliant firms by monitoring them with a higher frequency than previously compliant firms. This may permit – for given enforcement costs – the attainment of a higher compliance level overall.

A general point to be added is the finding that not only too high penalties but also too much control and enforcement may have detrimental effects. This is not only true for public but also for private enforcement; or, in particular, a combination of the two. Too much enforcement may induce regulated agents to spend more money on pollution abatement than is socially optimal.

1.4 Explaining Real Enforcement Practices: the Positive Approaches

The literature that has just been reviewed is normative in the sense that it aims at producing prescriptions on how enforcement schemes should be designed. Another stream of literature has tried to develop a more positive approach,[7] seeking to understand how enforcement schemes are working empirically, why they differ from the prescriptions developed above, and what can explain the empirically found behaviour of regulators and regulated agents.

1.4.1   Why do firms in reality comply more than would be expected according to the Becker based theory?

The question of why in reality firms actually comply was raised by Harrington (1988). He found that, for the USA, a large percentage of firms seemed to comply despite the fact that, when found to be non-compliant, firms are often not pursued and that the expected penalty is thus small compared to the compliance cost. Evidence for the 'Harrington-paradox' – compliance despite empirical evidence for comparatively low monitoring and enforcement effort and sanctions – has been noted for other countries as well (Heyes, 1998). Related publications offer a variety of possible reasons for this phenomenon.

The normative literature explains compliance behaviour over extrinsic motivation, following external cost incentives. But this description of a regulated agent's motivation may be too restrictive and several papers argue for the possibility of *voluntary compliance* or environmentally friendly behaviour due to intrinsic motivation, honesty or social norms, where compliance is independent of the compliance cost (Frey and Oberholzer-Gee, 1996; Bontems and Rotillon, 2000).

Other explanations for an unexpectedly high compliance rate may be linked to the firms' subjective expectations of the penalty they might incur. This may, on the one hand, explain compliance as a result of a simply wrong perception, i.e. an *over-estimation of the monitoring and sanctioning probability*, which points to the issue of perceived versus actual levels of inspections and sanctions (Cohen, 1998). On the other hand, compliance may be the effect of dynamic regulator-regulated relationships with *state-dependent enforcement schemes*, i.e. the expectation of becoming subject to stricter monitoring and sanctions if found non-compliant (Harrington, 1988; Harford, 1991).

Sanctions for environmentally unfriendly behaviour or non-compliance are not necessarily restricted to publicly enforced penalties. In addition, *market forces* may penalise firms and thus influence compliance. This issue is closely related to information available about a firm's environmental behaviour, and deals with the potentially adverse reactions of customers, investors, stock-market valuations or employees, to this information. Such information could also impact on the general public image of the firm concerned, or lead to community pressure being exerted on it (Heyes, 1998). There is some empirical research for the US which shows that declines in stock-market valuations as a reaction to sanctions of publicly-traded firms can exceed fines (Badrinath and Bolster, 1996).

Under the heading of *'regulatory dealing'* or 'issue linkage' Heyes (1998) points to the fact that enforcement agencies may interact with a firm in more than one context, because they meet in several regulatory settings or because of a firm having several plants. As a result, agencies may tolerate non-compliance in one setting if they judge it to be ameliorated by the firm's over-compliance in another. Regulatory dealing may thus explain cases where firms comply without a credible threat of sanctions. Finally, positive incentives should not be forgotten: *subsidies for compliance* may also add to firms' compliance.

1.4.2 The enforcer–polluter relationship: the bargaining models

Empirical literature has recognised for a long time that in reality the relationship between the enforcer and regulated agents is not only coercive but is also often characterised by negotiation and bargaining processes (see for example the sociological study of Hawkins, 1984[8]). This has been mirrored in recent economic research dealing with *bargaining* over environmental regulation. This literature gives up the traditional leader–follower relationship view of the firm–regulator interaction, where the regulator commands and the firm follows, by including the possibility of negotiations between the two agents and the fact that regulatory agencies sometimes make concessions that are forbidden by law. This literature investigates the bargaining incentives for both sides (Amacher and Malik, 1996 and 1998).

A reason for bargaining may reside in a firm's option to contest the stringency of regulation in court, which would lead to costs for both the firm and the regulator. The possibility to contest regulation is partly explained by the impossibility of covering all eventualities under environmental legislation; as a consequence, agencies have considerable discretionary power. In particular, plants that are responsible for complex environmental effects will be treated specifically and may try to force changes to the authorisation in court. This constitutes an incentive to bargain over the costs of pollution abatement, i.e. over the stringency of regulation, or the exact timing of investment (Amacher and Malik, 1996 and 1998; see Lehmann, 1997 for an investigation of German environmental legislation).

Scope for interpretation – and hence bargaining – is also introduced by concepts such as BAT or BATNEEC[9] (Peacock et al., 1984). The authors find empirical evidence of negotiated compliance solutions as the outcome of a bargaining process between regulator and regulated agent, for both the UK and (the former) West Germany, despite these countries' different regulatory systems.[10] Finally, 'regulatory dealing' (see above), linked to a multiple and continuous firm–regulator relationship, is a further example of an interaction that may lead to adjusted compliance objectives (Heyes, 1998).

1.4.3   What is the objective followed by the enforcer? The Political Economy's view on enforcement

Until now it has been assumed that the enforcer is a 'benevolent welfare maximiser' in the sense that his objective in every situation is to minimise the costs for society. However, the long established so-called Political Economy considers that this assumption needs to be relaxed in order to improve the understanding of actual political outcomes (Stigler, 1971; Peltzman, 1976; Olson, 1965; Buchanan et al., 1980). Political Economy is based on the assumption that the behaviour of political and administrative actors can be traced back to rational, self-interested individuals' decisions. It allows for influence of interest groups, thus dealing with the bargaining power of interest groups, coalitions and regulators.

As far as enforcement is concerned the major issue discussed in this literature has been the question of how the utility function of the regulatory agency can be specified (Cohen, 1998). Examples of assumed preferences and behavioural functions of the regulator, alternative to welfare maximisation, are a maximisation of:

- Political support (for example Peltzman, 1976; Gray and Deily, 1996). In this case, the regulator would adjust his activity so as to support interest groups in a way which guarantees him the maximal support and would perhaps not enforce environmental regulation towards plants that could mobilise political opposition, such as regionally important employers or plants for which compliance is particularly costly.
- Compliance (for example Laplante and Rilstone, 1995). The regulator's interest here would be to reach the highest level of compliance possible, independent of the costs this strategy entails.
- Environmental benefits (Cohen, 1998, citing Jones and Scotchmer, 1990). Here, the regulator would rather focus on plants with the highest environmental pay-off per monetary unit invested in compliance.
- (Discretionary) budget maximisation (for example Lee, 1983; Downing, 1981). In this case, an excessive agency activity is imaginable.

Finally, there are also attempts at more general models of implementation and enforcement. One example is Downing's (1981) political economy model of implementing pollution laws, including an agency bureaucrat, an emitting firm manager and a pro-environmental citizen interest group manager. The aim of this model is to understand the complex interactions at play in the implementation of pollution laws. The actors here try to affect policy through political pressure to affect the agency budget and through court action. Modelled are the resulting allocations of public funds towards pollution-control, i.e. the agency's budget, and the resulting environmental quality.

1.5 And What Are the Positive Literature's Lessons?

Investigating more closely why firms actually comply shows that, in certain cases of pollution control, there are alternatives to strict enforcement schemes and therefore opportunities for control cost savings. One example is the possibility of making use of information, and thus of market forces, as an incentive for firms to comply, be it in order to avoid negative publicity or stock market devaluation. The positive literature furthermore implicitly supports the usefulness of schemes which pass responsibility on to firms, such as self-monitoring schemes: if firms did not merely react to pure economic incentives, but actually had an intrinsic motivation for compliance and honesty, self-monitoring reports might become more reliable and therefore replace public monitoring to a certain extent.

The positive literature also stresses the fact that there are rarely just two options, compliance or non-compliance. In reality there is generally scope for adjustment of regulatory requirements. In this respect the bargaining literature points out that adjustments may be advantageous to both sides, the regulator and the firm: efficiency increases of regulatory outcomes are conceivable when a regulation is adjusted to better take into account specific features of a particular case.

A discussion of likely motivations and thus behavioural functions of the enforcer introduces objective functions that are distinct from welfare objectives, and therefore can be used as a basis for actual enforcement schemes. If the enforcement budget is limited, for example, it may be useful to maximise environmental benefits rather than compliance, as the former involves a targeting of firms where enforcement measures lead to the relatively highest achievable environmental effects.

By opening regulatory and enforcement activity to personal interests, that is by introducing the fact that enforcers may pursue personal objectives and thus be influenced by interest groups, the regulatory and enforcement system becomes endogenous (Horbach, 1992). Interests and actions of one agent may influence the behaviour of others. Interventions in the system may lead, as a side effect, to unwanted reactions of other systems' parameters and the effects of the application of policy measures are not necessarily straightforward. Taking endogeneity into account points at the need to carefully assess possible inter-relationships. To increase information about environmental issues and impacts may, for example, facilitate the implementation of environmental regulation by either making use of market forces or by increasing political support.

2.   IMPLEMENTATION AS A COMPLEX
      PHENOMENON – SOME INSIGHTS FROM
      POLITICAL SCIENCES

In the political sciences literature, two broad approaches to policy
implementation can be distinguished: the 'classical' top-down view and the
revisionist critique, generally subsumed under the title of bottom-up
approaches:

• Top-down models take policy as given (while admitting inter-
  relationships between policy decisions and implementation), and evaluate
  the subsequent implementation process with particular respect to the
  attainment of the policy's goals.
• Bottom-up approaches start from a policy problem and the affected
  actors' perceptions and interests, and investigate the complex interactions
  that occur between actors, rejecting the idea of a separability of policy
  making and implementation.

While discussions of the top-down literature centre on factors influencing
implementation, reasons for an implementation deficit, and conditions which
can help successful implementation, bottom-up literature is rather focused on
an analysis of processes that occur during implementation. Over recent years
there has, however, been a cross-fertilisation between the two approaches,
with authors traditionally associated with the top-down approach responding
to and incorporating parts of the critique into their concepts. The resulting
concepts, therefore, represent syntheses of the two approaches, where it is
not always easy to make a clear distinction between the two. For sake of
clarity, it is nevertheless useful to stylise to the two original broad views.

2.1   Requirements for an Effective Implementation – the Top-Down View

2.1.1 The Oakland Project study
The main elements of the top-down approach can be illustrated through the
famous Oakland Project study of Pressman and Wildavsky. It was first
published in 1973, and subsequently expanded (see for example the 1984
edition) taking into account criticism and discussions within public policy
analysis.[11] Although it does not constitute the first evaluation study, it is
generally considered as a starting point to implementation study and as a
prominent example of the top-down view on policy implementation. It
analyses the implementation of a federal development project aimed at the
construction of public works and the employment of long-term unemployed

in Oklahoma. As the full title of the book wryly indicates – *Implementation: How Great Expectations in Washington are Dashed in Oakland; Or, Why It's Amazing that Federal Programs Work at All, This Being a Saga of the Economic Development Administration as Told by Two Sympathetic Observers Who Seek to Build Morals on a Foundation of Ruined Hopes. The Oakland Project* – this study is about implementation failures and recommendations to implementers. Taking a top-down view, the authors consider *implementation* as the process of interactions taking place after the setting of goals, and after the initial conditions such as passing of legislation and committing of funds have been met; and as the ability to induce subsequent links in the causal chain so as to obtain the desired results. Implementation is defined as 'putting policy into effect' (Pressman and Wildavsky, 1984).

In this perspective, the authors' objective is to assess factors fostering or impeding effective implementation. With the 'Oakland Project' they chose an implementation case which largely failed despite seemingly favourable starting conditions: political agreement on the programme existed and projects were speedily approved by the federal agency. Initial local agreements were obtained, funds were secured, and there were no major conflicts. The problems that prevented successful implementation were of an everyday character, aspects assumed to be 'technical details' that would sort themselves out automatically (Pressman and Wildavsky, 1984).

A few years after launching the programme, it turned out that a negligibly low number of jobs had been created, and that although there had been a substantial amount of planning of public works construction, hardly any had been completed. Pressman and Wildavsky (1984) explain the failure of the programme by the failure to recognise that ordinary circumstances present serious obstacles to implementation.

First of all, the main cause for failure lies in *the number of actors and perspectives* involved in the implementation process and the related problem of *reaching agreement*. Unexpected complexity was introduced by the high number of approvals and decisions necessary. Actors who agree on objectives may still disagree on the way to reach them. Consequently, a high number of decision points results in many opportunities for disagreement, blockage, delay, modification or adaptation of agreements. Complexity increases with the length of the causality chain and a cumulative implementation deficit is possible. A related problem is that of *maintaining agreements*, when delays lead to a change in either the participants themselves, or the understandings they had with each other.

But reasons for failure were also found in *a policy design separated from implementation*, which was insufficiently tailored to the demands of execution and thus not able to prevent complex chains of reciprocal interaction. Furthermore, indirect instead of direct means for accomplishing the objectives were chosen, which were shown to have been based on wrong assumptions about causal relationships and which did not yield the expected results. The programme was thus based on an *inadequate causal theory*.

2.1.2 Preconditions for effective implementation

The top-down view offers criteria for the evaluation of an implementation process by comparing the original policy objectives with implementation results. Top-down analysts are interested in knowing to what extent the actions of implementing officials and target groups were consistent with the procedures and objectives outlined in the policy and to what extent the policy objectives were attained over time (Sabatier, 1986a). Top-down research thus studies goal attainment or policy effectiveness.

Several authors have attempted to develop a comprehensive list of factors supposed to act as preconditions for an effective policy implementation, and to be used as a yardstick against which to assess actual implementation processes (Hogwood and Gunn, 1984; Sabatier, 1986a; Sabatier and Mazmanian, 1979). Hogwood and Gunn (1984) explicitly name their list 'preconditions for perfect implementation', Sabatier (1986a) talks about sufficient and generally necessary conditions for effective implementation. The different lists largely overlap. Merging them leads to the kind of user's manual presented below, where policy design, available resources, organisation, hierarchy and control are considered as decisive for policy outcomes.

As pointed out by Pressman and Wildavsky's study, a first crucial factor for successful implementation is the policy itself: policy failure may be caused by poor policy design. Favouring successful implementation are therefore policies that are unambiguous and based on a valid theory of, and direct relationships between, cause and effect. Tasks should be fully and in sequence correctly specified. Clear policy objectives furthermore provide a standard for evaluation and an important legal resource to implementers. The availability of adequate time and sufficient resources as well as of the required combination of resources is the second pre-condition for successful implementation of policy.

Other conditions have to do with co-ordination and control, i.e. communication amongst and co-ordination of the various elements or agencies involved. Co-ordination is facilitated by a minimal number of dependency relationships and intervening links between the implementation agency and other agencies involved in the implementation structure. A minimal number of intervening links also furthers the necessary understanding of, and agreement on, objectives, i.e. the maintenance of political support throughout the implementation process. According to the top-down view of implementation as 'putting policy into effect', control of those in authority over implementing actors becomes a decisive factor for successful implementation. Where control is not possible, i.e. where discretion is unavoidable, control needs to be made up for by the commitment of implementation officials.

The possible influence of factors external to the implementation process on policy outcomes is also acknowledged. Successful implementation requires that external factors, such as changes in socio-economic conditions or political opposition, do not impose insurmountable constraints (Hogwood and Gunn, 1984; Sabatier, 1986a; Sabatier and Mazmanian, 1979).

2.2   The Bottom-Up Critique in Short

The theoretical basis of the top-down view has been criticised for some of its central assumptions by a variety of authors grouped together under the title of 'bottom-up' approaches. They share the view that 'the bottom matters' (Smith, 1997).

According to this strand of literature top-down analysis gives too much attention to (state) central decision-makers, ignoring the importance of other actors. It is seen to over-estimate the role of the official policy actors for policy outcomes and their control of the implementation process and of the performance of actors that carry out the tasks (Rhodes and Marsh, 1992; Hjern and Porter, 1981; Smith, 2000). Specifically, by neglecting the (necessary) discretion of street-level bureaucrats such as implementation agents (Lipsky, 1980; Hudson, 1989), the top-down approach is thought to risk ignoring the adaptive strategies of these actors. Bottom-up theorists believe discretionary power to have a high influence on implementation outcomes. Furthermore, with its focus on central objectives the top-down view is criticised for risking ignoring unintended consequences of government action (Rhodes and Marsh, 1992).

According to the bottom-up view it is, furthermore, not possible to completely plan a priori the implementation process. The conception of the implementation process representing a causal chain between conditions and consequences that can be planned is thus not supported. Instead of seeing implementation as a control or a 'management problem', the focus shifts to interactions between actors who seek to put policy into effect, i.e. to actors on whom implementation depends, and those whose interests are affected by the policy. Implementation, therefore, is viewed as an interactive process, the policy which is actually implemented will adapt to all these factors and differ from the policy originally formulated, with the bottom then taking part in policy (re-)formulation (Hjern and Porter, 1981; Barrett and Fudge, 1981; Smith, 2000). In the eyes of the bottom-up approach implementation shapes policy – as opposed to the top-down view of policy shaping implementation – and the theoretical distinction between policy formulation and implementation is considered as being inadequate (Barrett and Fudge, 1981; Ham and Hill, 1993; Majone and Wildavsky, 1979).

2.3   Issues Arising from the Bottom-Up Critique

If a restriction of the analysis to actors who are part of the administrative (functional) hierarchy charged with the implementation of a policy is rejected as being too narrow; if policy makers are denied a strong influence on implementation outcomes, who then are the actors relevant for implementation and its analysis? And what shapes their interaction? What are the reasons for actors to bargain? What role does learning play? And what does all this imply for policy evaluation?

2.3.1   Discretion of the local implementer

As to the question of which actors are decisive for implementation outcomes, a predominant role was assigned to a specific actor type, the street-level bureaucrat, by Lipsky (1980). This term describes the agents directly interacting with the target group of a policy; in the case of environmental policy these are usually pollution control inspectors. Street-level bureaucrats' discretion relates for example to whether or not they apply sanctions and how much and to whom, which behaviour they overlook, how they allocate resources, whether they delay decisions or withhold information. Lipsky suggests that these actors enjoy considerable power due to discretion and are thus of central importance for policy outcomes (Hudson, 1989).

While this discretion was also acknowledged by the top-down view, differences between the two approaches consist in its assessment. Whereas in a top-down view efficient implementation requires control of discretion, more bottom-up orientated authors consider street-level discretion not only as inescapable but also as desirable.

Discretion is considered as *unavoidable* for various reasons: simply because it is impossible to completely control behaviour but also due to a frequent lack in resources of street-level actors, be it financial means, information or time. Discretion is also unavoidable due to uncertainties, as the reaction of clients may be unpredictable. Agents must therefore deal with ambiguous situations, weigh up alternatives and are likely to develop routines of coping with their work (Hudson, 1989).

Discretion at the local level is also *desirable* in order to use the skill, expertise, knowledge, specialised problem-solving capabilities, and better information level of those who are closest to a problem and who are assumed to have a greater ability to influence the problem. Leaving them some discretionary power allows them to react to a complex and changing environment, to adapt to unanticipated situations, as well as to deal with contradictory objectives placed upon them by the top (Elmore, 1979). Street-level bureaucrats are assumed to adjust their activities and objectives to better match their overall ability to perform. Efforts to more strictly control street-level bureaucrats may have negative effects such as evasive behaviour (Hudson, 1989).

2.3.2 The role of interaction, negotiation and bargaining

In practice, implementation and enforcement of regulations involve a continuation of complex processes of bargaining, and negotiation between actors from the top and the bottom. They do not primarily depend on prescriptions and control (Barrett and Fudge, 1981; Hanf, 1982; Hill, 1997a). Elmore (1979) even considers bargaining as a key element of implementation, since the resources of those affected by a policy must be mobilised.

Bargaining during the implementation phase of a policy may be also necessary because of lack of control over implementers, remaining interest conflicts or limited resources, necessary adjustments to changes in the environment or to make policy more concrete. The latter refers to policy not being completely specified, which could have several reasons: conflicts that could not be resolved during the formulation phase or a lack of information at that stage. Or it may be due to the belief that implementers may be in a better position to make decisions, and that day-to-day decisions need to involve negotiation and compromise with powerful groups (Ham and Hill, 1993).

Literature on implementation dealing with networks of actors stresses interactions of actors from all levels, instead of giving most emphasis to either actors at the top or at the bottom (street-level). In this view negotiation is necessary to cope with the complexity of the numerous independent actions involved in implementation (Hjern and Porter, 1981). This is also in line with empirical findings of implementation studies showing that the development and execution of policy involves numerous agencies and interest groups at all levels of government (Sabatier, 1991). In this literature the view is thus enlarged from authoritative relationships and single implementation entities to partly self-selected clusters of public and private actors coming together in an implementation process (Jordan, 1995). The emphasis shifts to studying the interactions between the actors involved, to what is actually going on (Barrett and Fudge, 1981) and implementation is thus modelled as a process where policy makers and implementers negotiate, bargain and make compromises.

Issues of co-ordination are addressed without recourse to hierarchical concepts (Fudge and Barrett, 1981). Different drivers behind the co-ordination of behaviour are suggested: actors may view the policy as an (instrumentally) important interest (Hjern and Porter, 1981), they may share beliefs (values and causal assumptions) (Sabatier, 1988) or they might be connected by resource interdependencies (Smith, 1997). Resource interdependencies may lead to exchange relationships, where actors perceive mutual benefits from interaction, or to power dependency relationships, where relations are formed when the motivated party is powerful enough to induce the other to interact (Hjern and Porter, 1981; Zafonte and Sabatier, 1998). It is likely that participants have various motives; even if actors share a general interest they participate partly for their own reasons and self-interest (Hjern and Porter, 1981; Sabatier, 1998). It can be assumed that consensus among actors needs to be constantly renewed through negotiations redefining the expected gains and the conditions of participation (Hanf and O'Toole, 1992).

Once negotiation and bargaining between agencies and actors involved is acknowledged, policy can no longer be seen as fixed but rather as a series of intentions which may be modified whenever actors bargain. Implementation then can no longer be characterised as a distinct and sequential process from policy formulation to goal attainment but rather as a continuum of policy and action in which an interactive and negotiative process is taking place over time. Policy and action influence each other reciprocally. Policy decisions can be seen as taken by the top, but decisions of lower level actors may effectively limit hierarchical influence and by this alter policy (Barrett and Fudge, 1981). In this view, the implementation process becomes fluid and indistinct (Jordan, 1995).

2.3.3 The role of learning and policy change

Some authors suggest that for a policy to be effective it may be more important to make learning processes possible than to make the best decision in advance (Eberg, 1997, citing Kaufmann, 1986). Learning may be relevant in terms of the ability to test the environment and to correct mistakes or in order to adjust to or overcome unforeseen obstacles. But once policy learning is acknowledged – just as was the case with bargaining – original policy objectives or the means to reach them may be re-defined, with implementation becoming a dynamic and evolutionary concept.

A model offering an explanation of how policy learning and policy change come about was suggested by Sabatier (1988) with his 'Advocacy Coalition Framework'. Sabatier considers policy-oriented learning as aiming at a better understanding of causal relationships, consequences of policy alternatives as well as perceptions about external dynamics. He assumes that actors co-operate in coalitions[12] based on their shared beliefs, defined as a set of basic values, causal assumptions, normative beliefs and problem perceptions, concerning a specific policy issue, such as air pollution control, in order to influence policy. The author's focus on belief systems is explained by his assumption that public policies or programmes involve implicit theories about how to achieve their objectives. They involve for example value priorities, perceptions of causal relationships, the magnitude of a problem or the effectiveness of policy instruments. Policies can therefore be conceptualised in the same way as belief systems, and consequently policy change can be conceptualised as changes in dominant belief systems (Sabatier, 1988).

Actors aim to reach their policy goals over time by seeking to influence government decisions in a policy area, i.e. by trying to translate their belief into public policy (Sabatier, 1988; Eberg, 1997). Generally, there exist one or several competing advocacy coalitions for a policy issue. Each coalition will adopt a strategy believed to further its policy objectives. According to Sabatier (1988), policy change and evolution are induced by a) the efforts of advocacy coalitions to influence government programmes according to their belief system, which may be induced by policy learning and b) changes in factors external to the policy sub-system. How exactly programmes are implemented is not the direct focus of this model but appears to be taken for granted (Lane, 1987). This seems to assume a mechanism where, once a consensus about policy objectives is reached, implementation of these objectives poses no significant problems.

2.4   What does the Political Science Analysis tell us about Policy Evaluation?

The separate elements of the bottom-up based view, discretion, bargaining and learning, can be seen as related to the impossibility of ex ante planning. When it is considered impossible to completely foresee, plan and control all steps of the implementation process, when discretion is not only necessary but also desirable, when bargaining and negotiation are considered necessary to reach compliance, then adaptations to the policy to be implemented and divergence from original objectives are likely. Authors supporting this view consider such policy adaptation not only as necessary but also as desirable in order to allow for learning, correction of mistakes and adaptation to unexpected events and changes in conditions or context. But adaptability involves a trade-off: the more adaptable an idea or a policy is, the more likely is its realisation in some form but the less likely is it that it will emerge as originally intended (Majone and Wildavsky, 1979).

Unlike the top-down approach which offers a clear benchmark for evaluation of actual implementation processes, focusing on intended outcomes (Hill, 1997b), the introduction of a dynamic view, of notions such as learning, evolution, change and adaptability under the bottom-up approaches therefore leads to the problem of against which objective to actually measure implementation processes and outcomes (what is a success or failure? What is compliance?).

When objectives change due to adaptation and evolution of policy, the measure for what is successful implementation gets lost and it becomes unclear as to how to evaluate the implementation of a policy. Implementation is then no longer solely about achieving original objectives but also about what has since been learned, and implementation becomes a moving target (Majone and Wildavsky, 1979; Browne and Wildavsky, 1983b). This has repercussions on learning as well: it is difficult to learn from experience when performance gaps are difficult to assess (Sabatier, 1988). It is suggested that when policy is evolutionary or when the objective is to assess whether policy adapts well to its environment, evaluation should take place during implementation and become continuous as well. Continuous evaluation furthermore makes continuous learning processes possible (Pressman and Wildavsky, 1984; Browne and Wildavsky, 1983a).

The earlier direct confrontation between bottom-up and top-down views seems to have been overcome (Sabatier, 1986b; O'Toole, 2000) and has given way to a more pragmatic treatment by acknowledging that either approach or combinations of both may have advantages in certain situations. A top-down approach to implementation study, for example, may be justified in cases where clear policy objectives exist.[13] Furthermore, instead of only focusing on original policy objectives an implementation analysis may study where and when objectives of which the effects are measurable are formulated. Evaluation would here have to evolve with policy and its implementation. Furthermore, not a priori distinguishing between the two frameworks may open the view for both implementation outcomes in accordance with original objectives and unplanned events and effects as well as the factors explaining these results.

However an increasing difficulty in deriving results stems from the high number of potential explanatory variables that are covered by political science models of implementation (O'Toole, 2000) that become more and more sophisticated. The related danger is that these variables are not observable, and that analyses may remain descriptive.

3. CONCLUSIONS

With the disciplines Economics and Political Sciences two rather complementary views on implementation were presented here.

Normative economics focuses on the enforcement step within implementation and takes an optimality view. Its concern is thus efficiency. Under the economist's view perfect control is possible but may be undesirable because of the compliance or enforcement costs it may entail. In the economics of enforcement, the issue is socially efficient enforcement and the existence of an implementation gap does not therefore pose a problem in itself. The positive economics approaches are concerned with real world cases. What is efficient under the normative view may not necessarily be efficient under a view taking into account the influence of pressure groups and political processes.

Political Science deals with effectiveness and sees policy as a process. It treats the implementation issue in a less homogeneous way than Economics. One strand of literature, presenting the top-down view of policy implementation, focuses on an analysis of the level of goal attainment or policy effectiveness and factors explaining implementation deficits. Implementation is seen as 'putting policy into effect' where compliance with central objectives is the yardstick of success and failure. Under this view maximal compliance with policy objectives is desirable independent of the costs it may entail, and the question is rather how maximal compliance can be reached. Control becomes a central issue. Successful implementation is seen as depending, next to an adequate policy design and sufficient resources, upon the linkages between the actors in the implementation chain, on control and perfect co-ordination, and on a monitoring of local discretion.

A second and increasingly used strand, the vast literature subsumed under the heading of 'bottom-up approaches', tends to be much more descriptive, being rather concerned with understanding the interactions in a particular policy sector than with implementation of a specific policy (Sabatier, 1986a). The effectiveness view here becomes softer. The definition of what implementation is changes from 'putting policy into effect' to 'getting something done'. This literature takes a more negative view on the possibility of controlling and planning implementation processes and gives up the notion of goal attainment and its assessment. Instead, it focuses on the question of why and how actors interact in order to mobilise resources necessary to reach objectives and in how far this interaction leads to adjustments of the original policy. Other issues than control, such as the adaptability of policy to local requirements or a changing context and the ability of actors involved in implementation to learn, become central. Discretion here is desirable. Policy objectives are subsequently much less clear. By allowing for learning, for policy adaptation and change, the benchmark for an evaluation of effectiveness becomes less obvious, policy is no longer seen as a fixed starting point but becomes evolutionary.

Although the research agendas of Economics and Political Science differ, bottom-up approaches show similarities to positive economics approaches by putting emphasis on interest group influence on policy and policy outcomes and by this allowing for bargaining. What Economics could learn from Political Science is a necessity to give more room to positive approaches by putting more emphasis on discretionary power and adjustments of policy during implementation, and to enlarge the perspective to the policy formulation step by including questions of the implementability of a policy.

NOTES

1. This is strictly correct only in the case of risk neutral agents (see below). Otherwise, the effect of raising either variable on deterrence depends on the polluter's specific risk behaviour (i.e. on the elasticities of response of offences to changes in p and f).
2. Here, harm is reflected by x, where the exact level of harm is dependent on the level and the kind of offence committed.
3. As a second positive effect, fines can be used to compensate victims.
4. The threat of a third group for firms repeatedly found non-compliant condemning them to perpetual monitoring without possibility of escape from this state is estimated to provide an even higher deterrence effect and to lead to considerably lower monitoring costs.
5. As a second advantage, self-reporting may reduce the risk for firms, as pay-offs become more certain, i.e. firms reporting their behaviour bear certain rather than uncertain sanctions (Kaplow and Shavell, 1994).
6. Over-deterrence characterises for example a situation where the regulated agent spends more resources on abating pollution than is socially optimal.
7. The division between normative and positive theory is not very strict: various papers look at certain issues from a positive and a normative point of view. The bargaining literature, just to give one example, starts from the empirical finding of negotiated results. By this it takes positive aspects into account, although it models them in a normative way.
8. In his study on the environment and enforcement of water regulations in the UK, focusing on the enforcement work at a street level and on compliance behaviour of plants, the author finds a predominance of what he calls a compliance strategy. Such a strategy is preventive and aims to attain the broad objectives of legislation, gives emphasis to remedial measures rather than to punishment and is reluctant to exploit enforcement opportunities provided by formal law.

Hawkins (1984), furthermore, finds evidence for the use of indirect forms of control and for enforcement agents aiming at efficiency in the sense of goal attainment at least cost to them and their work. This leads to a case to case treatment of plants.

9. BAT denotes 'best available technology' and BATNEEC 'best available technology not entailing excessive costs'.

10. As a positive side effect they furthermore find that bargaining between plant personnel and inspectors helps to acquire information.

11. With this, the authors' view on implementation is qualified by some points closer to the bottom-up view.

12. Relevant actors come from different institutions interested in the policy issue, i.e. actors from various levels of government active in policy formulation and implementation, but also journalists, researchers, interest groups and policy analysts.

13. This may more frequently be the case of environmental regulation than of social programmes, which were often the object of Political Sciences based implementation studies.

REFERENCES

Amacher, G.S. and A.S. Malik (1996), 'Bargaining in Environmental Regulation and the Ideal Regulator', *Journal of Environmental Economics and Management*, **30**, pp. 233–253.

Amacher, G.S. and A.S. Malik (1998), 'Instrument Choice When Regulators and Firms Bargain', *Journal of Environmental Economics and Management*, **35**, pp. 225–241.

Badrinath, S.G. and P. Bolster (1996), 'The Role of Market Forces in EPA Enforcement', *Journal of Regulatory Economics*, **10** (2), pp. 165–181.

Barrett, S. and C. Fudge (1981), 'Examining the Policy–Action Relationship', in S. Barrett and C. Fudge (eds), *Policy and Action. Essays on the Implementation of Public Policy*, London: Methuen.

Baumol, W.J. and W.E. Oates (1988), *The Theory of Environmental Policy*, Cambridge: Cambridge University Press.

Becker, G.S. (1968), 'Crime and Punishment: An Economic Approach', *Journal of Political Economy*, **76**, pp. 169–217.

Bontems, P. and G. Rotillon (2000), 'Honesty in Environmental Compliance Games', *European Journal of Law and Economics*, **10** (1), pp. 31–41.

Browne, A. and A. Wildavsky (1983a), 'Implementation as Mutual Adaptation', in J.L. Pressman and A. Wildavsky (eds) (1984), *Implementation: How Great Expectations in Washington Are Dashed in Oakland; Or, Why It's Amazing that Federal Programs Work at All, This Being a Saga of the Economic Development*

Administration as Told by Two Sympathetic Observers Who Seek to Build Morals on a Foundation of Ruined Hopes. The Oakland Project, Third Edition, Expanded, Berkeley, Los Angeles, London: University of California Press.

Browne, A. and A. Wildavsky (1983b), 'What Should Evaluation Mean to Implementation?', in J.L. Pressman and A. Wildavsky (eds) (1984), *Implementation: How Great Expectations in Washington Are Dashed in Oakland; Or, Why It's Amazing that Federal Programs Work at All, This Being a Saga of the Economic Development Administration as Told by Two Sympathetic Observers Who Seek to Build Morals on a Foundation of Ruined Hopes. The Oakland Project*, Third Edition, Expanded, Berkeley, Los Angeles, London: University of California Press.

Buchanan, J.M., R.D. Tollison, and G. Tullock (1980), *Towards a Theory of the Rent-Seeking Society*, College Station Texas: A & M University.

Cohen, M.A. (1998), *Monitoring and Enforcement of Environmental Policy*, Owen Graduate School of Management, Nashville: Vanderbilt University.

Downing, P.B. (1981), 'A Political Economy Model of Implementing Pollution Laws', *Journal of Environmental Economics and Management*, **8**, pp. 255–271.

Eberg, J. (1997), *Waste Policy and Learning – Policy Dynamics of Waste Management and Waste Incineration in the Netherlands and Baravia*, Delft, The Netherlands: Uitgeverij Eburon.

Elmore, R.F. (1979), 'Backward Mapping: Implementation Research and Policy Decisions', *Political Science Quarterly*, **94**, pp. 601–616.

Frey, B.S. and F. Oberholzer-Gee (1996), 'Zum Konflikt zwischen intrinsischer Motivation und umweltpolitischer Instrumentenwahl', in H. Siebert (ed.), *Elemente einer rationalen Umweltpolitik: Expertisen zur umweltpolitischen Neuorientierung*, Tübingen: Institut für Weltwirtschaft an der Universität Kiel.

Fudge, C. and S. Barrett (1981), 'Reconstructing the Field of Analysis', in S. Barrett and C. Fudge, *Policy and Action. Essays on the Implementation of Public Policy*, London: Methuen.

Gabel, H.L. and B. Sinclair-Desgagné (1993), 'Managerial Incentives and Environmental Compliance', *Journal of Environmental Economics and Management*, **24**, pp. 229–240.

Gray, W.B. and M.E. Deily (1996), 'Compliance and Enforcement: Air Pollution Regulation in the US Steel Industry', *Journal of Environmental Economics and Management*, **31**, pp. 96–111.

Ham, C. and M. Hill (1993), *The Policy Process in the Modern Capitalist State*, Hemel Hempstead: Harvester Wheatsheaf.

Hanf, K. (1982), 'Regulatory Structures: Enforcement as Implementation', *European Journal of Political Research*, **10**, pp. 159–172.

Hanf, K. and L.J. O'Toole (1992), 'Revisiting Old friends: Networks, Implementation Structures and the Management of Inter-organizational Relations', *European Journal of Political Research*, **21**, pp. 163–180.

Harford, J.D. (1991), 'Measurement Error and State-Dependent Pollution Control Enforcement', *Journal of Environmental Economics and Management*, **21**, pp. 67–81.

Harrington, W. (1988), 'Enforcement Leverage when Penalties are Restricted', *Journal of Public Economics*, **37**, pp. 29–53.

Hawkins, K. (1984), *Environment and Enforcement. Regulation and the Social Definition of Pollution*, Oxford: Oxford Socio-Legal Studies, Clarendon Press.

Heyes, A. (1996), 'Cutting Environmental Penalties to Protect the Environment', *Journal of Public Economics*, **60**, pp. 251–265.

Heyes, A.G. (1998), 'Making Things Stick: Enforcement and Compliance', *Oxford Review of Economic Policy*, **14** (4), pp. 50–63.

Heyes, A. (2000), 'Implementing Environmental Regulation: Enforcement and Compliance', *Journal of Regulatory Economics*, **17** (2), pp. 107–129.

Hill, M. (ed.) (1997a), *The Policy Process in the Modern State*, London et al.: Prentice Hall.

Hill, M. (ed.) (1997b), *The Policy Process – A Reader*, London et al.: Prentice Hall.

Hjern, B. and D.O. Porter (1981), 'Implementation Structures – A New Unit of Administrative Analysis', *Organization Studies*, **2**, pp. 211–27.

Hogwood, B. and L. Gunn (1984), 'Why "Perfect Implementation" is Unattainable', in B.W. Hogwood and L. Gunn (eds), *Policy Analysis for the Real World*, Oxford: Oxford University Press.

Horbach, Jens (1992), *Neue Politische Ökonomie und Umweltpolitik*, Frankfurt/New York: Campus Verlag.

Hudson, B. (1989), 'Michael Lipsky and Street Level Bureaucracy – A Neglected Perspective', in L. Barton (ed.), *Disability and Dependency*, London: Falmer Press.

Jones, C.A. and S. Scotchmer (1990), 'The Social Cost of Uniform Regulatory Standards in a Hierarchical Government', *Journal of Environmental Economics and Management*, **19**, pp. 61–72.

Jordan, A. (1995), *Implementation Failure or Policy Making? How Do We Theorise the Implementation of European Union (EU) Environmental Legislation?*, CSERGE Working Paper GEC 95-18, Italy/Milano: Fondazione Eni Enrico Mattei.

Jost, P.-J. (1997), 'Monitoring, Appeal and Investigation: the Enforcement and Legal Process', *Journal of Regulatory Economics*, **12**, pp. 127–146.

Kaplow, L. and S. Shavell (1994), 'Optimal Law Enforcement with Self-Reporting Behaviour', *Journal of Political Economy*, **102** (3), pp. 583–606.

Kaufmann, F.X. (1986), 'The Relationship between Guidance, Control and Evaluation', in F.X. Kaufmann, V. Ostrom and G. Majone (eds), *Guidance, Control and Evaluation in the Public Sector*, Berlin: De Gruyter.

Lane, J.E. (1987), 'Implementation, Accountability and Trust', *European Journal of Political Research*, **15** (5), pp. 527–46.

Laplante, B. and P. Rilstone (1995), *Environmental Inspections and Emissions of the Pulp and Paper Industry: The Case of Quebec*, http://www.worldbank.org/html/dec/Publications/Workpapers/wps1447.

Lee, D.R. (1983), 'Monitoring and Budget Maximization in the Control of Pollution', *Economic Inquiry*, **21**, pp. 565–575.

Lee, D.R. (1984), 'The Economics of Enforcing Pollution Taxation', *Journal of Environmental Economics and Management*, **11**, pp. 147–160.

Lehmann, M. (1997), *Eine ökonomische Theorie informalen Verwaltungshandelns im Umweltschutz*, Diskussionsbeiträge des Fachbereichs Wirtschaftswissenschaft an der Freien Universität Berlin, Volkswirtschaftliche Reihe, Nr. 23/1997, Berlin.

Lipsky, M. (1980), 'Street-level Bureaucracy – An Introduction', in M. Lipsky, *Street-level Bureaucracy: Dilemmas of the Individual in Public Services*, New York: Russel Sage Foundation.

Majone, G. and A. Wildavsky (1979), 'Implementation as Evolution', in J.L. Pressman and A. Wildavsky (eds) (1984), *Implementation: How Great Expectations in Washington Are Dashed in Oakland; Or, Why It's Amazing that Federal Programs Work at All, This Being a Saga of the Economic Development Administration as Told by Two Sympathetic Observers Who Seek to Build Morals on a Foundation of Ruined Hopes. The Oakland Project*, Third Edition, Expanded, Berkeley, Los Angeles, London: University of California Press.

Malik, A.S. (1990), 'Markets for Pollution Control when Firms Are Noncompliant', *Journal of Environmental Economics and Management*, **18**, pp. 97–106.

Malik, A.S. (1992), 'Enforcement Costs and the Choice of Policy Instruments for Controlling Pollution', *Economic Inquiry*, **XXX**, pp. 714-721.

Malik, A.S. (1993), 'Self-Reporting and the Design of Policies for Regulating Stochastic Pollution', *Journal of Environmental Economics and Management*, **24** (3), pp. 241–257.

Naysnerski, W. and T. Tietenberg (1992), 'Private Enforcement of Federal Environmental Law', *Land Economics*, **68** (1), pp. 28–48.

Nowell, C. and J. Shogren (1994), 'Challenging the Enforcement of Environmental Regulation', *Journal of Regulatory Economics*, **6**, pp. 265–282.

Oh, Y. (1995), 'Surveillance or Punishment? A Second-Best Theory of Pollution Regulation', *International Economic Journal*, **9** (3), pp. 89–101.

Olson, M. (1965), *The Logic of Collective Action: Public Goods and the Theory of Groups*, Oxford: Harvard University Press.

O'Toole, L.J. (2000), 'Research on Policy Implementation: Assessment and Prospects', *Journal of Public Administration – Research and Theory*, **10** (2), pp. 263–288.

Peacock, A., M. Rickets and J. Robinson (eds) (1984), *The Regulation Game. How British and West German Companies Bargain with Government*, New York: Basil Blackwell.

Peltzman, S. (1976), 'Towards a More General Theory of Regulation', *Journal of Law and Economics*, **19**, pp. 211–248.

Polinsky, A.M. and S. Shavell (1979), 'The Optimal Trade-off Between the Probability and Magnitude of Fines', *American Economic Review*, **69** (3), pp. 880–891.

Polinsky, A.M. and S. Shavell (2000), 'The Economic Theory of Public Enforcement of Law', *Journal of Economic Literature*, **XXXVI** (March), pp. 45–76.

Pressman, J.L. and A. Wildavsky (eds) (1984), *Implementation: How Great Expectations in Washington Are Dashed in Oakland; Or, Why It's Amazing that Federal Programs Work at All, This Being a Saga of the Economic Development Administration as Told by Two Sympathetic Observers Who Seek to Build Morals on a Foundation of Ruined Hopes. The Oakland Project*, Third Edition, Expanded, Berkeley, Los Angeles, London: University of California Press.

Rhodes, R.A.W. and D. Marsh (1992), '"Thatcherism": An Implementation Perspective', in D. Marsh and R.A.W. Rhodes (eds), *Implementing Thatcherite Policies. Audit of an Era*, Buckingham, England; Philadelphia: Open University Press.

Sabatier, P.A. (1986a), 'Top-down and Bottom-up Approaches to Implementation Research: A Critical Analysis and Suggested Synthesis', *Journal of Public Policy*, **6**, pp. 21–48.

Sabatier, P.A. (1986b), 'What Can We Learn from Implementation Research?', in F.X. Kaufmann et al. (eds), *Guidance, Control, and Evaluation in the Public Sector. The Bielefeld Interdisciplinary Project*, Berlin, New York: Walter de Gruyter.

Sabatier, P.A. (1988), 'An Advocacy Coalition Framework of Policy Change and the Role of Policy-oriented Learning Therein', *Policy Sciences*, **21**, pp. 129–168.

Sabatier, P.A. (1991), 'Towards Better Theories of the Policy Process. Political Science and Public Policy', *Political Science & Politics*, **XXIV** (2), pp. 144–156.

Sabatier, P.A. and D. Mazmanian (1979), 'The Conditions of Effective Implementation: A Guide to Accomplishing Policy Objectives', *Policy Analysis*, **5**, pp. 481–504.

Segerson, K. and T. Tietenberg (1992), 'The Structure of Penalties in Environmental Enforcement: An Economic Analysis', *Journal of Environmental Economics and Management*, **23**, pp. 179–200.

Shavell, S. (1985), 'Criminal Law and the Optimal Use of Non-monetary Sanctions as a Deterrent', *Columbia Law Review*, **85**, pp. 1232–1262.

Sinclair-Desgagné, B. (1994), 'La mise en vigeur des politiques environnementales et l'organisation de la firme', *L'Actualité Economique – Revue d'analyse économique*, **70** (2), June, pp. 211–224.

Smith, A. (1997), *Integrated Pollution Control – Change and Continuity in the UK Industrial Pollution Policy Network*, Studies in Green Research, Aldershot et al.: Ashgate Publishing Limited.

Smith, A. (2000), *Fitting in with Brussels: Implementing the Urban Waste Water Treatment Directive in England and Wales*, SPRU research paper in the framework of the TEP – Technology and Environmental Policy project funded under European Commission DGXII Framework IV Environment and Climate Programme, University of Sussex, Brighton.

Stigler, G.J. (1971), 'The Theory of Economic Regulation', *Bell Journal of Economics and Management Science*, **2**, pp. 3–21.

Swierzbinski, J.E. (1994), 'Guilty until Proven Innocent – Regulation with Costly and Limited Enforcement', *Journal of Environmental Economics and Management*, **27**, pp. 127–146.

Zafonte, M. and P. Sabatier (1998), 'Shared Beliefs and Imposed Interdependencies as Determinants of Ally Networks in Overlapping Subsystems', *Journal of Theoretical Politics*, **10** (4), pp. 473–505.

4. The Large Combustion Plant Directive (88/609/EEC): an effective instrument for SO$_2$ pollution abatement?

Malcolm Eames

1. INTRODUCTION

The Large Combustion Plant Directive 88/609/EEC (here referred to as the LCP-Directive) was one of the most high profile and controversial pieces of European environmental legislation of the 1980s. First proposed by the European Commission in 1983, negotiation of the Directive was a long drawn out, highly politicised and contested process. Despite these difficulties, and a number of 'gaps' in the implementation of the LCP-Directive's administrative requirements, we found substantial over-compliance with the Directive's national emission ceilings for sulphur dioxide (SO$_2$) in all four of the countries considered: i.e. Germany, the Netherlands, France and the United Kingdom. How can this picture be explained? What role have the monitoring and enforcement activities of national regulatory agencies played? What other factors are important in determining environmental goal attainment, and what can the story of this Directive tell us about the cost effectiveness of the various national implementation processes?

This chapter seeks to answer these questions. A number of key variables are identified including: regulatory context and choice of policy instrument; public and political awareness; interactions with both other environmental and non-environmental policies; market structure and dynamics; and technology choice and path dependency. At the same time, however, the LCP-Directive itself is found to have had little direct impact on the various national outcomes obtained.

First of all, however, the principal requirements of the LCP-Directive are described, and placed in context with respect to the development of the broader European regulatory framework for the control of sulphur emissions. The following section details distinct and contrasting national case studies of the implementation of the LCP-Directive or, where appropriate, the equivalent prior national legislation for the four countries considered. Environmental goal attainment with the Directive's national SO_2 emissions ceilings, as well as with sectoral, national and UNECE objectives are reviewed. Compliance with the Directive's administrative requirements is then briefly discussed, and the relative cost effectiveness of the various national policy processes analysed. Finally, the concluding section of this chapter draws particular attention to the importance of policy interactions, market structure and dynamics of regulated industries, and technology choice and path dependency with respect to the environmental outcomes and costs of implementing European environmental policies.

2.   BACKGROUND

2.1   Directive (88/609/EEC) and Scope of Research

A 'daughter' Directive to the 1984 Air Framework Directive (84/360/EEC), the LCP-Directive regulates emissions to air from new and existing large combustion plant: defined as boiler plant with a thermal input equal or greater than 50MWth (Art 1). The approach taken by the Directive to the regulation of emissions from new plant was classic 'command and control'. Establishing uniform emission limits values (by plant size and fuel type), for a range of pollutants: sulphur dioxide (SO_2), nitrogen oxides (NO_x) and dust (Art 4 & Annexes III to VII).[1]

By contrast the approach taken to the regulation of 'existing plant', i.e. those licensed before 1 July 1987 (Art 2, 10), was far more flexible. The Directive established staged aggregate national emissions reduction targets (or national emissions ceilings), for SO_2 and NO_x, for each Member State (see Table 4.1). These national targets were differentiated to take into account variations in national circumstances, including abatement costs. What is more, the choice of policy instruments to achieve these targets was left to Member States.

Table 4.1 LCP-Directive SO_2 and NO_x reduction targets for case study
*   countries*

	SO_2% reduction over 1980 emissions			NO_x% reduction over 1980 emissions	
	1993	1998	2003	1993	1998
Germany (West)	40	60	70	20	40
Netherlands	40	60	70	20	40
France	40	60	70	20	40
United Kingdom	20	40	60	15	30

Article 17 of the LCP-Directive required Member States to 'bring into force the laws, regulations and administrative provisions necessary to comply with this Directive no later than 30 June 1990', whilst Article 3 required Member States to draw up 'programmes for the progressive reduction of total annual emissions from existing plant' by 1 July 1990. Articles 16, and Annex IX, imposed various monitoring and reporting requirements. Member States were required to inform the Commission of the details of their national emissions reduction programmes by 31 December 1990. They were also required to ensure appropriate monitoring of emissions, to prepare annual national emissions inventories, for SO_2 and NO_X, and submit periodic progress reports to the Commission.

Implementation of the Directive's requirements with respect to existing plants is of particular interest from a theoretical perspective because of the freedom of choice provided to Member States in the selection of policy instruments. By contrast the requirements with respect to new plants left relatively little room for differences in implementation practice. The analysis presented in this chapter therefore focuses upon implementation of the Directive's existing plant requirements, with particular emphasis upon the electricity supply industry (ESI): historically the largest single sectoral source of SO_2 emissions from LCP in all four of the countries considered. Furthermore, given the differing abatement options and technologies, as well as national and international (UNECE) regulator contexts involved, this analysis is restricted to developments with respect to SO_2 emissions from existing plants. Implementation of the Directive's requirements with respect to NO_X emissions from existing plants are therefore excluded from this analysis.

2.2   European SO_2 Policy: a Dynamic Patchwork of Regulatory Demands

Sulphur dioxide is an acid gas at normal temperatures and pressures. As an anthropogenic pollutant, it is formed principally by the combustion of fossil fuels containing sulphur, such as coal, lignite and heavier petroleum/oil products. Sulphur dioxide emissions are known to cause damage to human health, and the degradation of both natural and built environments.

There is a long history of local controls on SO_2 emissions in many industrialised countries. Historically such regulation has chiefly concerned the height and location of chimneys, the aim being to disperse and dilute the emissions, so avoiding acute local pollution problems. More recently the long-range transport of SO_2 which resulted from the construction of taller chimneys, has been linked to the problem of 'acid rain': resulting in the degradation of forests, lakes, buildings and other man-made structures. These concerns can be traced back to the 1960s, when scientific studies first linked sulphur emissions from continental Europe and the acidification of Scandinavian lakes.[2] Sweden first placed the issue on the international environmental policy agenda in a paper tabled at the 1972 United Nations Conference on the Human Environment in Stockholm (Boehmer-Christiansen, 1995, p. 22). Further studies in the mid-1970s supported the hypothesis that the long-range transport of air pollutants was possible.[3] This underlined the need for international co-operation to tackle the acidification problem. At the same time concern began to grow in West Germany over the so-called 'Waldsterben' or dying of the forests. In 1979, in response to these problems, thirty-four national governments and the European Community signed the United Nations Economic Commission for Europe (UNECE) Convention on Long-range Transboundary Air Pollution in Geneva. The Convention, which entered into force in 1983, was the first legally binding international agreement to deal with air pollution on a broad regional basis.

Since 1979 a host of further national, European and international (UNECE) policies, specifically aimed at abating sulphur emissions, have followed. Furthermore, the strictness of the regulatory objectives embodied in these policies has progressively ratcheted up over time, as both scientific knowledge of the damage caused by SO_2 and the availability and scope for abatement measures have improved. This ongoing process of policy formulation and target setting, often operating simultaneously, by several levels of governance, has provided ample scope for the emergence of both regulatory uncertainty and the strategic anticipation of future regulatory demands. Table 4.2 provides a selective illustration of the dynamic nature and increasing complexity of the European regulatory environment for the control of sulphur emissions over the period 1979-1996.

Table 4.2 Selective chronology of regulatory provisions affecting sulphur emissions in the case study countries

Regulatory Instrument	Date	Key Elements
UNECE Convention on Long Range Transboundary Air Pollution	1979	Signed by 34 Governments and the European Community. Set up institutional framework to bring together research and policy. Entered into force in 1983.
Directive on air quality standards for smoke and SO_2 (80/779/EEC)	1980	Limit and guide values for sulphur concentration in ambient air.
German GFA-VO	1983	German national emission control law included SO_2 emission limits for both new and existing large (>50MW) combustion plant.
Air Framework Directive (AFD) (84/360/EEC)	1984	Framework Directive for control of air pollution from industrial plant. Introduced the 'best available technology not entailing excessive cost' BATNEEC concept.

Regulatory Instrument	Date	Key Elements
1st UNECE Sulphur (Helsinki) Protocol	1985	Required 30% reduction in national SO_2 emissions cf. 1980 levels by 1993. Germany, Netherlands and France were all signatories. The United Kingdom was not.
Dutch Bees WLV (Stb., 1987)	1987	Dutch national legislation included SO_2 emission limits for both new and existing large (>75MW) combustion plant.
Large Combustion Plant Directive (88/609/EEC)	1988	Included new plant emission limits for SO_2 and national emission ceilings for existing plant.
Dutch National Plan for Fighting Acidification	1989	Established an 80% reduction target for SO_2 emissions for the year 2000 (cf. a 1980 baseline) as the objective domestic Dutch policy.
UK Environmental Protection Act 1990	1990	UK national legislation: implemented the 1984 AFD and established UK system of Integrated Pollution Control (IPC). No SO_2 emission limits specified for LCP but required application of BATNEEC.
French Arrêté of 27 June 1990	1990	Transposed new plant requirements of the 1988 LCP-Directive into French law.
French Decree of 25 October 1991	1991	Amended earlier French decree of 13 May 1974 controlling polluting emissions to air, which provided for the creation of special protection zones and procedures for alerts. Transcribed the ambient air quality Directives for SO_2 and dust (80/779/EEC), NO_X (85/203/EEC) and lead (82/884/EEC) into French law.
Large Combustion Plant (New Plant) Directions 1991, England and Wales	1991	Secondary legislation under the EPA 1990 transposing the 1988 LCP-Directive new plant requirements in UK law (for England and Wales).
Directive on the sulphur content of liquid fuels (93/12/EC)	1993	Limited sulphur content of gasoil to 0.3%.
2nd UNECE Sulphur (Oslo) Protocol	1994	Differentiated national targets for sulphur reduction from all sources for 2000, 2005 and 2010. New plant emission limits and fuel specifications based on EU Directives.
Amendment to the LCP-Directive (94/66/EC)	1994	Revised emission limit values for SO_2 for new (solid fuel) plant.
EU Directive on Integrated Pollution Prevention and Control (IPPC)	1996	Closely modelled on the UK IPC system, this framework Directive requires the adoption of Best Available Techniques (BAT) to prevent or minimise pollution of the environment as a whole. Qualifying installations require permit to operate and existing plant (pre-1997) required to upgrade to BAT standards by October 2007.
EU Directive on the assessment and management of ambient air quality (96/62/EC)	1996	Provides framework for ambient air quality management. To be followed by 'daughter' Directives specifying limit values for individual pollutants.

For the purposes of this chapter the most important European and international requirements, other than the LCP-Directive, are the 1984 Air Framework Directive (84/360/EEC), the first 1985 UNECE Sulphur Protocol, and the second 1994 UNECE Sulphur Protocol. These are briefly described below:

1. **The 1984 Air Framework Directive (84/360/EEC):** This Framework Directive does not specify emission limits for any particular class of plant, but lays out the circumstances under which certain types of plant (including large combustion plant) may be authorised to operate and which plants and substances will be subject to controls. The Directive also introduced the concept of *best available technology not entailing excessive costs* (BATNEEC) into EU legislation. New plants must conform to BATNEEC, whilst existing (pre-1987) plants must gradually be adapted to BATNEEC or closed down. Excessive costs are defined in relation to the sector as a whole, not the economic circumstances of individual plant.

2. **The 1985 UNECE Helsinki Protocol on the Reduction of Sulphur Emissions or their Transboundary Fluxes by at least 30 per cent:** Twenty-one countries, including Germany, the Netherlands and France, are Parties to this Protocol which, established uniform 30% national emission reduction targets for 1993 (cf. 1980 baseline). The UNECE targets cover all sulphur emissions, not simply those from large combustion plant. The United Kingdom refused to sign this protocol.

3. **The 1994 UNECE Oslo Protocol on Further Reduction of Sulphur Emissions:** The aim of this Protocol was to base national emission reduction targets on the contribution each country made to acid deposition on sensitive ecosystems. As a result the Protocol established a series of differentiated national emission reduction targets, for the years 2000, 2005 and 2010. It also set emission standards for new sources and details of the 'best available technologies' to be used by plant operators. Germany, the Netherlands, France and the UK all signed this Protocol. As with the 1985 Protocol, the reduction targets cover all sulphur emissions, not simply those from large combustion plant. The emissions reductions required for the four countries considered are set out in Table 4.3.

Table 4.3 1994 UNECE Oslo Protocol sulphur emission ceilings and percentage emission reductions for case study countries

	Emission levels (kt SO_2)		Emission Ceilings (kt SO_2)			Percentage Reductions (cf. 1980 base year)		
	1980	1990	2000	2005	2010	2000	2005	2010
France	3348	1202	868	770	737	74	77	78
Germany	7494	5803	1300	990	-	83	87	-
Netherlands	466	207	106	-	-	77	-	-
United Kingdom	4898	3780	2449	1470	980	50	70	80

Source: The 1994 UNECE Oslo Protocol on Further Reduction of Sulphur Emissions Annex II, http://www.unece.org/env/lrtap/protocol/94sulp_a/annex2.htm#a July 2000

3.   IMPLEMENTATION STORIES: FOUR CONTRASTING NATIONAL EXPERIENCES OF THE LCP-DIRECTIVE

Four distinct and contrasting national case studies of the implementation of the LCP-Directive, or where appropriate the equivalent prior national legislation, are presented below. Each describes the principal features of a national 'implementation story' and is structured as follows. Firstly a brief account of the national context of implementation is given, summarising: relevant aspect of the country's energy policy; the structure of its electricity industry; the national regulatory and policy context; and a qualitative assessment of public and political awareness of the environmental issues and acid rain. Each national implementation process is then described, e.g.: formal transposition; choice of regulatory instrument; interaction with other policies; monitoring and enforcement; and the policy outcomes achieved. Tables 4.4 and 4.5 summarise the key aspects.

Table 4.4 Legislation transposing the LCP-Directive 'existing' plant
requirements and type of regulatory instrument employed

	Germany	Netherlands	France	United Kingdom
Legislation transposing LCP-Directive existing plant requirements, (or pre-existing equivalent national legislation)	GFA-VO 1983	Bees WLV (1987 and 1991) and the 1990 Covenant with the Dutch electricity sector	Initially none. Subsequently existing EDF-programme submitted	'UK Plan for the Reduction of Emissions into the Air of Sulphur Dioxide and Oxides of Nitrogen from Existing Large Combustion Plants' 1990
Type of regulatory instrument	Uniform plant-based emission limits and upgrading timetable	Uniform plant-based emission limits and upgrading timetable, plus voluntary agreement	Voluntary agreement	Individual plant-based annual emissions quotas, with constrained company 'bubbles' operated in electricity sector

3.1 Germany: Command and Control Strategy Adopted by Environmental Pioneer

3.1.1 The German context of implementation

Spurred on by domestic public and political concern over the 'Waldsterben', Germany played a pivotal 'first-mover' role, enacting demanding national legislation to control acid emissions from large combustion plants in 1983 GFA-VO.[4] By 1988 West Germany had retrofitted flue gas desulphurisation (FGD) to more than 70 fossil fuelled power stations with a total capacity of 109,792 MWth (roughly 75% of the 145,000 MWth total capacity of the ESI).[5]

One of the largest electricity producers in the European Union, Germany is heavily reliant upon coal (both hard coal and lignite) for power generation.[6] The structure of the German electricity industry is fragmented and complex. Eight large companies own and operate the national high voltage grid and the majority of the generating capacity. Approximately one thousand regional and local distribution companies also generate small amounts of electricity. Prior to the liberalisation of European electricity markets (following the 1997 European Regulation on a single electricity market) German electricity suppliers enjoyed regional monopolies and were exempt from competition and anti-cartel laws.

Table 4.5 The implementation of the LCP-Directive: summary of contextual factors

	Germany	Netherlands	France	United Kingdom
Previous equivalent national legislation	Yes	Yes – although required minor amendments	No	No
Generating mix in ESI	Stable: coal and lignite predominate	Stable: coal and gas	Declining coal and oil, increasing nuclear	Increasing gas and nuclear, declining coal
Market structure of ESI	Stable: regional monopolies (some recent liberalisation)	Stable: nationally co-ordinated oligopoly (some recent liberalisation)	Stable: effective monopoly	Unstable: privatisation leading to increasingly open and competitive market
Political importance of acidification issue	High: 'Waldsterben' a national electoral issue already at the beginning of the 1980s	High: environment a national electoral issue	Low	Medium: significant for international relations. Uncertainty re: abatement costs potentially damaging to 'flagship' privatisation of electricity industry
Public awareness of acidification issue	High	High	Low	Low: but growing environmental awareness from late 1980s
National energy policy	Generators tied into long-term coal contracts (until 1995)	Policy of energy security through fuel diversity	Policy of energy security and independence through expansion of nuclear power	Liberalisation and privatisation energy markets. Political hostility to coal industry

As Ikwue and Skea (1996) have pointed out, given the transboundary nature of the acid rain problem and a desire to prevent its industry suffering a competitive disadvantage as a result of its strict domestic legislation,

Germany played a critical 'first mover' role in promoting the development of both EU and broader international (UNECE) policies to control acidification. Germany not only signed the 1985 UNECE Helsinki protocol, but was also the principal proponent of the LCP-Directive. Following passage of the LCP-Directive, the 1983 GFA-VO was judged by the European Commission to comply with its requirements. The Directive did not therefore require specific transposition into German law. This case study therefore examines the political evolution and implementation of the GFA-VO.[7]

3.1.2 Public alarm forces a precautionary approach

The political evolution of the GFA-VO began in the late 1970s and accompanied growing public concern over damage to Germany's forests. The initial development of the legislation was characterised by intense and prolonged political conflict between on the one hand the German Interior Ministry (BMI), which was responsible for the legislation, and on the other German electricity suppliers and coal industry and the Ministry of Economics. The Interior Ministry pushed for a tough limit of 400mg SO_2/m^3, whilst the industrial side argued that the necessary abatement technology was untested, and that the proposed limit and timetable for its introduction were impractical. The industry also argued that the proposed legislation would damage the German coal industry, impose higher costs threatening Germany's international competitiveness, and that furthermore there was no clear scientific evidence to show that SO_2 emissions were actually responsible for the forest damage.[8] As the scale of the 'Waldsterben' became apparent, public concern led the governing Liberal/Social Democrat coalition to intervene decisively in favour of the BMI, and its proposed tough 400mg/m^3 SO_2 emission limit, in the run up to the 1983 German elections. As a result the GFA-VO was enacted on 1 July 1983.

The GFA-VO was a classical piece of command and control legislation, setting uniform emissions limits and upgrading timetables for existing plant. New plants were required to comply with a limit for SO_2 of 400mg/m^3, or 650mg/m^3 SO_2 for plants using high sulphur coal. In addition new plants were required to achieve an 85% rate of desulphurisation. Differentiated interim emissions limits were set for existing plant, depending upon their capacity and remaining operating time, which were required to meet the new plant SO_2 standards by the end of June 1988 and at latest at 1 April 1993. In effect these ambitious standards meant that all German large combustion plants were required to fit flue gas desulphurisation (FGD) equipment by April 1993 or close down.

3.1.3 Regional voluntary agreement seeks to secure early gains

In North Rhine-Westphalia, the German state with the highest number of large combustion plant, the Regional Government also negotiated a voluntary agreement with the electricity industry: the 'Emission Reduction Plan for Large Combustion Plants of the Electricity Supply Industry in North Rhine-Westphalia' (or North Rhine-Westphalia EMP).[9] Although this agreement did not alter the emission limits set under the GFA-VO, it did establish a staged timetable for the early achievement of the emissions reductions required by the GFA-VO. The North Rhine-Westphalia EMP is therefore considered in more detail below.

According to Bültmann and Wätzold (2000) the North Rhine-Westphalia government's efforts focused upon the electricity sector for two reasons. Firstly, the electricity sector contributed 85% of the State's total SO_2 emissions from large combustion plant. Secondly the electricity companies held local monopolies and were therefore able to pass on their abatement costs to their consumers. However, the North Rhine-Westphalia government had no legal power to impose additional controls on the industry above and beyond those set out in federal legislation. Therefore, in order to achieve further environmental gains, the State Government negotiated a voluntary agreement with the industry. For their part the electricity suppliers sought to protect their reputations and demonstrate good faith, in the event it should prove impossible to meet their statutory objectives.

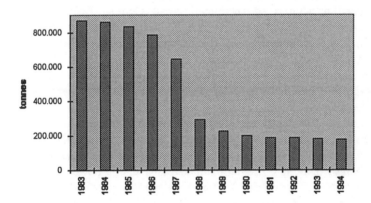

Source: EMP, p. 12: cited in Bültmann and Wätzold (2000).

Figure 4.1 Annual emission ceilings for SO_2 for the NRW electricity supply industry under the EMP

The EMP provided a timetable for achieving SO_2 and NO_X emission reductions, prior to the June 1988 federal deadline for implementing the GFA-VO emission limits. It took the form of an emission reduction schedule, with annual emission ceilings for each plant negotiated in 'working level' meetings with the electricity suppliers (see Figure 4.1). These negotiations were completed in November 1984. For the North Rhine-Westphalia electricity suppliers the EMP provided an additional impetus to complete retrofitting as soon as possible. About 90% of the electricity sector LCP in North Rhine-Westphalia were large coal-fired plant (>300 MWth). The GFA-VO emission limits for these plants could only be met by installing FGD, construction of which required official authorisation. To encourage industry's participation in the EMP, the regional government expurgated the licensing procedures for the FGD equipment, by temporarily transferring a significant number of licensing authority personnel from other duties. In total the industry faced the following SO_2 emission targets.[10]

3.1.4 Retrofitting completed early but at a price

As Bültmann and Wätzold (2000) note, at the time the GFA-VO was enacted, knowledge of desulphurisation technologies was fairly limited, being mainly restricted to the use of additive techniques and wet flue-gas scrubbing (in Japan). Furthermore in order to meet the GFA-VO and North Rhine-Westphalia EMP deadlines, operators had to plan, construct and commission FGD facilities much more quickly than would normally have been the case, and in parallel with their licence application. As a result many experienced difficulties. Furthermore, as all German LCPs had to be retrofitted more or less at the same time, FGD suppliers were overburdened. This led to a loss of quality and the subsequent need for additional repair work. It also resulted in a failure to optimise the operation of the FGD systems across the entire fleet of power stations, as there was no opportunity to learn from earlier mistakes, such as equipment faults that might otherwise have been avoided.

As a result of the EMP many large combustion plants in the North Rhine-Westphalian electricity sector were retrofitted well before the GFA-VO deadline. Other than a few exceptions retrofitting was completed between mid-1987 and mid-1988. In North Rhine-Westphalia 30 power stations with a total capacity of approximately 62,000 MWth (roughly 75% of the total 82,540 MWth of the ESI) were retrofitted with FGD systems. In West Germany as a whole more than 70 power stations with a total capacity of 109,792 MWth (roughly 75% of the total 145,000 MWth of the ESI) were retrofitted with FGD (MURL, 1992, p. 3 and Bertram and Karger, 1988, p. 98: cited in Bültmann and Wätzold, 2000). Only a minority of the electricity industry's large combustion plant were closed, or had their capacity reduced, as a consequence of the new limits and most of the plants that were closed in the 1980s would have done so in any case due to their age.[11] Between 1983 and 1990 the North Rhine-Westphalia electricity sector reduced its annual SO_2 emissions by 886,000 tonnes, compared with a reduction of 1,300,000 tonnes for West Germany as a whole. To achieve this the North Rhine-Westphalia electricity industry invested over 8 billion DM in FGD plant. In total West Germany invested some 14.3 billion DM in FGD (MURL, 1992, p. 4 and Jung, 1988, p. 268).

To sum up, the tight schedule laid down in the GFA-VO and the North Rhine-Westphalia EMP resulted in significant rapid emission reductions. However, these early environmental gains were sometimes achieved at the expense of optimal planning and construction processes and hence cost-effectiveness.

3.1.5 Sophisticated monitoring system developed

The GFA-VO not only prescribed emission limits but also monitoring and reporting requirements for plant operators. Besides retrofitting FGD, operators were required to install approved continuous monitoring and recording equipment and make regular reports to the supervising authority. In practice the German emissions monitoring system has been characterised by its increasing sophistication, automation and reliability (Bültmann and Wätzold, 2000). Monitoring devices have undergone a remarkable evolution. Originally monitoring data was simply written on punched paper tape. From early 1990s electricity suppliers installed computers that not only recorded, but also processed the data (i.e. automatically calculated half-hourly and daily mean values). The process was further automated in 1998 when North Rhine-Westphalia began connecting plants to a remote monitoring network. As a result it is now effectively impossible for a plant to exceed its emissions limits without detection.

The GFA-VO provides for plants to run without FGD for up to 72 successive hours, or a total of 240 hours in any one year, in the event of problems occurring with the abatement equipment. According to Bültmann and Wätzold (2000), problems with FGD systems initially occurred fairly frequently. However, in recent years operators have rarely needed to make use of the 72/240 hours rule. In failure-free operation SO_2 emissions are typically well below the limits set in the GFA-VO, and power stations frequently emit less than 200 mg SO_2/m^3. There have been only two incidents, in North Rhine-Westphalia, where electricity plant operators were unable to repair their FGD systems within the stipulated time. In both cases the operators applied for exemptions under §33 of the GFA-VO (to allow the plant to run without FGD whilst the abatement system was repaired) but these were refused. Where cases of non-compliance do occur informal sanctions usually suffice. However, where they fail the regulator has a range of formal sanctions available under German law. These range from a fine, to temporary closure of the plant or permanent revocation of the operators' licence. Apart from the two cases mentioned above, the North Rhine-Westphalian regulatory authorities have not had recourse to employ formal sanctions.

The development of a sophisticated monitoring system was necessary in Germany to enforce the GFA-VO's concentration-based emissions limits. However, although the increasing sophistication of the North Rhine-Westphalian monitoring system has effectively made it impossible for breaches of these limits to go undetected, this does not explain the degree of over-compliance obtained. It can only explain why plants complied with those limits.

3.2   The Netherlands: Co-operation Reduces Abatement Costs

3.2.1   The Dutch context of implementation

Motivated in part by growing domestic awareness of environmental concerns, and in part by the fact that approximately 75% of the acid deposition in the Netherlands was caused by transboundary emissions, the Dutch Government also played a progressive role in the development of European and international acidification policy (Lulofs, 2000), including the 1985 UNECE Helsinki protocol.

According to Lulofs (2000) Dutch energy policy, as formulated in the late 1970s, initially anticipated that the use of both coal and oil would increase. In practice, however, in the early 1980s uncertainties over security of supply and increased prices limited oil consumption. The expansion of nuclear power was considered, but ruled out following the 1986 Chernobyl disaster. Coal continued to be prioritized as a secure, cheap fuel. However, its cost advantage has progressively been undermined by increased pollution abatement costs. Likewise, post-1985 the use of gas, in gas/oil-fired plant, increased as the pollution abatement costs for oil increased. Throughout the 1990s, however, the relative inputs of these different fuels to the Dutch generating mix remained reasonably stable.

Throughout the 1980s and 1990s, the structure of the Dutch electricity sector could best be described as a co-ordinated oligopoly: effectively a monopoly, controlled by the 'NV Samenwerkende Electriciteitsproduktie-bedrijven' (or SEP). SEP was a private organisation controlled by the four Dutch electricity producers in charge of co-ordinating and planning Dutch electricity production. To achieve these goals, SEP ran a sophisticated cost-pooling mechanism. In essence, the system was a co-ordinated oligopoly, with SEP exempted from certain competition and anti-cartel laws. However, as in the case of Germany, the privileged position of the Dutch industry disappeared as a result of the liberalisation of the European electricity market, and in 1999 SEP was dissolved.

From the mid-1980s environmental issues, and acidification in particular, achieved a high public and political profile in the Netherlands. Awareness of the 'Waldsterben' in neighbouring Germany resulted in the initiation of a substantial Dutch research programme, and the introduction of tough domestic legislation to combat acidification, the Bees WLV (Stb., 1987). Like the German GFA-VO, the Dutch Bees WLV (1987) was a classical piece of command and control legislation, setting uniform emissions limits for SO_2, NO_X and dust, and upgrading timetables for existing plant. As in Germany, new plants were required to comply with a SO_2 emissions limit of 400mg/m^3 and to achieve an 85% rate of desulphurisation. Differentiated interim emissions limits were set for existing plant, depending upon their capacity, fuel and remaining operating time, which were required to meet the new plant SO_2 standards by either 1994 or 1999 depending upon the type of plant.

The mid-1980s also saw the preparation of the 'Brundtland' Report, by the World Commission on Environment and Development. A parallel in-depth study, by the National Institute of Public Health and the Environment (RIVM), was extremely influential in shaping both Dutch public opinion and environmental policy. Indeed, as a direct result of this study the first integrated Dutch National Environmental Plan was published in May 1999. One objective of this was to reduce acid emissions by 70–80% (cf. a 1980 baseline) by the year 2000 in order to preserve woodlands and nature reserves.

This objective was clarified under the National Plan for Fighting Acidification (Second Chamber of Parliament, 1988–1989, 18225, nr.31), which established an 80% reduction target for SO_2 emissions for the year 2000 (cf. a 1980 baseline). This Plan included both emissions and environmental quality targets for 2000 and 2010. Emission targets were given for various sectors including the electricity sector. These were implemented through the Dutch practice of establishing sectoral Covenants (or negotiated agreements) between the Government and industry. In the case of the electricity sector the Government signed a Covenant with industry in 1990. According to Lulofs (2000), it was these domestic national targets, rather than those set out in the LCP-Directive or the UNECE Protocols, which provided the underlying drivers of Dutch acidification policy. Indeed, this 80% domestic reduction target exceeds both the LCP-Directive's targets and the 77% SO_2 reduction target that the Netherlands signed up to under the second UNECE Sulphur Protocol.

3.2.2   Transposition requires minor amendments

Following the passage of the LCP-Directive, a number of technical changes were required to the Bees WLV 1987 in order to transpose fully the Directive. Most of the new plant standards specified under the Bees WLV 1987 were actually stricter than those prescribed by the Directive.[12] However, a number of minor discrepancies had to be dealt with, such as adjusting the definition of large combustion plant used in the Bees WLV 1987 down from 75MW to 50MW to bring it into line with the Directive. The Directive was therefore formally transposed into Dutch law by an amendment to the Bees WLV on 5 July 1991 (Stb. 354). With respect to Article 3 of the LCP-Directive requiring Member States to draw up national programmes for the reduction of emissions from existing plant, the Netherlands cited the Bees WLV (1987 and 1991) and a 1990 Covenant with the Dutch electricity sector (discussed below).

3.2.3   Domestic policy places public/private co-operation centre stage

The 1990 Covenant was agreed by the Dutch central government (represented by the Ministry of Housing, Physical Planning and the Environment), the twelve Dutch Provinces, SEP and the individual electricity plants. In negotiating the Covenant, the Ministry of the Environment regarded the goals to be reached as non-negotiable and used the threat of further formal regulation to achieve its objectives. The electricity industry was reluctant to commit to specific end-of-pipe measures and tried to gain as much flexibility as possible over how to achieve the specified emission ceilings (Lulofs, 2000). However, the Bees WLV (1987 and 1991) already required the use of FGD for new plants and made retrofitting FGD or closure inevitable for existing plants. Negotiation of the Covenant therefore centred upon the degree of flexibility to be provided to the plant operators regarding the desulphurisation technologies to be used, and on NO_x emissions. The outcome satisfied both sides. The Covenant established aggregate SO_2 emission ceilings for the electricity sector (of 30 kt/SO_2 for 1994 and 18 kt/SO_2 for the year 2000) in line with the Dutch National Plan for Fighting Acidification, whilst no new SO_2 emission limits were specified at the plant level.

Under the 1990 Covenant SEP was required to produce a plan, the principal elements of which were: the closure of five coal-fired plants and the planned closure of a sixth plant (Maascentrale 6) in 1999/2000; the commissioning of two new coal-fired plants (Amer 91 and Hemweg 8); all remaining coal-fired plant to be retrofitted with FGD by the year 2000; FGD equipped plant to achieve greater than 90% desulphurisation rates; the use of low-sulphur coal; and measures to ensure fewer malfunctions of abatement equipment. The emission reductions forecast under the SEP plan are set out in Table 4.6.

Table 4.6 Projected emissions from the Dutch electricity sector LCP, as forecast under the 1991 SEP plan

Year	1991	1992	1993	1994	1995	1996	1997	1998	1999	2000
Planned SO_2 emissions kt/yr	54	45	43	30	33	32	31	33	33	26

Source: Lulofs (2000).

In fact, 'Maascentrale 6' was closed in 1997 three years earlier than planned, whilst the two new FGD-equipped coal-fired plants were commissioned in 1993 and 1994 respectively, and SO_2 emissions from the sector's LCP were just 18.7 kt in 1996 compared with the 32 kt forecast under the 1991 plan (Lulofs, 2000).

In the Netherlands air emissions from large combustion plant are monitored by the Province. If abatement equipment malfunctions the plant operator must also report this to the Province. Under certain conditions the plant may, as in the German case, continue to operate for up to 72 hours, if the fault is not repaired within this time limit other measures, such as fuel switching or temporary closure, must be taken. In practice, SEP was able to step in and exercise its co-ordinating function should such a closure prove necessary. Thus the co-ordinating role of SEP, together with stricter objectives of the Covenant, meant that electricity plants did not exceed the national emission limits set out in the Bees WLV (1987 and 1991) (Lulofs, 2000).

3.3 France: Nuclear Strategy Means Business as Usual

3.3.1 The French context of implementation

In the early 1980s acidification did not have a high public profile in France. Furthermore, this was not a country that was generally considered to be in the vanguard with respect to the development of European environmental policy. Despite this France signed the 1983 Helsinki Protocol and supported the proposed national emission ceilings during negotiation of the LCP-Directive. However, France's apparently progressive international stance on this issue can be quite easily explained. In response to the oil shocks of the 1970s France had embarked on a policy of energy security through a massive programme of investment in nuclear power. As result France was able to sign up to the 1983 Helsinki Protocol, privately confident that its increasing reliance on nuclear power would allow it to meet its obligations without additional measures (at the time other countries did not know the precise impact of the nuclear programme on France's SO_2 emissions). A similar view was taken with respect to the national emission ceilings imposed by the LCP-Directive, which France again considered unproblematic.

The French electricity industry is essentially a monopoly: Electricité de France (EDF), the dominant producer, has the monopoly on electricity distribution. In addition Charbonnages de France (CDF), a former coal-mining company, runs several power stations and sells the electricity to EDF. Both companies are government-owned. EDF is extraordinarily dependent on nuclear power as an energy source. By the mid-1990s about 80% of its electricity was produced by nuclear generation. Coal and fuel-oil-fired plants are now only used to complement nuclear (and some hydro-electricity) production at peak demand. EDF's thermal plants are relatively old, the majority having been built before the nuclear programme was started.

Table 4.7 shows the increase in EDF's nuclear energy production and the consequent decrease in its classic thermal electricity production. The related SO_2 emission reductions were sufficient to ensure France would more than comply with its SO_2 emission ceilings under both the Helsinki Protocol and the LCP-Directive. Despite this comfortable position France was to find itself in conflict with the European Commission over its failure to properly implement the LCP-Directive.

Table 4.7 ED's power production in TWh

	1980	1997	Change
Nuclear	26	82	+215%
Thermal	43	4	-91%

Source: EDF-homepage/internet: http://www.edf.fr

3.3.2 Voluntary measures cited for administrative compliance

The LCP-Directive was transposed into French law by an 'arrêté' on the 27 June 1990.[13] Two major differences arose at this stage. Firstly the definition of 'new plant' used in the arrêté specified 19th August 1990 as the qualifying date rather than 1 July 1987 as specified in the Directive.[14] Secondly and more importantly existing plant were not covered by the arrêté. As noted above the French government expected to achieve over-compliance with the Directive's national emission reduction targets without further policy measures. It therefore did not see any need to define a specific emissions reduction programme as required by Article 3 of the LCP-Directive. When challenged over this omission by the European Commission, the French Ministry of the Environment cited an existing EDF-programme to reduce local air pollution and indicated that it was discussing equivalent emission reduction objectives for CDF's existing plants (Schucht, 2000).

However, the EDF-programme had not been intended to implement the LCP-Directive. Rather it was a unilateral voluntary commitment to manage SO_2 and NO_X emissions, intended to enhance EDF's public image and portray the company as environmentally pro-active. Schucht (2000) identifies three factors underpinning EDF's commitment and provides a detailed account of the programme's implementation. Firstly EDF had just appointed a new environmental Director. Secondly, EDF's nuclear programme had been put into practice and the company wanted to demonstrate that it was still concerned with its thermal stations. Finally a new five-year programme between the State and EDF was agreed. The Ministry of the Environment negotiated several alterations to the company's initial proposals, and the EDF-programme was formalised in a 1993 government circular (12 January). Planned measures to reduce SO_2 emissions included: switching to the use of low sulphur fuel oil in all nineteen oil-fired plants; trials of lime injection primary desulphurisation equipment (at La Maxe and Loire sur Rhône) and its possible installation at Le Havre and seven 250 MW coal-fired plants; retrofitting of FGD to EDF's three newest 600 MW plants; and limits on average annual utilisation times for various stations.[15] A circular is, however, essentially an administrative guideline. It is only binding on the administration. It does not have the legal force of an 'arrêté' and cannot be enforced by the Ministry. In practice EDF has largely failed to fulfil the voluntary commitments given in its 1993 programme. The use of primary desulphurisation was not continued after the trial phase, and the only measure systematically adopted was the switch to low sulphur fuel oil. EDF subsequently abandoned the programme's remaining objectives. However, the planned retrofitting of FGD to three large coal-fired plants was eventually completed in 1999.[16]

Despite the electricity industry's failure to implement many of these planned measures unexpected reductions in thermal energy production have ensured that France has more than met its LCP-Directive SO_2 reduction targets. In essence then, it may be said that EDF respects the 'spirit' of the LCP-Directive with respect to the reduction of emissions from existing plant. But not the 'spirit' of French domestic policy (e.g. the EDF-programme), as this was also intended to deal with local air quality concerns. However, when the Ministry tried to push through the EDF-programme in 1997, EDF made it clear that it would close plants rather than retrofit abatement equipment. Both the Ministry and EDF now consider the EDF-programme to be obsolete (Schucht, 2000).

3.4   The United Kingdom: the 'Dirty Man of Europe' Proves Remarkably Efficient

3.4.1 The UK context of implementation

In the early to mid-1980s the United Kingdom (UK) gained the reputation as the 'dirty man of Europe' in part at least for its refusal to sign the Helsinki Protocol and history of opposition to the LCP-Directive. Indeed, the UK's opposition was one of the main reasons it took five years for the Directive to be agreed. This opposition was based on the belief that compliance would require an expensive programme of retrofitting FGD to much of UK's coal-fired generating plant. As Ikwue and Skea (1996) note, at the time the UK electricity industry, in the form of the Central Electricity Generating Board (CEGB), was operating within a technological paradigm committed to building large nuclear and coal-fired plant. This paradigm had developed over the CEGB's previous thirty years as a highly centralised publicly-owned monopoly. Compliance with the LCP-Directive was expected to require the retrofitting of FGD to some 12GW of plant (approximately 17% of the UK's total generating capacity) at a total cost of £1.8bn (1989 prices). This total included an existing commitment to retrofitting 6GW of plant with FGD, previously announced by the CEGB in 1986. Boehmer-Christiansen (1995) argues that this previous commitment was largely the result of bilateral political pressure from the Scandinavian countries, particularly Norway. Indeed, the 1986 decision was announced just prior to a visit to Norway by the then British Prime Minister, Mrs Thatcher.

Table 4.8 Thermal input to electricity generation 1989-96 (% of total)

Fuel	1989	1990	1992	1994	1996
Coal	64.6	65.3	61.3	50.3	43.0
Oil	9.4	11.0	10.5	5.5	4.6
Gas	0.7	0.7	2.0	13.4	21.5
Nuclear	23.6	21.3	24.1	28.8	28.9
Hydro	0.5	0.6	0.6	0.6	0.4
Other	1.2	1.1	1.4	1.4	1.7
Total	100.0	100.0	100.0	100.0	100.0

However, shortly after the LCP-Directive was finally agreed in 1988, the British Government announced its intention to privatise the UK electricity industry. The CEGB's non-nuclear generating capacity was split between two new companies, National Power and PowerGen and, once opened to increasing competition, the privatised industry soon adopted a radically different technological strategy. In the event, fuel switching, the construction of combined cycle gas turbine (CCGT) stations and an increase in nuclear output ensured an unexpectedly rapid decrease in SO_2 emissions. Table 4.8 illustrates changes in the UK generation mix between 1989 and 1996.

Implementation of the LCP-Directive also co-evolved with the restructuring and modernisation of the UK pollution control regime. In 1987 Her Majesty's Inspectorate of Pollution (HMIP) was established, as a Directorate of the Department of the Environment, to provide an integrated national pollution regulator.[17] This was the first of a number of radical reforms, the context of which was: growing environmental activism; industry lobbying for 'defensive' reform to restore the credibility of the regulatory system; the desire of the Department of the Environment to strengthen its executive control over the regulation of industrial pollution; and the need to implement the formal requirements of EU legislation and to resolve outstanding tensions with the traditional flexible British regulatory approach (Smith, 1997). Indeed, implementation of the 1984 Air Framework Directive (84/360/EEC) was one of the principal driving forces behind the introduction of the UK Environmental Protection Act 1990, which established the UK system of Integrated Pollution Control (IPC). This Act in turn provided the legal framework for the transposition and implementation of the LCP-Directive.

3.4.2 UK regulatory framework modernised
Formal transposition into UK law was achieved through secondary legislation made under the 1990 Act. The 'Large Combustion Plant (New Plant) Directions 1991' set out the minimum emissions standards the regulator must apply when issuing authorisations for new plant, in accordance with the requirements of the LCP-Directive.

With respect to the LCP-Directive's requirements for Member States to draw a national programme for the reduction of emissions from existing plant by 1 July 1990 (Article 3), the UK was a few months late achieving formal compliance. This it did through publication of the 'UK Plan for the Reduction of Emissions into the Air of Sulphur Dioxide and Oxides of Nitrogen from Existing Large Combustion Plants' (the National Plan) on 20 December 1990. This National Plan was the subject of extensive closed negotiations between the government and the about to be privatised electricity industry, prior to it being published for public consultation, as the government sought to minimise the industry's environmental liabilities at flotation.

3.4.3 Flexible approach adopted for electricity generators
The UK National Plan allocated emission reductions geographically (i.e. between England and Wales, Scotland and Northern Ireland) and by sector between the 'electricity supply industry', 'refineries' and 'other industry'.

Under the Plan annual reduction targets were allocated to each sector up to 2003. As can be seen from Table 4.9, the overall reductions required by the National Plan were slightly stricter than those required by the LCP-Directive. Furthermore, the reductions were not evenly distributed between sectors, as both the refinery and other 'industry sectors' had already achieved proportionately much greater emissions reductions (largely through the retirement and closure of plants) since 1980 than had the electricity sector.

The Plan envisaged the use of a mixture of measures to achieve the required SO_2 reductions from the electricity sector. These included: retrofitting 8 GW of FGD equipment; the construction of some new low-polluting plant, such as CCGT plant; and the use of low-sulphur coal in existing plant. The National Plan also included special arrangements providing a significant degree of operational flexibility for companies in the English and Welsh electricity sector, where the sector's reduction targets were subdivided into company quotas or 'bubbles' for National Power and PowerGen.

Table 4.9 UK National Plan sectoral SO_2 quotas for selected years –
expressed as % reduction required from 1980 baseline

UK National Plan Sector	1991	1993	1998
Total UK ESI	- 4%	-10%	-40%
Total UK Refineries	-59%	-63%	-65%
Total UK Other Industry	-50%	-56%	-63%
Total UK National Plan	-15%	-21%	-45%
LCP-Directive Targets	-	-20%	-40%

Source: DoE (1990).

The National Plan was implemented by HMIP under the central direction of the Department of the Environment. National Power and PowerGen plants were assigned a fixed BATNEEC limit and a separate plant quota allocation (the quota allocation generally being lower than the BATNEEC limit). The sum of each company's plant quotas was equal to its annual 'bubble' under the National Plan.[18] Each company was allowed to allocate emissions between their plants so long as neither the company bubble nor the individual plant BATNEEC limits were exceeded. In effect, National Power and PowerGen were allowed to operate constrained company emissions bubbles, so facilitating the cost-effective dispatch of each company's plant (Sorrel, 1999). In the other sectors covered by the National Plan the approach taken was much less flexible. The distinction between BATNEEC limits and quota allocations did not appear, and plants were assigned single fixed annual SO_2 emissions limit.

In 1992, the Department of the Environment proposed a wider 'sulphur switching' or trading scheme. In part at least to overcome what it perceived to be some of the geographical and sectoral inflexibilities of the National Plan, particularly with respect to the Northern Ireland electricity and other industry sectors. Despite repeated government pronouncements in favour of a wider trading scheme, a series of informal and formal consultations, and a strong ideological commitment to the use of market instruments on the part of the Conservative government of the time, the idea was eventually dropped in 1996. Sorrell (1999, p. 170), who undertook a detailed study of this episode, identified six main reasons for this failure: 'Namely: independent developments in energy markets; a conflict of regulatory principles; a conflict of regulatory culture; a conflict over quota allocation; persistent regulatory uncertainty; and inadequate political support'. The UK National Plan was, however, amended on a number of occasions before being subsumed within the UK's strategy for meeting its obligations under the UNECE Oslo Protocol in December 1996. The Plan now consists of a series of aggregate annual national emissions targets.[19]

3.4.4 Compliance proves remarkably easy

As noted above compliance with the LCP-Directive was originally expected to require the retrofitting of FGD to some 12GW of plant. By the time the UK National Plan was published in December 1990 this estimate had been reduced to 8GW, in combination with other measures. By the mid-1990s, however, the industrial context had changed completely. The principal driver of this change was the privatisation of and introduction of competition into the UK electricity supply industry.[20]

The introduction of competition into electricity generation, together with an expectation of tighter future regulation of sulphur emissions if the UK signed up to the second UNECE sulphur protocol (Eames, 2000), had a dramatic impact. Plans to build new large coal-fired plant were abandoned in the face of high capital costs and expected difficulties in obtaining planning consents (Ikwue and Skea, 1996). A new technology strategy emerged based upon the rapid construction of Combined Cycle Gas Turbine (CCGT) plant. CCGT capacity increased from zero in 1989 to 13GW in March 1997 (Watson, 1998), whilst between 1990 and 1995 National Power and PowerGen together closed a total of 18,960 MWth of coal-fired plant.[21] These new CCGT stations were built both by National Power and PowerGen, and by new entrants into the generation market. These structural changes led to a rapid decline in sulphur emissions, making further expensive investment in FGD largely unnecessary. As a result, only 6GW of coal-fired plant was actually retrofitted with FGD, and the UK has so far met its LCP-Directive SO_2 emissions reductions targets with ease. Indeed, total SO_2 emissions from existing UK large combustion plant fell by some 37% between 1990 and 1995, with emissions from electricity sector large combustion plant declining by 42% over the same period.

3.4.5 Simple monitoring suffices for annual limits

Compliance with the UK National Plan is monitored by the Environment Agency (previously HMIP) on the basis of monthly returns provided by plant operators. Sulphur dioxide emissions are calculated on the basis of the sulphur content and mass of fuel used except in the case of plant fitted with FGD, where a combination of emission factors and continuous flue gas monitoring are used to calculate monthly emissions. Whilst this type of monitoring, based on emission factors and fuel consumption, may at first sight appear weaker than the German system of continuous monitoring, it is perfectly adequate for enforcing the UK's annual emission limits. The monthly returns are then used to compile the annual UK emissions inventories submitted to the Commission. According to the Environment Agency no breaches of relevant plant annual emission limits have actually occurred.

4.   ENVIRONMENTAL GOAL ATTAINMENT AND ADMINISTRATIVE COMPLIANCE

In addition to examining attainment of the LCP-Directive and UNECE Protocol national emissions reduction targets, where possible the following section also considers environmental goal attainment with respect to the various national policy objectives and sectoral targets outlined above.

4.1   The LCP-Directive's SO_2 National Emissions Reduction Targets

Remarkably, in 1993 all four case study countries achieved greater than 95% over-compliance with the Directive's 'Phase 1' SO_2 emission reduction objectives, although of course the target for the UK was less stringent than that of Germany, the Netherlands and France. West Germany initially achieved the greatest degree of over-compliance: 128.5% in 1993. The 1996 over-compliance figure for Germany is somewhat anomalous as it reflects amendments to the national targets following German unification. Overall, however, the pattern of massive initial over-compliance with the Directive's requirements in all of the countries considered is clear.

Table 4.10 National SO₂ emissions (kt/yr) from 'existing' large combustion plant

Year	Germany (West)	Germany	Netherlands	France	United Kingdom
1980	2225	3803	299	1910	3883
1993	236	1967	76.6	412.8	2329
1996	-	1144	56.9	389.8	1468
1998	N/A	N/A	N/A	382.8	1207

Note: N/A denotes not applicable or data unavailable.
Sources: Schucht (2000); Lulofs (2000); Eames (2000); Bültmann and Wätzold (2000).

At the time of writing SO₂ emissions data for 1998 was not available for Germany or the Netherlands. However, in the case of the UK and France, both countries continued to over-comply with their respective national SO₂ emission reduction targets in 1998, although for both there was a significant reduction in the degree of over-compliance achieved (to 14.8% and 14.2% over-compliance respectively). See Tables 4.10 and 4.11.

Table 4.11 Percentage over-compliance achieved

Year	Germany (West)	Germany	Netherlands	France	United Kingdom
1993	123.5%	-	95.75%	95.75%	100%
1996[22]	-	231.3%	60.2%	59%	107%
1998	-	N/A	N/A	14.2%	14.8%

Note: N/A denotes not applicable or data unavailable.

4.2 Goal Attainment with UNECE Protocols

As previously noted, the 1985 Helsinki Protocol required signatories, including Germany, the Netherlands and France to achieve a 30% cut in their sulphur emissions by 1993 cf. a 1980 baseline.[23] UNECE data indicates that Germany, the Netherlands and France all massively over-complied with this target (with 61%, 67% and 68% reductions respectively). In the event, the UK also over-complied (achieving a 35% emissions reduction), although not a signatory to the Protocol. All four countries are also expected to comply with the 1994 Oslo Protocol's more ambitious reduction targets for the year 2000. However, in this case only the UK, which was once again allocated a relatively lenient reduction target, is expected to achieve a significant degree of over-compliance. See Table 4.12.

Table 4.12 UNECE sulphur emissions data for Germany, the Netherlands, France and the UK

	1980 emission level (kilotons)	1993 emission level kilotons (% reduction cf. 1980)	1996 emission level (kilotons)	2000 projected* emission level (kilotons)	Target level for 2000 (kilotons) (% reduction cf. 1980)
Germany	7514	2938 (61%)	1543	1300	1300 (83%)
West Germany	3164	-	-	-	-
East Germany	4350	-	-	-	-
Netherlands	490	164 (67%)	135	92	106 (77%)
France	3338	1061 (68%)	1031	868	868 (74%)
United Kingdom	4863	3143 (35%)	2017	1290	2449 (50%)

Note:* denotes based on current reduction plans.
Source: Data obtained from http://www.unece.org/env/lrtap/ 6 May 2000.

4.3   Goal Attainment with National Policy Objectives

4.3.1   Germany: the GFA-VO and NRW EMP

As noted above, the LCP-Directive sets national ceilings for emissions from existing large combustion plant whereas the GFA-VO specified concentration-based emission limits (in mg/m^3) for individual plants. Most German large combustion plants were required to comply with an emission limit of 400mg/m^3 SO$_2$ from 1 April 1993. Table 4.13 illustrates changes in average SO$_2$ emissions from large combustion plant in the West German electricity sector over the period 1980–95. As one can see this indicates a significant degree of both early and over-compliance with the 400mg/m^3 GFA-VO.

Table 4.13 Average SO$_2$ emissions from large combustion plant in the West German electricity sector and resulting indicators (1980-95 selected years)

	1980	1982	1985	1988	1989	1990	1992	1995
Average emissions SO$_2$ in mg/m^3	2154	2160	1847	582	270	290	250	154
% reduction cf. 1980	-	-0.3	14.3	73.0	87.5	86.5	88.4	92.9
% over-compliance with GFA-VO 400 mg/m^3 limit	-	-	-	-	-	-	37.5	61.5

Source: Bültmann and Wätzold (2000).

With respect to the NRW emission reduction plan (EMP), the EMP SO$_2$ emissions targets and actual emission levels achieved are given in Table 4.14. As one can see the EMP targets were met each year, with varying degrees of over-compliance. Indeed, in 1989 actual emissions where almost 60% lower than specified in the EMP.

Table 4.14 Goal attainment with North Rhine-Westphalia EMP

	1983	1984	1985	1986	1987	1988	1989	1990
Actual SO_2 emissions in kt/yr	870	845	750	745	640	205	90	95
EMP Emission targets in kt/yr	870	860	833	786	645	289	224	197
% reduction achieved cf. 1980	-	2.9	13.8	14.4	26.4	76.4	89.6	89.1
% over-compliance with EMP targets	-	1.7	10.0	5.2	0.8	29.1	59.8	51.8

Source: Bültmann and Wätzold (2000).

4.3.2 The Netherlands

As noted above the Dutch National Plan for Fighting Acidification (Second Chamber of Parliament, 1988–1989, 18225, no.31) established a national target of an 80% reduction in SO_2 emissions for the year 2000 (cf. 1980). The electricity sector Covenant, implementing this national target, established annual emissions ceilings of 30 kt/SO_2 for 1994 and 18 kt/SO_2 for the year 2000. Table 4.15 provides details of actual emissions from the Dutch electricity sector and goal attainment with the Covenant's 1994 target.

Table 4.15 SO_2 emissions from the Dutch electricity sector and goal attainment with the Covenant targets

	1980	1990	1991	1993	1994	1996
Electricity sector actual emissions SO_2 (kt/yr)	196	43.7	37.5	22.1	14.6	18.7
% reduction cf. 1980	-	77.7	80.9	88.7	92.6	90.5
Electricity sector Covenant target (kt/yr)	-	-	-	-	30	
% over-compliance with Covenant target	-	-	-	-	51.4	-

Source: Lulofs (2000).

As one can see, the picture is again one of significant over-compliance. Indeed, the sector achieved more than 50% over-compliance with the Covenant's 1994 SO_2 target. Furthermore, by the early 1990s the sector had already achieved a 90% reduction in SO_2 emissions, compared with the aggregate national target of an 80% reduction by the year 2000.[24]

4.3.3 United Kingdom

Table 4.16 illustrates the percentage SO_2 emissions reduction required of the electricity supply industry in England and Wales under the UK National Plan, for the years 1993 and 1998, compared with the actual percentage reductions and the degree of compliance achieved. Again the pattern is one of significant, although declining, over-compliance.

Table 4.16 England and Wales ESI: over-compliance with UK National Plan (selected years)

Year	Emissions SO_2 kt	% reduction required by National Plan	Actual % reduction achieved	% over-compliance
1980	2776	-	-	-
1993	1958.2	10	29.5	195
1998	969.5	40	65.1	62.8

Source: Eames (2000).

4.3.4 France

Table 4.17 compares actual emissions with the achievable reductions forecast from implementation of the EDF-Programme. As one can see, despite failure of the industry to implement many of its planned abatement measures, SO_2 emissions from the French electricity sector are significantly lower than originally forecast.

Table 4.17 Forecast and actual SO_2 emissions (kt) from LCP in the French electricity sector

	1993	1996	1998	2003
Forecast achievable emission level	400	-	350	280
Actual emissions of all (new and existing) CDF and EDF LCPs ≥ 50MW	158.3	167.1	-	-

Source: Schucht (2000).

In summary then, the analysis presented above shows a consistent pattern of over-compliance with sectoral, national, EU and UNECE SO_2 policy objectives for all four of the countries considered. The economic literature has largely viewed legal compliance and environmental goal attainment as a function of the monitoring and enforcement. With respect to the implementation of the LCP-Directive, however, monitoring and enforcement appears to have played a relatively minor role in the four countries considered. Indeed, only in the case of Germany, where the regulatory authorities have invested considerable effort in the development of an increasingly sophisticated emissions monitoring system, does monitoring and the threat of enforcement action appear to have acted as a real constraint. However, by itself this factor would not be sufficient to explain German over-compliance.

One general way of interpreting such over-compliance would be to argue that the policy objectives were not in fact demanding. However, only in the case of France is there evidence to suggest that this was known at the time the relevant objectives were agreed. In particular, France signed up to both the first UNECE Sulphur Protocol and the LCP-Directive privately confident of meeting her reduction targets, without the need for additional policy measures, as a result of the planned expansion of nuclear generation: a fact that France chose not to disclose to her negotiating partners. This explains why the other countries involved, which had accepted the principal of differentiated national objectives, agreed to the undemanding French targets.

With hindsight it may be argued both that the UK could easily have signed up to the first UNECE Sulphur Protocol's 30% reduction target, and that the sulphur targets negotiated by the UK under the LCP-Directive and Second Sulphur Protocol were excessively cautious. However, in this case it was the unexpected and rapid restructuring of the electricity sector (the so-called 'dash for gas'), which followed privatisation, which underpinned over-compliance. In both the French and UK cases over-compliance can then be largely attributed to, more or less expected or unexpected, interactions with national energy policy.

In Germany and the Netherlands the early introduction of demanding domestic legislation was clearly driven by the high degree of public and political awareness of the acidification problem (and of environmental issues in general). Furthermore, one can assume that such high public awareness also tended to make individual electricity consumers more willing to pay for abatement measures.

Bültmann and Wätzold (2000), argue that in Germany the effective requirement to use what was at the time a largely untested abatement technology (e.g. FGD), together with a short deadline for compliance, not only promoted an initial over-specification of FGD plant but also precluded any opportunity for technological learning. They also argue that the cost structure of FGD also contributed to over-compliance in the German case. The costs of building and operating an FGD system are heavily front-loaded. Most of the costs relate to the systems installation. Once the FGD unit is operational, SO_2 emissions (over a certain range) depend on the amount of lime added to the flue gases. The marginal cost of adding additional lime is relatively small. Hence, once FGD had been installed, the marginal cost to the plant operator (who as part of a regional monopoly will have been protected from price competition) of responding to public pressure to reduce emissions as far as technically possible, thereby over-complying with the GFA-VO limit, will have been relatively low. Finally they suggest that the strict and increasingly automated German monitoring system also promoted over-compliance, as plant operators needed to allow a margin of safety to prevent minor exceedences of tightly enforced concentration-based emission limits.

Table 4.18 Factors explaining over-compliance

Germany	Netherlands	France	United Kingdom
High public and political awareness	High public and political awareness	Undemanding policy objectives	Interaction with national energy policy
Compliance plus negotiated agreement	Compliance plus negotiated agreement	Interaction with national energy policy	Unexpected restructuring of energy sector
Initial over-specification of FGD and absence of technological learning effects	Regulatory anticipation	Expected restructuring of energy sector	Regulatory anticipation

In Germany and the Netherlands the use of negotiated agreements, i.e. the North Rhine-Westphalia Emission Reduction Plan (NRW EMP) and the 1990 Dutch Electricity Sector Covenant, also appear to have contributed to the patterns of over-compliance found. The North Rhine-Westphalia EMP successfully delivered early emissions reductions prior to the GFA-VO coming into force, whilst the Dutch Electricity Sector Covenant played a rather different role, delivering additional emissions reductions beyond those required by the LCP-Directive and the Bees WLV (1987 and 1991). In France, however, EDF failed to implement its voluntary agreement. Why then were the German and Dutch agreements successful, whilst the French EDF-programme was not? Well of course the national contexts of the three agreements were very different. In Germany, the NRW EMP was successful, because public and political opinion considered acidification a national ecological disaster. The Dutch electricity sector Covenant was negotiated under the threat of additional legislation. In France, neither of these drivers underpinned the failed EDF-programme.

Given the dynamic, multi-layered (local, national, EU and UNECE) and often overlapping character of the regulatory framework for controlling sulphur emissions, it is reasonable to assume that an element of regulatory anticipation will also have contributed to the patterns of over-compliance found. For example, all of the countries signed up to more demanding and longer-term SO_2 reduction targets, under the Second UNECE Sulphur Protocol, just four years after finally agreeing the LCP-Directive. This factor clearly influenced UK electricity generators, technology strategies and long-term investment decisions (Eames, 2000).

4.4   Administrative Compliance

By contrast to the record of substantial over-compliance with the LCP-Directive's SO_2 emissions reductions targets presented above, the picture with respect to administrative compliance has been far more mixed. The Netherlands, France and the UK have at times all failed to comply with various aspects of the Directive's administrative requirements. For example:

1. The French legislation transposing the Directive, e.g. the 'arrêté' of 27 June 1990, specified a different qualification for 'new plant' to that given in the Directive: i.e. 19 August 1990 compared with 1 July 1987 cited in the LCP-Directive.
2. The Dutch Bees WLV interpreted Article 8 of the Directive, which deals with procedures in the case of malfunction, interruption of the supply of low-sulphur fuel or sudden interruption in the gas supply, incorrectly with respect to new plants. This and a number of other minor anomalies were rectified when the Bees WLV was amended on 6 January 1995.
3. France initially failed to produce a national emissions reduction programme as required under Article 3 of the Directive.
4. The UK was 6 months late producing its national emissions reduction programme.
5. The UK was also late in bringing into force the secondary legislation necessary to transpose the Directive's new plant requirements (in accordance with Article 17).

However, none of these administrative infringements actually prevented attainment of the Directive's environmental goals, thus illustrating the importance of clearly distinguishing between administrative compliance and policy goal attainment when considering the implementation of EU environmental legislation.

5.   COST EFFECTIVENESS

Cost effectiveness refers to the ability to achieve a given level of environmental quality at low cost. Comparable figures on compliance costs are not readily available for implementation of the LCP-Directive (or equivalent pre-existing national legislation) for the four countries considered owing to the radically different compliance strategies adopted and the extended time period over which implementation effectively took place. However, by considering the degree of flexibility afforded to plant operators by the various policy instruments employed, together with any other external constraints upon their freedom to reduce their abatement costs, it is possible to make a number of well-founded deductions concerning the relative cost performance of the four national implementation processes examined. In this case we see that the overall ranking with respect to cost effectiveness is principally determined by the choice of policy instrument.

In Germany and the Netherlands the specification of a relatively inflexible policy instrument in pre-existing national legislation (i.e. the requirement to upgrade existing plant to meet a plant-based emissions limit of $400mg/SO_2/m^3$), meant that the cost effectiveness of implementing the LCP-Directive in these countries would inevitably be low. In effect, this limit meant that existing plant would either be required to retrofit FGD or close.

German electricity generators were also constrained by long-term domestic coal contracts, thereby ruling out the switching fuels and generating technologies as an abatement strategy, and further reducing the potential scope for cost effectiveness gains. Finally, in North Rhine-Westphalia forest damage was treated as an environmental emergency and cost effectiveness was further traded-off for early environmental gains under the State's Emissions Reduction Plan. Overall then one can conclude that the cost effectiveness of the implementation process in Germany was relatively low.

In the Netherlands, the electricity sector Covenant also further traded-off cost effectiveness for environmental gains. However, the particular market structure of the Dutch electricity sector (e.g. a nationally co-ordinated oligopoly controlled by SEP) provided the flexibility necessary for these additional environmental gains to be achieved in a relatively cost effective manner. Prior to its dissolution in 1999, SEP was responsible for: co-ordination of electricity supply and demand; import and export of electricity; collective purchase of fuels; pooling of fuel and production costs; and, operational rank ordering of individual plants. As a result SEP was effectively able to operate a system of cross-company subsidies to exploit the limited opportunities for cost effectiveness gains, through a differential allocation of abatement efforts, available under the Covenant. Hence, the cost effectiveness of the implementation process in the Netherlands was somewhat better than that in Germany.

By contrast, the choice of a relatively flexible policy instrument, e.g. sectoral targets with constrained company bubbles, to implement the LCP-Directive in the UK electricity sector, suggests that the UK implementation process was relatively cost effective, as the two dominant generating companies, National Power and PowerGen, were largely free to optimise their internal allocation of abatement costs. Furthermore, the low number and large size of these companies would have meant that the flexibility provided by their 'company bubbles' allowed them to exploit a very large part of theoretical potential for 'gain from trade'. This deduction is supported by several pieces of circumstantial evidence. Firstly, the UK government's proposals to establish a fully-fledged national sulphur trading scheme failed, in part at least, because National Power and PowerGen did not see that it was in their commercial interests to support such a scheme. Secondly, an analysis of UK emissions inventories (Eames, 2000) shows that the average mean capacity of the 16 large combustion plants closed in the UK electricity sector between 1990 and 1995 was 1291.25 MWth, compared with an average mean capacity of 6175.41 MWth for plant in this sector in 1990 as a whole. Hence it follows that the plants closed were considerably smaller than average.[25] This period therefore saw the concentration of the UK's remaining coal-fired generating capacity in the larger, and one would therefore assume, more economically efficient plant.

Finally, in the case of France, the government's policy of increasing reliance on nuclear power meant that implementation was almost entirely a case of business as usual. No additional constraints on the electricity sector (EDF and CDF) were required to ensure compliance with the Directive's national emission reduction targets. Furthermore, no such constraints were implemented by the French government, which instead chose to cite an existing voluntary agreement (the EDF-programme) to achieve administrative compliance with the Directive. Strictly speaking the process for implementing the LCP-Directive in France may therefore be regarded as highly cost-effective. However, it should also be noted that the construction, operation and decommissioning of nuclear plant is far from cost free.

One can therefore rank the relative cost performance of the various national processes for implementing LCP-Directive (or equivalent pre-existing national legislation) in the four countries considered, as shown in Table 4.19.

Table 4.19 Cost effectiveness of implementation of the LCP-Directive (in electricity sector) in selected countries

	Germany	Netherlands	United Kingdom	France
Relative cost effectiveness	Low	Medium/low	High	Very high
Explanatory factors	Uniform plant-based emissions limit ($400mg/SO_2/m^3$)	Uniform plant-based emissions limit ($400mg/SO_2/m^3$)	Very flexible pollution abatement allocation (company bubbles)	Implementation largely 'business as usual'
	NRW Negotiated agreement provided for additional environmental gains (on basis of environmental emergency)	Negotiated agreement provides for additional environmental gains	Dynamic market structure (impact of privatisation)	State monopoly (market structure – facilitates investment in nuclear power)
	Long-term coal contracts	Intra industry co-ordination via SEP (market structure: national co-ordinated oligopoly)	Phasing out of long-term coal contracts	

6.   SUMMARY AND CONCLUSIONS

The European regulatory framework for abating sulphur emissions that has evolved over the last two decades has been characterised by significant uncertainty, increasing complexity and overlapping requirements. Each of the countries considered has international obligations both as a member of the European Union and as a signatory to the UNECE Convention on Long Range Transboundary Air Pollution (CLRTAP). Each also possesses its own distinctive body of national regulation, developed in accordance with its own legal and administrative traditions.

A wide variety of different regulatory instruments have been deployed at various times, across varying geographical spaces. These include national and sectoral emissions ceilings and reduction targets, plant-based emission limit standards, technology-based standards, ambient air quality standards, voluntary or negotiated agreements, and controls on the sulphur content of various types of fuel. Furthermore, the strictness of the regulatory objectives embodied by these various instruments has generally been ratcheted-up over time, as both scientific knowledge of the environmental damage caused by SO_2, and the practical scope for abatement have improved.

Only in the case of Germany has no evidence of 'gaps' in the implementation of the Directive's administrative requirements come to light. Despite this all four countries considered (Germany, the Netherlands, France and the United Kingdom) have to date achieved substantial over-compliance with the LCP-Directive national SO_2 emission reduction targets. Furthermore, this is part of a broader picture, for these countries, of over-compliance with sectoral, national and international (UNECE) SO_2 emissions reduction objectives. In each case, however, the environmental outcomes observed were the product of quite distinct national implementation processes. Strictly speaking the LCP-Directive itself has had very little effect on the environmental outcomes achieved. Indeed, in the cases of Germany, the Netherlands and France there was no causal link between the SO_2 emission reductions achieved and the LCP-Directive.

In Germany and the Netherlands SO_2 emission reductions were driven not by the Directive but by (pre-existing) domestic policy initiatives, underpinned by the high public and political profile of acidification and environmental issues more generally. This finding is not particularly surprising as it reflects the well-known 'leader–laggard' dynamic of some EU policies, whereby a European policy cycle starts when a new policy problem is tackled by domestic legislation in an environmental 'leader' such as Germany, the Netherlands or other Nordic countries. Concerns about transboundary pollution, or attempts to seek national competitive advantage, then result in the initiation of an EU policy-making process, leading ultimately to the diffusion of the policy in less advanced countries (Liefferink and Andersen, 1998; Héritier, 1995).

In the French case, implementation was almost entirely a case of 'business as usual' as the reduction of classic thermal electricity production, and associated SO_2 emissions, which resulted from the expansion of nuclear power was sufficient to comply with the Directive's targets. Only a minor part of the emission reductions achieved in the 1990s can be attributed to voluntary action by EDF which was in any case not causally linked to implementation of the LCP-Directive, but to promotion of the company's image and local air quality concerns.

Furthermore, even in the UK case a significant proportion of the emission reductions achieved can also be attributed to other drivers; such as bi-lateral pressure from Norway and the other Scandinavian countries; anticipation of further regulation under the second UNECE sulphur protocol; and, perhaps most significantly the switch to CCGT generation with the introduction of competition into the UK electricity market. This work therefore demonstrates that the implementation of European environmental policies depends upon far more than simply effective transposition, monitoring and enforcement, as is often assumed. Indeed, only in the case of Germany is monitoring and enforcement seen to have played a significant role, and even the sophisticated monitoring system employed cannot explain the pattern of over-compliance found.

Crucially, this chapter illustrates the importance of policy interactions; market structure and dynamics; and technology choice and path dependency, to both the environmental outcomes obtained and cost effectiveness of implementation processes. Such policy interactions may be with parallel domestic environmental policy initiatives, as for example was the case with the implementation of the LCP-Directive in the Netherlands. Or they may be with non-environmental policies, as was most clearly illustrated in the case of the interactions with national energy and competition policy in France and the UK. Without the policy-push development of the French nuclear sector in the 1980s, and the dash to build CCGT plant unleashed by the privatisation in UK in the 1990s, compliance in both of these countries would have required much greater investment in retrofitting expensive FGD. This second example also illustrates the link between market structure and dynamics, and technology choice and path dependency. The French drive to expand nuclear power relied upon EDF's effective public monopoly. In the UK case, liberalisation of the electricity market played a positive role promoting a radical shift to a cleaner less capital-intensive generating technology (CCGT), thereby reducing compliance costs. The likely impacts of such interactions currently receive little explicit consideration in the policy process. Furthermore, the dynamics of such interactions could equally well be either mixed or negative, i.e. acting either to reduce environmental goal attainment or increase abatement costs, or both. Given current global trends towards market liberalisation, this is clearly an issue that deserves much greater consideration by researchers and policy makers alike.

NOTES

1. The LCP-Directive was subsequently amended by the Council Directive 94/66/EC in December 1994.
2. http://www.unece.org/env/lrtap/, July 2000.
3. That is not to say that the results of these studies were not disputed. In the UK in particular scientific dispute over the role of the long-range transport of pollutants and the mechanisms through which acidification actually took place continued well into the 1980s.

4. In German, the 'Dreizehnte Verordnung zur Durchführung des Bundes-Immissionsschutzgesetzes' (Verordnung über Großfeuerungsanlagen – 13. BimSchV).

5. See Bertram and Karger (1988, p. 98), cited in Bültmann and Wätzold (2000), IMPOL case study report.

6. For example, in 1997 Germany generated 549.7 billion kWh electricity and consumed 545 billion: source, Statistisches Bundesamt (1999, p. 225) and VDEW, www.strom.de/zf_sz_15.htm, 03/23/99.

7. Implementation of West German law (i.e. the GFA-VO) in the former East Germany, following reunification, is excluded from this analysis, as this concerns the transformation of a former communist country into a market economy and is therefore beyond the scope of this current work.

8. Bertram and Karger (1988, p. 99) and Dose (1997).

9. In German, the 'Emissionsminderungsplan für Großfeuerungsanlagen der öffentlichen Energieversorgung'.

10. As noted above, the GFA-VO emission limits had to be met from June 1988. Consequently, the EMP provided for outstanding reductions in that year; however, a remarkable decline of emissions was in fact achieved before that date. This can be explained by a special agreement between the North Rhine-Westphalia government and one electricity supply company, the Rheinisch-Westfälische Elektrizitätswerke (RWE), which dated back to 1982. Thus was neither a direct consequence of the GFA-VO nor part of the EMP. Rheinisch-Westfälische Elektrizitätswerke promised to decrease its SO_2 emissions by about 110,000 tons between 1984 and 1987 through application of a dry lime additive technique called 'Trocken-Additiv-Verfahren' (TAV). This simple technique allows for a rapid reduction in SO_2 emissions, but only to a limited extent. The demands of the GFA-VO could not be met by means of TAV. Nevertheless, the technique was useful to bridge over the period of time necessary to install FGD. The EMP itself did not prescribe or promote the application of any particular desulphurisation technique.

11. In fact, according to Bültmann and Wätzold (2000), the ordinance sometimes had the effect of prolonging the operational life of plants. When the GFA-VO came into force, a number of existing LCPs were rather old, but not old enough to be closed and were therefore retrofitted. However, the installation of expensive FGD facilities was only economic if they were operated for at least 10 years. Consequently, some combustion plants were overhauled to stay in operation for this period of time. Hence, the construction of new plants and development of cleaner, more efficient combustion techniques was postponed.

12. There was one exception: new coal-fuelled combustion plants that were permitted before 1 August 1988 were allowed to emit up to 800 mg of NO_x/m^3 according to Bees WLV cf. the 650 mg/m^3 NO_X limit specified in Directive 88/609/EEC.

13. 'Arrêté du 27 juin 1990 relatif à la limitation des rejets atmosphériques des grandes installations de combustion et aux conditions d'évacuation des rejets des installations de combustion' published in the Official Journal of the French Republic on 19 August 1990.

14. In order to solve this problem and comply with the LCP-Directive, the French Government eventually had to issue additional arrêtés covering those plants built between the two dates.

15. In 1993 the EDF sector consisted of 15 sites, totalling 28 plants using coal and 19 plants using fuel oil.

16. The five-year plan also made funds available to finance the installation of desulphurisation equipment at two of CDF's plants. However, these measures were dependent upon the satisfactory completion of EDF's primary desulphurisation trials, and hence these too have never been implemented.

17. HMIP was subsumed within the Environment Agency with its establishment as a fully independent Agency on 1 April 1996.

18. The BATNEEC limit was designed to protect local air quality and to ensure that critical load effects from individual power stations were addressed.

19. In all, the following amendments were made to the Plan: i) July 1994, adjustment to the limits for NO_X between the refinery and electricity sectors in England and Wales; ii) October 1995, transfer of quota allocation from the English to the Northern Ireland electricity sector; iii) June and July 1996, quota allocation in England and Wales ESI adjusted following sale of National Power and PowerGen combustion plant to Eastern Merchant Generation Ltd; iv) December 1996, sectoral and geographical allocations of emissions quotas removed. These amendments had no effect on the overall UK SO_2 and NO_X emission limits under the Plan.

20. The England and Wales electricity supply industry was restructured in 1989 and transferred to private ownership in 1991. Generation competition was introduced immediately, whilst supply competition was phased in over a nine-year period.

21. At the time of privatisation, the 80 Mtonnes of coal taken by the electricity generators accounted for 75% of the UK coal market. UK deep-mined coal prices were significantly higher than world prices. To protect the industry, the government brokered contracts between the generators and British Coal for a transitional period until 1998. Under these contracts, the volume of coal supplied to the electricity generators fell steadily to 30 Mtonnes in 1997.

22. The 1996 emissions targets have been interpolated as no reduction target was set in the LCP-Directive for this year, except in the case of Germany where the 3000kt/yr emission target, which the unified Germany was required to meet by 1 January 1996, under Directive 90/656/EEC was used.

23. According to the UNECE, in total the 21 Parties to the 1985 Protocol had reduced their sulphur emissions by more than 50% by 1993 and all individually complied with the Protocol's objective of a 30% reduction. Furthermore, eleven

Parties achieved reductions of at least 60% (http://www.unece.org/env/lrtap/ 6 May 2000).

24. Table 4.15 also shows that the sector's SO_2 emissions actually increased slightly between 1994 and 1996. At the time of writing more recent data was not available to show whether this trend has continued.

25. In fact none of the sector's 24 largest combustion plants was closed, whereas 16 of the 30 plants with a capacity of 2800 MWth or less were closed.

REFERENCES

Bertram, Jürgen and Robert Karger (1988), 'Entscheidungen gefordert. Planung, Bau und Inbetriebnahme von REA-Anlagen in Steinkohlekraftwerken', *Sonderdruck aus Energie*, 40 (7), pp. 98–109.

Boehmer-Christiansen, S. (1995), 'The Domestic Basis of International Agreements', SPRU contribution to EC contract EVSV-CT 930.85.

Bültmann, A. and F. Wätzold (2000), 'The Implementation of National and European Legislation Concerning Air Emissions from Large Combustion Plants in Germany', European Project IMPOL – The Implementation of EU Environmental Policies: Efficiency Issues, UFZ-Centre for Environmental Research Leipzig-Halle, August 2000.

Department of the Environment (1990), 'The United Kingdom's Programme and National Plan for Reducing Emissions of Sulphur Dioxide (SO_2) and Oxides of Nitrogen (NO_X) from Existing Large Combustion Plants', Annex A, London: DoE.

Dose, N. (1997), *'Die verhandelnde Verwaltung. Eine empirische Untersuchung über den Vollzug des Immissionsschutzrechtes'*, Baden-Baden.

Eames, M. (2000), 'The Implementation of the Large Combustion Plant Directive: Over Compliance but at what Cost?', SPRU, University of Sussex: in M. Glachant, *How can the Implementation of EU Environmental Policy be more Effective and Efficient? Lessons from Implementation Studies*, CERNA, Ecole des Mines de Paris, Research Paper 2000-B-7, September.

Héritier, A. (1995), 'Leaders and "Laggards" in European Clean Air Policy', in F. van Waarden and B. Unger (eds), *Convergence or Diversity? Internationalisation and Economic Policy Response*, Aldershot: Avebury, pp. 278–305.

Ikwue, A. and J. Skea (1996), 'Energy Sector Responses to European Combustion Emission Regulations', in F. Lévêque (ed.), *Environmental Policy in Europe*, Cheltenham UK, Edward Elgar, pp. 75–112.

Jung, J. (1988), 'Die Kosten der SO_2- und NO_X-Minderung in der deutschen Eletrizitätswirtschaft', *Elektrizitätswirtschaft*, 5, pp. 267–270.

Liefferink, D. and M.S. Andersen (1998), 'Strategies of the "Green" Member States in EU Environmental Policy-making', *Journal of European Public Policy*, 5(2), pp. 254–70.

Lulofs, K. (2000), 'Adjustments in the Dutch Electricity Producing Sector in the Context of the European Directive 88/609/EEC', European Project IMPOL – The Implementation of EU Environmental Policies: Efficiency Issues, Research Paper 2000-B-4, CERNA.

MURL-Ministerium für Umwelt, Raumordnung und Landwirtschaft des Landes Nordrhein-Westfalen (1992), Bilanz und Erfolg des Emissionsminderungsplanes für Großfeuerungsanlagen der öffentlichen Energieversorgung in NRW (EMP), Düsseldorf.

Schucht, S. (2000), 'The Implementation of the EU Large Combustion Plant Directive (88/609) in France', European Project IMPOL – The Implementation of EU Environmental Policies: Efficiency Issues, Research Paper 2000-B-3, CERNA.

Smith, A. (1997), *Integrated Pollution Control*, Studies in Green Research, Aldershot, UK: Ashgate Publishing Ltd.

Sorrell, S. (1999), 'Why Sulphur Trading Failed in the UK', in S. Sorrell and J. Skea, *Pollution for Sale: Emissions Trading and Joint Implementation*, Cheltenham UK: Edward Elgar, pp. 170–210.

Watson, J. (1998), 'Advanced Fossil Fuel Technologies for the UK Power Industry', Submission to the UK government's review of power station fuels, Brighton: Science Policy Research Unit, University of Sussex.

5. Implementing Command and Control Directives: the case of Directive 89/429/EEC

Kris Lulofs[1]

1. INTRODUCTION

For a long time incineration was considered to be a 'clean' method of waste disposal, but in the 1970s and 1980s the incineration of municipal waste was shown to be a significant source of air pollution. This became a political issue in some countries, the most notorious aspect being the emissions of dioxins, which may cause cancer and birth defects (Eberg, 1997; EC, 1997). In 1989 the European Union issued two European Directives on the control of atmospheric emissions from municipal waste incinerators: Directive 89/369/EEC applies to new incinerators licensed after 1 December 1990, and Directive 89/429/EEC applies to existing incinerators licensed before 1 December 1990.

This chapter is a discussion of the implementation of the 1989 European Directive 89/429/EEC on existing plants. It focuses on the emission limits for a number of pollutants, which apply to individual plants and thus provides an analysis of a traditional command and control approach. It highlights the interaction between actors and factors in national implementation arenas and answers a number of questions: what were the dynamics of implementation in national arenas? Were good results achieved? Was the desired environmental quality achieved at the lowest possible cost?

Section 2 of this chapter examines the negotiations on the 1989 European Directives. An assessment is made of the characteristics of municipal waste incineration and the pre-existing national regulations in individual Member States to determine whether these played a decisive role during negotiations on the content of the Directives. In the European arena, waste policy is usually about knowledge, perceptions, uncertainties and negotiations (Weale, 1992); arguments are about the necessary level of environmental protection and the fine-tuning of precautionary measures (EC, 1997).

Section 3 analyses how the countries coped with the 1989 European Directives. When the 1989 Directives came into force, their provisions had to be incorporated into the national legislation of Member States of the European Union. Germany and the Netherlands have proved to be the most ambitious, followed at a respectable distance by the United Kingdom; France adopted the minimum European requirements into French law. The question of whether the waste incineration sectors in the four countries have been restructured to ensure compliance with the national regulations is also answered in section 3.

Section 4 evaluates the outcomes of the national implementation processes. In section 4.1 the criteria used for evaluation are the level of goal attainment and the contribution made by the European Directives in achieving the goals. In section 4.2 the cost effectiveness of implementation is assessed. Some conclusions and observations concerning the implementation of the 1989 regulation on existing plants are presented in section 5.

The analysis is based predominately on the national case studies by Bültmann and Wätzold (2000), Eames (2000), Lulofs (1999) and Schucht (2000). The findings on environmental and efficiency outcomes are limited to Directive 89/429/EEC (on existing incinerators). The analysis of individual plants is based on the 400 or so existing municipal waste incinerators in the four countries. The research relates to the period 1989–1999, focusing on the years 1989–1996.

2.   NEGOTIATING THE EUROPEAN DIRECTIVES

2.1   The Pre-Existing National Contexts

Table 5.1 presents some key characteristics of national waste policies, waste markets, the incineration sector and pre-existing national regulations. These characteristics explain the positions taken by Member States in the negotiations and demonstrate that landfill was and still is an important option in European countries. In this respect, Germany, France and the Netherlands, in that order, were to be found in the middle ground, incinerating between 30 per cent and 40 per cent of their waste. The United Kingdom lagged behind, incinerating 10 per cent of its municipal waste. The share of waste incinerated in the front-running European countries was in the 60–80 per cent range (Hartenstein and Horvay, 1996).

Table 5.1 Some characteristics of national waste policies, waste markets and waste incineration sectors

	France	Germany	Netherlands	United Kingdom
Number of incinerators	302 in 1989, 297 in 1993	42 in 1980, 48 in 1990, 61 in 1999	13 in 1989, 7 early 1990s, 11 in 1999	40 in 1987, 4 in 1996, 10 in 1999
Landfill (1990)	52% of waste	70% of waste	52% of waste	90% of waste
Capacity of incinerators	Around 1993 80% < 6 t/h, 20% > 6t/h	Around 1989 almost all > 6 t/h	Around 1989 all but one > 6 t/h	Around 1990 all but 4 > 6 t/h
Ranking of waste management options	Since 1992 equal status for materials and energy recycling; materials recycling prioritised in 1998	In 1998 re-use and recycling was given a higher priority over energy recycling	In 1998 organic recycling and materials recycling given a higher priority than energy recycling	Poorly articulated until 1995. In 1995 energy from waste was given an equivalent status to recycling and composting
Opportunities of passing on retrofitting costs	Small, due to budget constraints and local democracy	Large, due to political debate and a rather high public environmental awareness and willingness to pay	Large, due to political debate and a rather high public environmental awareness and willingness to pay	Small, due to budget constraints of decentralised actors and competition from cheap landfill
Trend in incineration and landfill	Incineration favoured over landfill and of considerable importance; landfilling of combustibles to be banned in 2002	Proportion of waste incinerated is increasing, but there is still more waste landfilled than incinerated	Incineration favoured from 1989 and of considerable importance, landfilling of combustibles banned from 1996	Continuing emphasis on cheap landfill option, Non-Fossil Fuel Obligation has revitalised large scale incineration since 1995
Market structure	Regional monopolies	Regional monopolies	Regional monopolies	Regional monopolies
Existing national emission limits compared with 1989 EU-Directives	In general lax; moderate for new incinerators starting from 1986	Strict	Strict	Lax

Source: Data on landfill (Buclet and Godard, 2000).

Germany and the Netherlands developed waste management policies that gave priority to re-use and recycling relatively early, in the mid to late 1980s. These policies favour incineration over landfill as disposal options. Although the share of incineration increased in Germany, more waste was still landfilled than incinerated. French waste policies favoured incineration for a long time, but from 1992 to 1998 French policy was somewhat ambiguous. Emphasis was first placed on reducing the amount of waste landfilled in favour of materials and energy recycling, which led to an increase in the amount of waste incinerated with energy recovery, but only limited materials recycling. In the late 1990s policies were adjusted, leading to an increase in the amount of materials recycling, with landfill as an option of last resort, i.e. only where necessary. UK waste policy was developed relatively late on. The decentralised waste disposal operators were given considerable discretion and could choose the relatively cheap landfill option.

Table 5.1 illustrates that the effects of the European Directives were likely to be marginal in Germany and the Netherlands. In Germany the political debate and a rather high public environmental awareness and willingness to pay made it possible to pass on retrofitting costs if incineration was chosen within the regional monopoly. Although in the Netherlands landfill was also cheaper compared with incineration, the chosen waste policy priorities, strict national regulations and ability to pass on retrofitting costs made the European Directives a marginal issue. For France and the United Kingdom the draft Directives were likely to have substantial impacts because of the considerable number of older incinerators and the rather lax regulations (Loader et al., 1991). For the United Kingdom this was not a big threat because national waste policy did not favour incineration over landfill. Closing these incinerators down would not lead to political controversy. French waste policy, however, did favour incineration, but was accompanied by cheaper landfill, relatively lax regulation of incinerators and limited opportunities to pass on the costs (Bertossi et al., 1994; Buclet and Godard, 2000, p. 211).

2.2   The Negotiation Process

When the drafts of the 1989 Directives were discussed, the French government realised that implementing the Directives would be a very ambitious project for the French waste incineration sector. It is therefore not surprising that France participated in a coalition that tried to limit the requirements contained in the draft Directives by objecting to the proposed standards for dioxin emissions. It also tried to prolong the deadlines for compliance and introduce a range of deadlines for plants of different capacities so that investment costs – often to be borne by regional and local government – could be spread out over a longer period. The estimated costs were huge and the idea behind the progressive deadlines was to start by bringing the larger incinerators into compliance and postponing work on the smaller plants until 2000. This would allow the municipalities to keep the small plants running and amortise their investments (Schucht, 2000).

The negotiations resulted in differentiated emission standards according to the capacity and age of the plant. Such standards are more cost-efficient compared with uniform emission limits if the appropriate categories are chosen. On 1 December 1996 existing large incinerators had to comply with more or less the same emission standards as new incinerators. For small incinerators there was a transitional arrangement from 1 December 1995 to December 2000, at which point they had to meet the same standards as new incinerators. The indirect requirements to reduce dioxin emissions were also eased for existing incinerators. The emission standards are set out in full in Table 5.2.

Table 5.2 Emission limits in mg/m³ for the various incinerator capacities.
Standard conditions: 273 degrees K, 101.3 Kpa, 11% oxygen or
9% CO₂

	Emission limits per 1 December 1996 for existing incinerators with a capacity > 6t/h; per 1 December 2000 for other existing incinerators; and per 1 December 1990 for new incinerators			Emission limits from 1 December 1995 to 1 December 2000 for existing incinerators with a capacity < 6t/h (transitional arrangement)	
	< 1 t/h	1 t/h–3 t/h	> 3 t/h	< 1t/h	1–6t/h
Pb+Cr+Cu+Mn		5	5		
Ni+As		1	1		
Cd+Hg	250	100	50		
HF	'divided'	4	2		
SO₂		300	300		
CO	100	100	100	100	100
Compound	20	20	20		

Research related to municipal waste incineration carried out for the European Commission (EC, 1997) has shown that the emission limits in Belgium, Italy and Spain are largely comparable with those in France, while the national regulations on waste incineration in Sweden and Austria are roughly comparable with those in Germany and the Netherlands. The United Kingdom is broadly representative of countries whose standards lie somewhere in between these two groups. It should also be noted that the European Commission decided to prepare a new Directive on waste incineration and published a draft in 1994. This has still not been adopted because of continuing negotiations on issues such as the comprehensiveness and severity of the regulations. This new Directive would raise the standards to roughly the level already in force in Germany and the Netherlands.

3.   FRONT RUNNERS AND LAGGARDS ANALYSED

How did Germany and the Netherlands, as front runners, and France and the United Kingdom, as relative laggards, cope with the European Directives? Two questions are relevant. First: how did national governments enact the laws and regulations and establish the administrative provisions necessary to comply with the Directives before 1 December 1990? And second: how were the national waste incineration sectors restructured to meet the requirements of national standards? A number of options were available for restructuring. The first choice was between compliance and non-compliance. Choosing compliance implied three possible courses of action: to close incinerators down, to downgrade the capacity of plants or to retrofit the plants. What choices were made and what were the factors, including national monitoring and enforcement activities that influenced these choices?

3.1   The Front Runners

The central issues and events that dominated implementation in Germany and the Netherlands are similar. In both countries the Directives did not lead to changes in domestic standards, which were already strict. But there were differences between the two countries. We turn first to the German case.

3.1.1 Germany
Germany was the only country studied that managed to integrate the European requirements on time – by 23 November 1990 in fact. The technical guideline German TA Luft 1986, issued under the Federal Emissions Control Act of 1974, was the relevant air pollution regulation in force at the time. By the 1980s the German public was highly concerned about emissions from waste incinerators, particularly about dioxin emissions, and when the TA Luft was adopted it was criticised by pressure groups and environmental organisations. The emission limit values set in the TA Luft were either equal to or stricter than the equivalent standards set by the European Directives. However, the TA Luft did not include an emission limit for dioxins, but only required plant operators to reduce dioxin emissions as much as possible.

Soon after the TA Luft 1986 was issued, the Federal Ministry of the Environment (Bundesministerium für Umwelt – BMU) wanted to set even stricter emission limits. This time an ordinance was prepared instead of a technical guideline. Ordinances have the same status as acts of parliament, while technical guidelines have the status of administrative guidelines and are binding only on the public administration and have no direct effect on citizens and the courts. However, it is widely accepted (in legal theory and practice) that the courts should take the provisions of the TA Luft into account when making their decisions (see Kahl and Voßkuhle, 1995, pp. 7–8 and 112–114). Incineration plants had to comply with the limits only after they were incorporated into the plants' individual licences.

The choice of an ordinance instead of a technical guideline was to a large extent the result of pressure groups and environmental organisations blocking the authorisation process, which hindered the disposal of municipal waste and led to lengthy authorisation procedures. In many cases, appeal proceedings were pursued through all the courts, delaying authorisation for up to eight years.

The first drafts of the ordinance were prepared by the BMU during 1988. Waste incineration plant operators, suppliers of incineration and emission abatement technologies and scientists were consulted on the technical possibilities for reducing emissions – German engineers were pioneers in both incinerator design and abatement technology. The 'typical' picture was observed: federal and state environment ministries, environmental organisations and pressure groups were in favour of strict emission limits; operators of waste incineration plants and the economic affairs ministry (Bundesministerium für Wirtschaft – BMWi) opposed tight limits. The German states, especially the Environmental Ministers' Conference (UMK), played a very active role, demanding much stricter emission limits than the TA Luft 1986. They wanted to respond to public concerns and remove their authorisation and enforcement authorities from the firing line. During the discussions the waste incineration plant operators adopted a fairly co-operative strategy, although they were not happy with the costs of the tighter emission limits. However, the waste incineration plant operators were able, quite easily, to transfer the costs to their clients by charging higher rates.

The most problematic emission limit value discussed was that for dioxins and furans. The BMU wanted an emission limit value of 0.1 ng TEQ/m^3 and referred to promising results from test operations, although it had to admit that it was only very likely, but not certain, that the limit value of 0.1 ng TEQ/m^3 could be met. Nevertheless it decided to set this value. Pressure groups and environmental organisations took part in the official inquiry that took place at the end of 1988 and the beginning of 1989. They declared that stricter limits were technically feasible, although some argued for abandonment of waste incineration. Some minor points of the draft ordinance were changed. The ordinance was incorporated into German law as the seventeenth ordinance under the Federal Emissions Control Act (BImSchG) and therefore referred to simply as '17.BImSchV'. The emission limits, scope and most of the measuring procedures of the German ordinance were, and still are, much stricter than the European Directives. The European Directives have not influenced the preparation of the ordinance.

Box 5.1 Stricter German national limits

All existing municipal waste incinerators had to comply with the same emission limits as new ones by 1 December 1996; there were no transitional arrangements for incinerators with a capacity of less than 6 tonnes/hour. Lenient emission standards were not introduced for small incinerators. Permitted concentrations in flue gases of dust and HCl were reduced by 67 per cent compared with the EU-limits. Permitted concentrations of HF, Cd and Hg were reduced by 50 per cent, allowed concentrations of HCl and SO_2 were reduced by 80 per cent. Limits for emissions of Pb, Cr, Cu and Mn were 90 per cent lower than the EU standards. Additional limits were set on NO_X and dioxins ($0.1 ng TEQ/m^3$).

Restructuring the municipal waste incineration sector in North Rhine-Westphalia, Germany. The empirical analysis for Germany focuses on the federal state of North Rhine-Westphalia (NRW), which, with Bavaria, has the highest number of waste incineration plants of all the German states.[2] Experts are of the opinion, though, that the outcomes in other federal states are comparable. The major issues concerning the Directives that were discussed in NRW were the technical possibilities and the costs of meeting the dioxin target. In August 1989, studies were carried out in NRW on dioxin abatement, the available techniques and their installation costs. Four suppliers of active coal filters had already tested their equipment in test plants and guaranteed they could meet the limit of 0.1 ng TEQ/m^3. The techniques were ready to be applied in large-scale incinerators and could be installed without entailing excessive additional costs (EUR 4–6 per tonne of waste).

The government of North Rhine-Westphalia negotiated a voluntary agreement with the waste incineration sector in the state, the 'Emission Reduction Plan for Dioxins from Waste Incineration Plants' (Emissionsminderungsplan für Dioxine aus Abfallverbrennungsanlagen – EMDA). The high level of public concern about dioxin emissions from municipal waste incinerators and the administrative delay tactics were the two decisive factors behind the EMDA, not the ordinance. The agreement covered not only the municipal waste incinerators, but also integrated incinerators for hazardous and industrial waste. The deadline for retrofitting the incinerators was 1 December 1995. The agreement was reached in February 1990, ten months before the 17.BImSchV was enacted. Although the agreement originally only covered dioxin emissions, it soon became clear that the equipment for cutting dioxin emissions could not be separated from equipment designed to reduce emissions of other pollutants covered by the 17.BimSchV already in force. This meant that the EMDA's deadline for retrofitting the plants for dioxin abatement (indirectly) applied to the entire abatement technology necessary to comply with the 17.BImSchV. The voluntary agreement was of strategic interest to both the NRW government and the incineration sector: both parties were interested in working for a more positive image. They were confronted by a great deal of pressure from the public and administrative delays to the authorisation procedures, caused by legal action taken by environmental groups, which were hampering waste management and business opportunities. The desire for a more positive image, therefore, had its basis in very material interests. The agreement speeded up compliance with strict emission standards. The NRW government established a co-ordination committee (Koordierungsstelle) to draft a text of the official agreement, to observe its implementation and to co-ordinate the retrofitting activities to ensure that there would always be sufficient incineration capacity available at any one time. The co-ordination committee presented the final agreement at the beginning of 1991. The agreement covered 14 municipal waste incineration plants, excluding only a few old or small plants (which were due for closure anyway). Three incinerators were exempted from the deadline because they had special site-related problems. All incineration plants were given an extra six months to optimise the abatement equipment after it had been installed.

Of the 14 municipal waste incinerators in NRW participating in the EMDA, 13 were retrofitted. Only one very small plant was closed down – and the 17.BImSchV was not even the decisive reason for the closure. The operators independently retrofitted their waste incineration plants. They chose and installed the flue gas cleaning techniques they considered to be appropriate for their individual plants. When the 17.BImSchV was enacted, German waste incinerators had either already been fitted with de-dusting systems (cyclones or electrostatic precipitators) and scrubbers to 'wash' acidic pollutants from the flue gases (dry, semi-dry, semi-wet or wet systems) or were about to be fitted with these cleaning systems. This meant that in effect the 17.BImSchV mainly required the waste incinerator operators to install deNO$_x$ systems and devices to reduce dioxin and furan emissions. DeNO$_x$ systems were already in use in other plants, such as large combustion plants. The retrofitting mainly took place between 1994 and 1996.

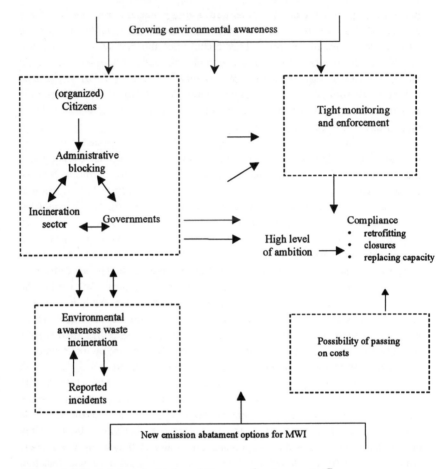

Figure 5.1 Explaining the high ambitions and outcomes in Germany

There is a strict monitoring and enforcement system in Germany. In general, incineration plants are equipped with computers that automatically record and process the emission data. Once the devices are installed, the whole system must be approved by the supervising authority. The 17.BImSchV requires plant operators to have their measuring equipment checked once a year and calibrated every three years. At the end of each year a report on all emission values for the preceding year is submitted to the supervising authority. As well as the pollution abatement retrofits, all plants in NRW were connected to a system for telemetric transfer of emissions data (Emissions-Fernüberwachung – EFÜ) by 1 December 1995. The processed and classified emission values are automatically transmitted to the supervising authority once a day. In addition, the system automatically alerts the authority if any emission limit values have been exceeded during the last 24 hours by means of a message on the computer monitor. The EFÜ makes it impossible to exceed emission limit values without the supervising authority knowing about it. The EFÜ even enables supervising authorities to log on to a plant's electronic emissions control system at any time and without prior notice to the operators. Moreover, supervising authorities are authorised to carry out on-site controls whenever they consider this to be necessary. In most cases the limits are exceeded only for a few minutes and can be put right by process optimisation. Municipal waste incinerators are still high on the supervision authorities' list of priorities and it seems to be almost impossible for waste incinerators to evade control. In principle, enforcement methods range from the imposition of fines to temporary closure of incineration units or revocation of the licence.

3.1.2 The Netherlands

The relevant series of events in the Netherlands started in the mid-1970s when the Seveso incident prompted research in the Netherlands into the sources of dioxins. In 1979 questions were raised in the Dutch parliament about the release of dioxins from waste incineration plants. Preparations were made to issue regulations. A small research project indicated serious emissions of heavy metals, mercury, cadmium and dioxins (Second Chamber of Parliament, 1983–1984, no. 18319), followed by a study into pollution abatement technology, which concluded that stricter limits were viable. This led to the Incineration Guideline 1985. The standards set for new plants were more or less comparable with the European Directives, but the issue of existing incinerators was left in the hands of the provinces, the licensing authorities in these cases. The government was afraid that the extra costs would push up the costs to households too much if existing incinerators had to meet the same requirements (Waque, 1990).

After stricter limits were issued in Germany and Sweden in 1986, work started on the preparation of a new Guideline. Hence, the Incineration Guideline 1985 did not require that incineration plants be fitted with state-of-the-art technology. In 1988 draft texts were available that referred to the German limits in the TA Luft 1986 and to ongoing discussions in Germany. The Germans, however, did not yet have limits on dioxin emissions. During the preparation of the Incineration Guideline 1989 growing environmental awareness led to a dramatic change in perceptions of the costs involved. As in Germany, these costs became legitimate: high concentrations of dioxins were found near incineration plants and measurements in three incinerators in 1989 showed that emissions varied from 1.5 ng TEQ/m^3 to 25 ng TEQ/m^3 (Sein et al., 1989). There was no real discussion about the need for strict emission limits to enable an increase in the volume of waste incinerated. In 1989 news broke that traces of dioxins had been found in dairy products made from the milk of cows that were grazed in the Lickebaertpolder. The milk and dairy products were immediately removed from sale. Once German suppliers of pollution abatement equipment were willing to guarantee that their equipment would keep dioxin emissions down to 0.1 ng TEQ/m^3 the draft Incineration Guideline 1989 was agreed. In response, though, the waste incineration sector began a publicity campaign arguing that they could not meet these limits. The limits for dioxins, dust, SO_2, heavy metals and NO_X were debated, but despite this opposition the Incineration Guideline 1989 was issued on 15 August 1989, only a month after the Lickebaertpolder affair had been made public. The emission limits were comparable with those in the German 'ordinance' issued in 1989.

So, as in Germany, the process of enacting the Incineration Guideline 1989 was driven by domestic concerns about dioxins and other pollutants. It led to requirements far stricter than the European demands. However, once the European Directives were adopted, the Dutch government faced huge problems in establishing the formal incorporation of the European requirements into Dutch law on time. On 25 April 1991 the European Commission found the Netherlands to be in default. This was owing to formal problems of implementation, not the environmental objectives and requirements of the Directives. The problem was that the Incineration Guideline 1989 gives the provincial administrations some discretion (see section 3.1.1). For formal compliance with the European Directives the emission limits had to be issued by an Order in Council (Algemene Maatregel van Bestuur – AMvB), which is comparable with a German ordinance. The Dutch law on waste treatment and disposal only authorised the minister to issue guidelines and not an AMvB, and so the law had to be amended. At the same time, the existing 'sectoral' environmental laws in the Netherlands were being revised and integrated within a new single-law framework. The initial idea was to integrate the Dutch law on waste treatment and waste disposal into this new framework law and at the same time establish the necessary authority to issue an AMvB. Because of all kinds of technicalities connected with such a drastic change in the legislation, the transformation process into a single-law framework was slow. The Dutch parliament discussed the issue with the environment minister and proposed an amendment to the existing law on waste treatment and waste disposal (Second Chamber of Parliament, 1990/1991, 1991/1992) which gave the environment minister the authority to issue general rules by AMvB (article 53a, Stb. 1992, no.378). The draft AMvB was pre-published on 3 April 1992. The scope and standards set by the requirements in the AMvB are in line with the Dutch Incineration Guideline 1989.

Box 5.2 Stricter Dutch national emission standards

There is no transitional arrangement for existing incinerators with a capacity of less than 6 tonnes/hour. These have to meet the same requirements as new incinerators on 1 January 1995. Lenient emission standards were not introduced for small incinerators. Compared with EU limits, permitted concentrations in flue gases of a group of heavy metals, HCl and SO_2 were reduced by 80 per cent. The permitted concentrations of organic compounds, HF, CO and Cd+Hg were reduced by 50 per cent. Additional limits were set on NO_x and dioxins. The time allowed for existing large incinerators to comply with the new regulations was also shortened by one year in the Netherlands compared with the European requirements.

The proposed time schedule prompted some discussion about the date existing waste incinerators had to comply with the same requirements as new incinerators. In the Incineration Guideline 1989 and the draft proposal this date was 30 November 1993 but was subsequently changed to 1 January 1995 to avoid foreseeable infringements that would have to be tolerated anyway. For the incineration of municipal waste the old Incineration Guideline 1989 was finally withdrawn on 7 January 1993 and replaced by the Air Pollution from Waste Incineration Decree (Besluit luchtemissies afvalverbranding). The emission standards set by this decree are identical to those in the Incineration Guideline 1989 and go far beyond the standards in the European Directives 89/429/EEC and 89/369/EEC. The Dutch case is also illustrated and summarised in Figure 5.1, which explains the German national ambitions and outcomes. An additional explanatory factor in the Dutch case was the clear choice in Dutch national waste policy to favour incineration over landfill. This was driven partly by the emerging large-scale contamination of soil near landfills, which was starting to pose a threat to groundwater quality.

Restructuring the municipal waste incineration sector in the Netherlands. In a process very unlike the normal Dutch tradition of consultation, the final decisions on the Incineration Guideline 1989 were made very quickly and not on a consensual basis. The decisions were driven by the political imperative of dealing with the dioxin crisis. In an initiative designed to settle conflicts with the incineration sector, co-ordinate implementation and find the best solutions, a study and advisory group was formed (Stuurgroep Uitvoering RV'89) consisting of representatives from the environment ministry, the provinces, the VEABRIN and some consultants. In its final report the Stuurgroup Uitvoering RV'89 disputed whether the limits for dioxins, mercury and NO_x were achievable, but the minister stuck to the Incineration Guideline 1989, with the exception of dioxins for existing incinerators. He decided that the 0.1 ng/m^3 limit should be considered not as an absolute standard but as a guideline for existing incinerators; an absolute standard of 0.4 ng/m^3 was set for existing incinerators. For two incineration plants the 0.4 ng/m^3 limit was applied but with an obligation to reduce this to 0.25 ng/m^3 in the future; the other plants had to comply with the 0.1 ng/m^3 limit. Techniques for reducing NO$_X$ emissions were granted subsidies totalling 39 million guilders and the NO$_X$ emission standards had to be met by 1 January 1995. The Stuurgroep Uitvoering RV'89 also considered four existing incinerators to be too poorly designed and old-fashioned to meet the requirements of the Combustion Guideline 1989. In the end, six incinerators were closed and the capacity replaced, although not all the plants were rebuilt on the same location. Emission reduction techniques employed include active coal injection or active coal filters to reduce emissions of dioxin and furans and NSCR or SCR techniques to reduce NO$_X$ emissions.

The strict system of monitoring and enforcement in the Netherlands must also be mentioned. The incineration plants are equipped with sensors and computers that automatically record and process emissions data on a number of substances. The system is part of the licensing procedure and is checked by the authorities, which inspect municipal waste incinerators frequently; it is not unusual for the provincial authorities to visit them every month. Enforcement measures are comparable with those in North Rhine-Westphalia. A large comprehensive inventory was carried out in 1995 for the Waste Board at the environment ministry as part of the monitoring of new standards for existing incinerators. Of the 212 measurements taken, 206 were within the limits set by the Dutch regulation and none exceeded the limits set by the European regulation (Hesseling et al., 1995). The authorities knew about the breaches and were working together with the incineration plants concerned to solve the problems. There was, however, one exception: the Dutch authorities tolerated the failure of one existing waste incinerator to meet the new Dutch regulations on 1 January 1995 and granted it an extension until 1 December 1996.

3.2   The Laggards – Catching Up?

The central issues and events that dominated implementation in France and the United Kingdom were quite different from those in Germany and the Netherlands. In the UK drastic changes occurred in the waste incineration sector. We examine the French case first.

3.2.1   France

Prior to the integration of the European Directives into national law, an 'arrêté' of 9 June 1986, authorised on 10 July 1986, regulated emissions to the atmosphere from new incineration plants and expanded plants. Standards for these plants were set for emissions of dust, HCl, gaseous hydrocarbon, Cu, Pb, Zn, Ni, Cr, Su, Ag, Co, Ba, Hg+Cd, As and O. The 'arrêté' was not quite as strict as the European Directives of 1989 and covered a different package of atmospheric pollutants and a greater number. No emission limits were set for HF, SO_2 and CO, and on average the limits were 30–50 per cent more lax. The limits set for heavy metals were comparable with the European standards. However, only few incinerators were authorised between 1986 and 1991, and until 1991 the only emission standards applying to existing incinerators were for dust, while there were virtually no regulations for incinerators with a capacity of less than 1 tonne/hour.

Box 5.3 French national standards

The 'arrêté' of 25 January 1991 sets standards as high as those in the European Directives. In some cases less frequent controls of emissions are required. Unlike the Directives, however, the French law takes an integrated approach. It defines requirements with respect to solid residues of waste incineration, such as slag, and residues of the flue gas treatment, in particular for their disposal (landfill), transport and elimination. Moreover, the 'arrêté' defines requirements and standards for the prevention of water pollution and noise.

At the time the European Directives were adopted there was basically no public concern in France about environmental or health effects of waste incineration. The French public viewed waste incineration as 'clean', whereas landfill was believed to be more problematic. Concern about dioxin emissions from incineration plants and its effects on health started to grow around 1997.[3]

The French environment ministry and the Agency for Air Quality (Agence pour la Qualité de l'Air, formerly ADEME) were aware that the policy for existing plants was not sufficient. At that time waste incineration had been identified as a major source of pollution of HCl, mercury and other pollutants. France believed it would be able to comply more or less with the differentiated emission limits decided upon in the European arena, even though the costs were expected to be very high, and so the subsequent transposition of the Directives did not lead to noteworthy discussions or any conflicts. France decided to integrate the minimum European requirements into an 'arrêté' issued on 25 January 1991.

Restructuring the municipal waste incineration sector in France. In the late 1980s, most French municipal waste incineration plants were only equipped with off-gas de-dusting facilities (Milhau and Pernin, 1994). Generally these were electrostatic precipitators for big incinerators and mechanic de-dusters (such as cyclones) for small incinerators. Only about 25 plants already had equipment installed to scrub combustion gases by the end of the 1980s, or were planning to.

In France about 134 furnaces of incinerators with a capacity of more than 6 tonnes/hour were retrofitted, although 61 of them were late in complying with the European standards, being retrofitted between 1997 and 2000. Only two furnaces still do not meet the standards. In the category of furnaces belonging to plants with a capacity of between 3 and 6 tonnes/hour, 19 had been retrofitted in 1997 and 24 had not yet been retrofitted. Few smaller plants have been retrofitted, if any. In general, quite a number of large plants were brought into compliance too late and a large proportion of smaller incinerators still do not meet the standards.

A number of factors have influenced emission abatement at French plants (see Figure 5.2). The first factor is the large number of plants, many of them of small capacity, contrary to the situation in the other countries studied. A second factor has been political uncertainty surrounding the implementation of the Directives owing to the still developing and unstable national waste policy: the market prospects for incineration were diffuse, a new waste law adopted in 1992 changed the hierarchy of waste treatment methods and new requirements for recycling packaging waste were also introduced in 1992. Investment decisions were slowed down. Choosing between the available options (closing plants, downgrading plant capacity or retrofitting) was further hampered by uncertainty about the possibilities and requirements for slag re-use and recycling ('valorisation de mâchefers') and the treatment and disposal of the off-gas cleaning residues of municipal waste incineration. Regarding the off-gas cleaning residues, discussions concerned the intensity of treatment required, which was not specified in the 'arrêté' of 1991.

Uncertainty arose again when in 1993 and 1994 discussions about a new European Directive for municipal waste incinerators began. Initially it was expected that the Directive would be adopted rapidly and, again, investment decisions were postponed. However, the adoption of the Directive was delayed and fresh uncertainty was added in April 1998 when the French environment minister criticised the emphasis given to waste incineration in the waste plans and demanded a revision of the waste plans.

Furthermore, a political dimension was introduced by the municipal elections in 1995. It can be assumed that during the year preceding municipal elections no new investment projects are undertaken that might induce tax increases, and projects are not restarted until about a year after the elections. Also, in the opinion of the public, waste incineration is clean and landfills are problematic. Therefore, contrary to the situation in Germany and the Netherlands, there was no public pressure for change. Another factor was the high investments needed to bring the incinerators up to the required standards, which many of the municipalities found difficult to cover. The problem was deepened by the integrated approach of the 1991 'arrêté', which included requirements for the treatment of solid and liquid residues, and by the large number of small municipalities, which meant that the construction of large plants required co-operation between municipalities, something which was not easy to bring about.[4] Ignorance may have played a decisive role with respect to the very small incinerators. In several cases municipalities might not even have known for a long time that their very small incinerators belonged to the 'installations classées' and/or believed that their mechanical filters met the legal requirements. Many of these plants were very small units indeed, often with a capacity below 1 tonne/hour and often only used a few days a week.

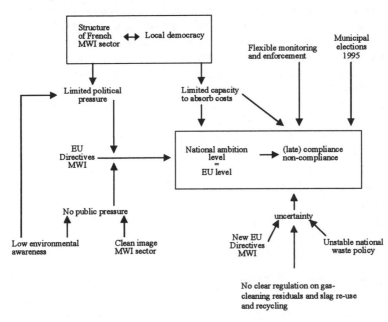

Figure 5.2 Explaining national ambitions and outcomes in France

Lastly, the regulatory style may be an important explanatory factor for the low level of compliance in France. Imperfect enforcement, including emission measurement and reporting requirements, is a characteristic of the French regulatory style, and application of the 1991 'arrêté' has not necessarily been a priority. The balance of power between local enforcers and politicians played a further decisive role in the low level of enforcement.

Prefects have to deal with strong elected representatives and some of them will not want to force the issue of implementation. Even if they are keen to enforce the law they cannot do much if the mayor opposes them. The general picture, therefore, is one of flexible monitoring and enforcement, with an emphasis on large incinerators. Enforcement actions were only found in 28 cases out of the 75 large plants that were late in complying or failed to comply. Moreover, the strictest enforcement measures were, on average, found to have been taken against older incinerators. Recently, the French environment ministry exploited dioxin incidents in 1998 to enforce the 'arrêté' of 1991. The fact that dioxins were put on the political agenda in France is partly due to a Greenpeace campaign in 1996 and subsequent campaigns run by another environmental lobby, CNIID (the National Centre of Independent Information on Waste). In early 1997, France initiated a new policy on dioxin pollution in the circular of 24 February 1997 which required new municipal waste incinerators to meet the emission standard of 0.1 ng TEQ/m^3. A further circular of 30 May 1997 required the measurement of dioxin emissions from large plants, including the municipal waste incineration plants with a capacity of at least 6 tonnes/hour. It should be noted here that a circular is not legally binding on the plants, but rather constitutes a recommendation to the prefect to include these requirements into the plant licences, and in doing this to anticipate the future Directive.[5] The measurement campaign following the circular and the generally rising concern about dioxin led to a media crisis. In January 1998 measurements revealed heavy contamination of milk in dairy cows in the vicinity of the Lille waste incineration plant.

The environment ministry clearly stressed that compliance with the Directives was perceived as a first step to reduce the emissions of dioxins. The new left-wing environment minister took a stricter attitude and summoned the prefects of the regions where there were delays in meeting the standards to ask them to take action. She asked them to bring the incinerators with a capacity above 6 tonnes/hour into compliance with the 1989 Directive, otherwise these plants would have to be closed down. This was written down in a 'circulaire' of 26 August 1998 (Desachy, 1999).

3.2.2 United Kingdom

In the United Kingdom there was little regulation of municipal waste incineration prior to 1989. The plants were not subject to prior authorisation, as required by the 1984 Air Framework Directive. There were no legally enforceable emission limits and no systematic monitoring of emissions. The government was aware of the laxity of the existing regulation and in 1986 proposed bringing the municipal waste incineration plants under the control of her Majesty's Inspectorate of Pollution (HMIP). This would have made them subject to prior authorisation and a requirement to use 'best practical means' for pollution abatement (House of Lords, 1989). The proposal was part of a Department of the Environment (DoE) consultation paper titled 'Air Pollution Control in Great Britain'. The paper proposed changes to UK legislation to make it compatible with existing and prospective EC environmental directives (DoE, 1986), but these were not implemented for several years. Eventually, under pressure from the EC, the 'stop-gap' Health and Safety Regulation 1989 (Emissions into the Atmosphere) (Amendment) brought all incineration processes, including municipal waste incineration plants with a capacity of more than 1 tonne/hour, under the regulatory responsibility of HMIP (Loader et al., 1991).

Few local authority associations were involved in the political process surrounding implementation of the 1989 Directives. The Association of District Councils expressed some concern that plant closures would lead to increased transport of waste to landfill in rural areas. The Association of Metropolitan Authorities lobbied unsuccessfully for the DoE to fund the necessary upgrading of existing plants. The politically influential National Society for Clean Air and Environmental Protection (NSCA) lobbied unsuccessfully for the DoE to build a state-of-the-art plant using foreign designs and technology to assist with implementation of the 1989 Directives (House of Lords, 1989). Both Friends of the Earth and Greenpeace UK have taken a much more hostile position with respect to waste incineration, but there is little evidence to suggest that either Friends of the Earth or Greenpeace have played an influential role in the implementation of the 1989 MWI Directives in the UK. However, a number of grass-roots community organisations, of which more than 50 are currently active in the UK, have campaigned against existing and proposed plants on human health and environmental grounds. These organisations became more active and more influential during the 1990s and have frequently used the opportunities in the British planning system for public participation and lodging objections to successfully oppose or significantly delay the construction of new incineration plants.

In a debate in the House of Commons it was concluded that the costs of upgrading the sector would also be broadly in line with costs incurred for domestic environmental reasons as set out in the 1986 consultation paper (Haigh, 1997). An important consideration was tight fiscal control of both local government and DoE expenditure, which limited their ability to invest in incineration plants.

The British government has consistently taken a more relaxed view of the risks associated with dioxins than the US EPA and a number of European governments. A 1989 report by the DoE found 'no convincing evidence of a link between exposure to dioxins and cancer'. In 1989 the Department of

Environment (on the basis of research commissioned with Warren Spring Laboratories) estimated that the municipal waste incineration sector contributed up to 25 per cent of British dioxin and furan emissions. Since 1995 Her Majesty's Inspectorate of Pollution has revised this estimate upwards, suggesting that the sector accounts for about 70 per cent of total UK dioxin emissions.

Box 5.4 National standards in the UK

All municipal waste incinerators with a capacity of more than 1 tonne/hour had to meet the same emission limits as new ones by 1 December 1996. For all incinerators with a capacity of 1 to 3 tonnes/hour the permitted concentrations of dust and HCl in flue gases were reduced by 70 per cent compared with the EU limits, the permitted concentrations of Pb+Cr+Cu+Mn were reduced by 80 per cent and the permitted concentrations of HF were reduced by 50 per cent. For all incinerators with a capacity of more than 3 tonnes/hour emissions standards for Pb+Cr+Cu+Mn were tightened by 80 per cent and for HCl by 40 per cent. In addition, an emission limit of 1 ng TEQ/m^3 was set for dioxins, with an obligation to reduce this further, and an additional limit was set on NO_x emissions.

The United Kingdom did not incorporate the European Directives into national regulation on time. The Commission took formal infringement proceedings in May 1991 and formal transposition was completed in November 1991 by issuing Municipal Waste Incineration Directives under section 7 of the Environmental Protection Act 1990, which introduced a more integrated and centralised approach. Incinerators with a capacity above 1 tonne/hour are required to meet the Integral Pollution Control regime (IPC), which includes prior authorisation and application of the Best Available Techniques Not Entailing Excessive Cost (BATNEEC). Detailed advice on what constitutes BATNEEC for a particular process is set out in 'process guidance notes'. For municipal waste incinerators the process guidance notes were issued in the 'Process Guidance Note IPR 5/3, Waste Disposal & Recycling Municipal Waste Incineration', published on 1 June 1992. These standards are more comprehensive and stricter than the European standards (see Box 5.4) but the European Directives were important in pushing forward these limits. The Municipal Waste Incineration Direction 1991 instructed the relevant regulatory agencies to include conditions in IPC authorisations. It also stated that no exemptions may be granted for plants with a nominal capacity of less than 1 tonne/hour or that burn waste-derived fuels.

Restructuring the municipal waste incineration sector in the UK. The existing incineration plants were generally designed in order to minimise incineration costs and no provisions were made for heat recovery.

Consequently, none of the existing plants would have met the requirements of the EU Directives without drastic upgrading; in fact, the Directives led to the closure of about 33 plants. A survey indicated that 12 existing plants would close by 1994 irrespective of the stricter rules (House of Lords, 1989, p. 52), due largely to the tight budgetary policy that prevented investments being made by local authorities, the availability of cheap landfill and the reasonably tight monitoring and control where the timely close down of non-retrofitted incinerators was at stake (see Figure 5.3). The survey also identified factors influencing decisions by local authorities to either upgrade or close incinerators. Among them was the cost of upgrading to new plant standards, the costs of closing plants down and converting them into waste transfer facilities, the availability and costs of landfill (including transport costs), the availability and terms of loans for capital expenditure and energy prices (House of Lords, 1989, p. 52).

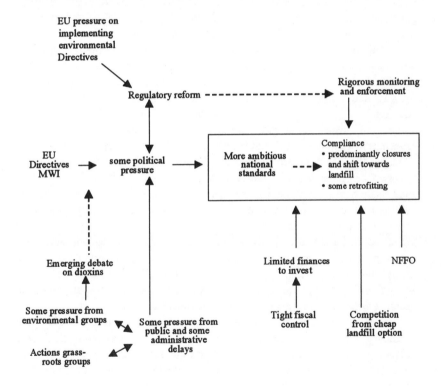

Figure 5.3 Explaining national ambitions and outcomes in the UK

After the 1 December deadline only four existing plants remained in operation. Three ceased operation temporarily for conversion and throughput at the other plant was reduced while upgrading work was carried out. Two new large plants were commissioned in the UK between 1989 and December 1996. These plants were subsidised under the Non-Fossil Fuel Obligation (NFFO), which significantly improved the financial viability of electricity generation by municipal waste incineration plants. The Electricity Act 1989 empowered the Secretary of State for Energy to require, by order, electricity companies to purchase specified capacity generated from non-fossil fuel sources on long-term contracts. The NFFO was designed to support the increased market penetration of renewable technologies and to subsidise the UK's existing nuclear industry. The electricity supply companies pay a premium price for electricity generated under the NFFO, the price being determined by a competitive bidding process among potential generators. The NFFO has significantly improved the financial viability of electricity generation from municipal waste incineration, but it has not helped the many old plants without energy recovery. Leaving these older plants in a state of non-compliance to avoid the upgrading costs was not an option because of the strict monitoring and enforcement of the actual closing down of old non-retrofitted plants. The Environment Agency's annual inspection programme for a typical incinerator consists of four to six planned visits and up to six additional visits to investigate complaints and operational problems. The number of visits could rise significantly where major problems arise, especially where 'public interest is generated' (House of Lords, 1999).

Under the UK's Integrated Pollution Control (IPC), operators are required to report any breaches of their authorisation to the regulator. Breach of an authorisation condition renders an operator liable to prosecution under the 1990 Act. The maximum penalty is a £20,000 fine on summary conviction, or an unlimited fine and up to 2 years, imprisonment on conviction in a higher court. Failure to comply with a court order could result in action for contempt of court, rendering the operator liable to sequestration of assets and an unlimited term of imprisonment. Corporate liability applies under Section 157 of the Act. However, the regulator has considerable discretion in deciding whether to prosecute in any particular case.

Almost 500 breaches of emissions limits were reported to the EA between 1 January 1996 and November 1998 by operators of incinerators (including municipal waste, hazardous waste and sewage sludge incinerators) licensed under IPC. This figure is likely to be an underestimate as it is based on self-reporting by plant operators. The majority of these breaches are thought to have occurred at municipal waste incineration plants and relate to HCl, dust, No_x and CO. It has to be emphasised that most breaches are believed to be very short-lived. Offences have occurred both at new plants and existing plants. The absence of waste separation prior to incineration may contribute to these problems and substantial efforts have been made to overcom these problems. The Environmental Agency has used informal and formal sanctions to bring about changes and now believes that the problems have largely been solved.

The survival of the UK incineration sector. When the British domestic regulation was issued it was already known that the outcome would be a structural shift towards the cheap landfill option. Until 1994 there was no recognised trade association representing the municipal waste incineration sector as a whole. The Department of Trade and Industry (DTI) has played an important role in shaping the financial climate for MWI during the 1990s. The DTI encouraged the formation of the Energy from Waste Association which was formed in 1994. It brought together local authorities with an interest in municipal waste incineration with energy recovery, private sector waste management firms and incinerator equipment suppliers. Six new plants were built in addition to the four existing incinerators. Faced with competition from cheap landfill, it was this promotion of energy recovery technology that was the life insurance for a number of plants with energy recovery. The total capacity of the sector has now been restored to approximately the same level as in the late 1980s although concentrated in a much smaller number of plants.

4.   ENVIRONMENTAL AND EFFICIENCY OUTCOMES

We turn in this section to an assessment of the environmental benefits gained by upgrading the municipal waste incineration plants, followed by a discussion of whether the characteristics of implementation are in line with the assumption that countries are in favour of efficient implementation.

4.1   Environmental Outcomes

In this section the focus is on *the actual reduction of atmospheric emissions* from existing incineration plants. The assessment is linked to the goals of the 1989 European regulation. A number of pollutants need to be assessed in this context; just picking out one pollutant would not be a satisfactory approach. Where sufficient data were available an index has been calculated for existing incinerators that expresses average compliance with the European emission limits for dust, CO, HCl, SO_2, Cd + Hg and HF.[6] Detailed quantitative data on emissions from incinerators were available for Germany and the Netherlands.

A second relevant consideration in this section is the extent to which the European Directives have *contributed to the improvements* made in the four countries. Table 5.3 summarises the outcomes followed by some explanations.

4.1.1 The front runners: Germany and the Netherlands

The existing incinerators in North Rhine-Westphalia emitted only a very small share of the emissions permitted by the European limits. Data on Bavarian waste incineration plants show comparable low levels of emissions. There is even over-compliance compared with German national limits. However, it should be kept in mind that over-compliance with annual averages is necessary to avoid breaches for smaller periods of time.

Table 5.3 Environmental outcomes in 1996

	France	NRW (Germany)	The Netherlands	United Kingdom
Average emissions as % of EU limits	> 150% estimated	3.2% calculated	15.4% calculated	< 100% estimated
Emission reduction	25% estimated (1990–1996)	90% estimated (1990–1996) 57.6% calculated (1994–1996)	91% calculated (1990–1996)	90% (1990–1996) estimated
Contribution of EU Directives	High for large plants Low for small plants	None	None	High

The available data on improvements for North Rhine-Westphalia covers the period 1994–1996. The lower calculated percentage reduction compared with the Dutch outcomes presented in Table 5.3 can be explained by the period of measurement (1994–1996). By 1994 a considerable proportion of plants had already been retrofitted in North Rhine-Westphalia. Over the 1990–1996 period the emission reduction is probably equal to or better than the Dutch improvements over the same period. Of course, these averages conceal some variance. For instance, in the Netherlands emission reductions vary from 3.9 per cent of allowable emissions of SO_2 to 35 per cent of allowable emissions of CO according to European standards. Calculating annual averages for every pollutant separately does not imply that there are no short-term breaches in individual plants – minimal breaches of national limits have been reported in both countries – but breaches of the European limits must be considered to be negligible. Finally, data collected in the

Netherlands imply that upgraded existing plants perform almost as well as the new municipal waste plants. As discussed in the previous section, the improvements in Germany and the Netherlands cannot be attributed to the European Directives.

4.1.2   France and the United Kingdom

For France the available data was limited to whether furnaces of plants complied with the standards or not and to the technology applied in each case. Table 5.4 gives data on compliance; estimates of the level of over-compliance are not available.

Experts generally agree that none of the plants with a capacity of less than 3 tonnes/hour comply with the standards, and that any clean-up technology installed in these plants is limited to mechanical filters such as cyclones. Therefore they do not comply with the emission limits of the 1995 transitional arrangement and are clearly non-compliant with the 2000 limits. Many of these plants will be in breach of the regulations all the time they are in operation.

Table 5.4 Compliance of furnaces in France in 1996/1997

Capacity	Compliant	Non-compliant
> 6 t/h	61	75
3–6 t/h	24	19
< 3 t/h		All

Estimates of the environmental outcomes in France can be made, but these involve substantial levels of uncertainty.[7] Meanwhile the position of the larger incinerators has improved considerably over the position shown in Table 5.4. Almost all non-compliant large incinerators are in fact late compliance cases; 73 of the 75 are expected to be in a position to comply with the standards between 1997 and 2000. This means that actual performance is better than shown in Tables 5.3 and 5.4, which are based on the situation in 1996 and 1997. The situation of the smaller incinerators has not improved substantially. These figures indicate that in France emission reductions have been lower than the more impressive results in the other countries. In France the European Directive has been the key driver for emission abatement at large plants, but even here implementation has been slow. It is likely, therefore, that the recent tightening up of monitoring and enforcement efforts have been influential. Having said that, the European Directives have not yet had an effect on small incinerators in France.

In the United Kingdom 33 plants, or about 80 per cent of the incineration capacity, were closed in time. The closed plants were in compliance by default and the status of the four remaining incinerators remains to be decided. The large number of reported breaches indicate that there are problems with these incinerators. However, these breaches are often very short-lived. When we take the level of retrofitting into account and the effects of the monitoring and enforcement efforts described, it is plausible that the existing incinerators, on average, comply with the European requirements. Taking the retrofitting of the four remaining plants and the large number of closures into account it is likely that emission reductions in the United Kingdom are extremely large, if not the largest. Given the retrofitting and the large number of closures it may be safe to assume that emissions from waste incineration plants have been reduced by more than 90 per cent, as shown in Table 5.3. The European Directive led to the national regulation, the retrofitting and the closures in the UK. However it was known that about one third of the incinerators that were closed were going to be closed anyway.

4.2   Cost Effectiveness

Cost effectiveness refers to the ability to achieve a given level of environmental quality at the lowest costs. One important lesson of economic analysis is that effectiveness arises from taking proper account of local circumstances. Within the overall policy process, adjustments to local conditions typically take place at the implementation stage. This justifies an attempt to evaluate this aspect.

4.2.1   A method using two indirect cost indicators
Although relevant, assessing cost is a difficult task. The main challenge lies in cost data availability. The evaluation of cost effectiveness necessarily requires data at a plant level, given that the problem is one of efficiently coping with inter-source cost differences. Some figures on the generic level of costs of specific techniques can be found in the technical literature but quantitative data on real costs *at the plant level* are very difficult to obtain. This data problem probably largely explains why ex post policy evaluation is usually restricted to environmental impacts. To overcome this obstacle, we have developed a method that relies on indirect indicators that are more easily observed than costs but which reflect the level of costs involved. In the following, two indirect cost indicators are presented: the waste capacity of the incinerators and the incinerator's age.

The relationship between the size of incinerators and abatement costs is straightforward. According to the technical literature (see, for example, European Commission, 1997), economies of scale in pollution abatement are important in the case of domestic waste incinerators. Basically, this means that the larger the plant, the lower the marginal and average abatement costs.

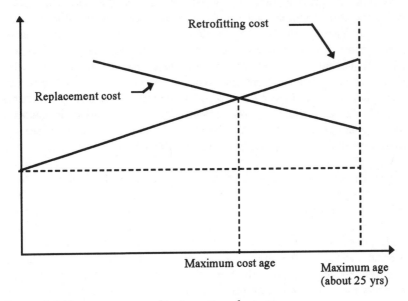

Figure 5.4 Abatement cost and incineration plant age

The relationship between cost and plant age is more complex. The starting point is that the lifetime of an incinerator is limited (about 30 years). To go further in identifying how the age of a given incinerator influences the level of abatement cost, it is necessary to consider the two possible routes to reducing pollution: (i) investing in abatement equipment to retrofit the plant, or (ii) closing down the plant and replacing it by a new retrofitted plant. The second solution is generally not considered in the textbooks, but was in fact chosen in our cases. In the Netherlands 6 of the 12 incinerators were closed and replaced, although not always at the same location. In North Rhine-Westphalia 14 of the 15 incinerators were retrofitted and one was closed – but not for reasons related to the costs of compliance. The analysis is presented in Figure 5.4, which shows two cost curves. The retrofitting cost curve exhibits a minimum when the age is nil, i.e. when the incinerator has just been built, because the remaining life of the plant during which the costs can be recovered is at a maximum. The replacement cost curve consists of two components: (i) the cost entailed by plant closure, which decreases with plant age until it is nil when the plant is at the end of its lifetime (when the plant has to be closed down anyway, even in the absence of a policy) and (ii) the cost of retrofitting the new plant, which is higher than the cost of retrofitting the existing plant because regulatory requirements for new plants are more stringent. The intersection of these two curves corresponds to a cost maximum at which replacement or retrofitting cost the same. Specialists claim that this maximum cost age for municipal waste incinerators is about 15 years. Based on this analysis, we can obtain the second indicator to be used according to the following rule of the thumb: the greater the deviation from the maximum cost age, the lower the abatement cost. Alternatively, this curve can be used to represent other types of substitution costs. For instance, one option may be to close down plants as part of a structural shift towards landfill. As an illustration, the implementation of the waste incineration directive in the UK led to the closure of about 33 of the 37 registered existing plants! These incinerators were not replaced.

4.2.2 The cost characteristics of the national sectors of regulated plants are very diverse

When considering cost issues, the first key consideration is related to the diversity of the national incinerator sector targeted by the Directive. In this regard, two related points are worth mentioning. First, due to the features of the national sectors, the *aggregate compliance cost* entailed by the Directive has differed very significantly from one country to another. Second, *the potential for cost savings* has differed a lot from one case to another or from one country to another. The two following sections develop the arguments using both of these indirect indicators.

4.2.3 The aggregate compliance costs are very heterogeneous

The average values of our two indirect cost indicators are given for waste incinerators in Table 5.5. Incinerator capacity in France was much lower than in the other countries. France is the only country to have many small incinerators with a capacity below 6 tonnes/hour. To compensate this cost disadvantage, the Waste Incineration Directive includes less stringent requirements for this category of incinerator. France adopted this differentiation unchanged into its national legislation. To be fully consistent, therefore, the comparison needs to be restricted to the incinerators belonging to the plant category with the same regulatory requirements, i.e. to the incinerators with a capacity larger than 6 tonnes/hour. If we do this, France remains the most disadvantaged country. As far as plant age is concerned, France is clearly in the worst position. In 1995, the year of the deadline for compliance with the Directives, the average age of French incinerators was 15 years, probably close to the maximum cost point. In comparison, the 1995 deadline was more in line with the investment cycles in Germany, the

Netherlands and the UK since the average age there was close to the incinerators' lifetime.

Table 5.5 Average capacity and age of existing waste incinerators

	United Kingdom	Netherlands	North Rhine-Westphalia (Germany)	France
Number of domestic waste incinerators in analysis	36	12	10	245
Average capacity (Kt/year)	145	260	288	40 for incinerators > 6t/h: 122
Average date of construction	1973	1972	1972	1980 for incinerators > 6t/h: 1978

4.2.4   The potential for cost savings differs very significantly

According to the microeconomic view, the cost effectiveness of a policy is above all an allocative issue: the main way a policy can minimise pollution abatement cost is to efficiently allocate pollution abatement efforts between the different pollution sources and over time. The challenge is related to cost heterogeneity: the abatement cost of each source is specific and the level of cost depends on the date at which the investment is made. Cost heterogeneity among sources and over time explains why the uniform 'one size fits all' allocation – in which sources would have to reduce pollution by the same amount at the same time – is not efficient. However, this reasoning also suggests that the lower the cost heterogeneity, the lower the detrimental impacts on cost effectiveness of a uniform allocation.

This point is crucial since the degree of cost heterogeneity is in fact very different in the countries studied. Table 5.6 presents two indirect indicators of heterogeneity in pollution abatement costs for municipal waste incinerators: the standard deviation value of plant capacity and age of the different national waste incinerator sectors. It suggests that the need for time flexibility was less important in the UK than in the other countries. If we consider the other cost indicator, plant capacity, the picture is different. For incinerators with a capacity greater than 6 tonnes/hour, the countries where the potential for cost savings are greatest are France and the Netherlands.

Table 5.6 Dispersion of waste incinerator capacity and standard deviation
*   age in the different countries*

	United Kingdom	Netherlands	North Rhine-Westphalia (Germany)	France
Number of municipal waste incinerators	36	12	10	245
Capacity dispersion (standard deviation/ average capacity)	0.63	0.89	0.65	1.88 for incinerators > 6t/h:1.06
Standard deviation age	3.1	5.6	7.7	7.2 for incinerators > 6t/h:7.3

4.2.5 Overall view on cost effectiveness

The above considerations are useful since they provide the background necessary to judge the genuine cost performances of different implementation processes. High expected compliance costs reinforce the *need* for a cost effective implementation: it is increasingly important to save costs when the overall cost becomes large. Inter-source heterogeneity provides the *possibility* for saving costs through flexible and tailored implementation solutions. In this regard, one could expect implementation to be more cost effective in the cases where both compliance costs and the potential for cost savings are important. As far as the implementation of Directive 89/429 on waste incinerators is concerned, Table 5.7 provides a synthesis showing whether the cost performance of different implementation processes is in accordance with the need for cost effectiveness (i.e. aggregate compliance cost) and the potential for cost savings. While evaluating the potential for cost savings, the emphasis was laid on the capacity indicator. The argument for this choice is that our data on the indicator 'capacity' are more reliable, bearing in mind that plants may have been modernised since the year of construction.

All in all, the picture looks consistent, in the sense that the search for cost effectiveness is in line with the need and the possibility for cost savings. For instance, it appears that France has strong reasons in this particular case for paying attention to cost aspects in implementation. At the opposite end of the spectrum, the rather uniform and inflexible implementation in Germany seems to be in line with the nature of the German waste incinerator sector. It is also conceivable that the limited potential cost savings in this country dampened any interest in a cost-effective strategy. In contrast the Netherlands, given the potential for cost savings, could have made more effort in this respect.

The general lesson that can be drawn from this discussion is that the need and the possibility for cost savings are different in each country. A very cautious approach should be taken when judging the cost performances of different countries and consideration should be given to the level of the costs entailed and the potential for cost savings. Although flexible implementation may be less crucial when compliance cost and/or cost heterogeneity is very low, it cannot have negative cost impacts if the differentiation is applied sensibly. In this respect, flexibility and differentiation in implementation can be viewed as an insurance against high costs. This does not negate the usefulness of flexibility for saving costs, but it is advisable to consider the context carefully when judging non-flexible processes.

Table 5.7 The consistency between national cost performances and two cost-related features of the national waste incinerator sectors

	United Kingdom	The Netherlands	North Rhine-Westphalia (Germany)	France
Some cost-related sector features				
-Aggregate compliance cost	ambiguous	small	small	large
-Potential for cost savings	(very) small	large	small	very large
Implementation cost-effectiveness variables				
- Compliance time-span	6 years	6 years	6 years	9 years (full compliance in 2000)
- Standard differentiation?	Yes - limited compared with EU Directive	No	No	Yes - through selective enforcement - specific standards for small incinerators

5.   CONCLUSIONS

With the new European Directive on waste incineration entering a new round of implementation, the implementation of the 1989 directives represents an important case.

This study demonstrates that it can be wrong to think of the implementation of European Directives as a top-down implementation process, even if a traditional command and control approach is taken. Implementation has proved to be a highly interactive process, and national characteristics that are not linked to the European Directives have played decisive roles.

The pattern of events in Germany and the Netherlands was strongly influenced by a relatively high level of public environmental awareness, expressed as concern about waste incineration, public action, incidents, media coverage and administrative delaying tactics. In a nutshell: this was an issue with a high political and public profile. This meant that retrofitting incineration plants as an issue had more to do with the overall image of waste incineration as a method of waste disposal rather than an issue related to compliance costs.

Although strict and non-flexible standards were used in Germany and the Netherlands, the importance of enforcement was almost irrelevant in North Rhine-Westphalia in Germany and in the Netherlands. Moreover, for a long time there was basically no monitoring and enforcement of waste incineration in France. This indicates that monitoring and enforcement do not automatically play an important role in a command and control approach.

The pattern of events in France and in the UK was strongly influenced by considerations of compliance costs, budget restraints and possibilities for cost savings. Awareness of the environmental risks of waste incineration among the public was less in the UK and almost absent in France. In France the regulatory style helped to keep many incinerators open, although some small French plants may be closed under the 1 December 2000 deadline. The United Kingdom national regulations are in an intermediary position between France and the front runners. The British case was largely influenced by the option to use cheap landfills, and to some extent by the pressure to close old incinerators before the deadline. The shift towards landfill may have caused other forms of pollution.

Flexibility and differentiation in implementation can be viewed as an insurance against high costs. However, a general lesson from this study is that the appropriate flexibility of implementation should not be judged solely on the basis of the presence or absence of differentiated emission limits and flexible compliance time-spans. The total compliance costs, the cost heterogeneity among sources, and therefore the potential for cost savings, should be included in the analysis. If there is very little cost heterogeneity, non-flexible implementation can be cost-effective.

The patchwork of factors influencing implementation should not be interpreted as a permanent feature. The patterns found in some countries have already changed during the research period. For instance, in France incidents involving dioxin emissions from incinerators were reported in the late 1990s and action by environmental pressure groups has led to more focused awareness of the environmental issues involved. In addition, a shift in the political background, with a new left-wing environment minister taking office, has led to a shift in the trade-off between environmental gains and costs. New forces are emerging that appear to be overcoming the French 'regulatory style', with a tendency towards increasing competition in markets. This may reinforce efforts to raise the efficiency of implementation.

NOTES

1. The author wishes to thank Olivier Godard, member of the scientific committee, for his coaching comments in several stages of the case study and Matthieu Glachant for his detailed and productive suggestions on drafts of this chapter.
2. For an analysis of the events see Eberg (1997).
3. With respect to dioxins, a French government circular of 24 February 1997 requires that all *new* municipal waste incinerators (licensed after that date) meet the emission standard of 0.1 ng TEQ/m³. This decision anticipates future European emission standards. As this concerns new plants only, it does not affect the research undertaken for this case study.
4. With this the legal uncertainty was solved. However, it took two more years to solve the technical problems related to the 'stabilisation' of the residues.
5. At the moment France does not regulate dioxin pollution in a binding law. A decision on dioxin emission standards was suspended until the publication of a toxicology report on waste incineration and public health published by the Société Française de la Santé Publique (French Society of Public Health) in November 1999. This report includes models for emissions and their behaviour in the food chain.
6. The first step was to calculate the actual emissions for every substance separately, expressed as a percentage of the allowable emission. The second step was to add up the calculated percentages and to divide the outcome by the number of pollutants in the analysis. Detailed quantitative data on emissions from incinerators were available for Germany and the Netherlands.
7. The estimate of the improvement in environmental performance in Table 5.3 is explained as follows: The plants that were late in complying are estimated to have caused approximately 60 per cent more emissions than allowable (Schucht, 2000). A reduction in emissions from large plants in the 40–50 per cent range in 1996 compared to 1990 is plausible. Estimates of the emissions of dust, HCl, Pb, Cd and Hg indicate that the share of the smaller non-compliant plants in total emissions is on average 56 per cent if all large incinerators are assumed to be in compliance (Schucht, 2000). Assuming a required, highly speculative,

abatement level of 80 per cent, it can be calculated that non-compliance of small plants brings about 45 per cent more emissions than allowable at the aggregate level for the country as a whole. For all plants, the improvement during the research period may therefore be in the order of 25 per cent in 1996 compared to 1990. These estimates are an average of two scenarios. The first scenario assumes that all plants with a capacity above 3 t/h comply with the Directive's requirements for 1996 and 2000 respectively, while plants with a capacity below 3 t/h are assumed not to comply (even with the requirements for 1995) but only to be equipped with mechanical filters. The second scenario assumes, like the first, that the plants with a capacity above 6 t/h comply with the Directive while those with a capacity below 3 t/h do not comply. The difference from the first scenario is that we assume that of the group of plants with a capacity of between 3 and 6 t/h only those plants that in 1997 complied with the Directive's 1995 requirements (equipped with fabric filters or electrostatic precipitators) will comply with the Directive's requirements for 2000, while the plants not complying in 1997/98 are assumed not to comply in 2000 (neither with the Directive's 1995 requirements nor with its 2000 requirements). The calculations and estimates take into account the number of French plants in the identified capacities, the data on installed technology and data on compliant and non-compliant incinerators. These are very rough estimates with high levels of uncertainty related to the assumptions involved, and the results have to be interpreted with due caution.

REFERENCES

Bertossi, P., S. Brusco and F. Tagliazucchi (1994), *The Municipal Waste Management Industry: Concentration, Technological Change and Regulatory Activity*, Bologna, Italy: Nomisma.

Buclet, N. and O. Godard (2000), 'Municipal Waste Management in Europe: a Comparison of National Regimes', in N. Buclet and O. Godard (eds), *Municipal Waste Management in Europe*, Dordrecht: Kluwer Academic Publishers.

Bültmann, A. and F. Wätzold (2000), *The Implementation of the European Directives 89/429/EEC and 89/369/EEC on Air Pollution from Municipal Waste Incinerators in Germany*, Leipzig Halle: UFZ.

Department of the Environment (1986), *Air Pollution Control in Great Britain: Review and Proposals – A Consultation Paper*, London: DoE.

Desachy, C. (1999), *L'histoire et l'évolution de la réglementation de l'incinération des déchets*, Paris: Technique & Documentation.

Eames, M. (2000), *Implementation of European Directives 89/369/EEC and 89/429/EEC, on the Incineration of Municipal Waste in the United Kingdom*, Brighton: SPRU.

Eberg, J. (1997), *Waste Policy and Learning Policy Dynamics of Waste Management and Waste Incineration in the Netherlands and Bavaria*, Delft: Eburan Publishers.

European Commission (1997), *Economic Evaluation of the Draft Incineration Directive*.

Haigh, H. (ed.) (1997), *Manual of Environmental Policy*, UK: Cartermill Publishing.

Hartenstein, H and M. Horvay (1996), 'Overview of municipal waste incineration industry in west Europe', *Journal of Hazardous Materials*, **47**, pp. 19–30.

Hesseling, W.F.M., G. Kuipers and J.W. Wormgoor (1995), *Emissiereductie gespecificeerd per AVI 1990–1995 (Reduction of Emissions Specified by Municipal Waste Incinerator 1990–1995)*, Delft: TNO.

House of Lords Select Committee on the European Communities (1989), *Air Pollution from Municipal Waste Incineration Plants*, HL Paper 17, London, UK: HMSO.

House of Lords Select Committee on the European Communities (1999), *Waste Incineration*, HL Paper 71, London, UK: HMSO.

Kahl, W. and A. Voßkuhle (eds) (1995), *Grundkurs Umweltrecht. Einführing für Naturwissenschaftler und Ökonomen*, Heiselberg/Berlin/Oxford: Spektrum.

Loader, A. et al. (1991), *Review of Pollution Control at Municipal Waste Incineration Plants*, DoE report no. DoE/HMIP/RR/91/038.

Lulofs, K.R.D. (1999), *Adjustments in the Dutch domestic waste incineration sector in the context of the European Directives 89/369/EEC and 89/429/EEC*, CSTM studies and reports no. 118, Enschede.

Milhau, A. and H. Pernin (1994), 'Traitement des gaz provenant de l'incinération de déchets', *Revue générale de thermique*, June.

Schucht, S. (2000), *The Implementation of the Municipal Waste Incineration Directives in France*, Paris: CERNA.

Sein, A.A, J.J. Sluijmers and E.J.H. Verhagen (1989), *Onderzoek emissies afvalverbrandingsinstallaties, Eindrapport*, Report no. 738473006, Bilthoven.

Waque, W. (1990), 'De richtlijn verbranden 1989', *Lucht en omgeving*, September, pp. 94–98.

Weale, A. (1992), *The New Politics of Pollution*, Manchester/New York: Manchester University Press.

6. The implementation of EMAS in Europe: a case of competition between standards for environmental management systems[1]

Frank Wätzold and Alexandra Bültmann

1. INTRODUCTION

The Council Regulation (EEC) No. 1836/93 on the Community Eco-management and Audit Scheme (EMAS) of 29 June 1993 is one of the market-based instruments that were introduced by the European Commission in the context of its Fifth Environmental Action Programme 'Towards Sustainability'. In short, EMAS is an environmental management system (EMS) standard which opens voluntary participation to companies in the industrial sector. In contrast to other standards, EMAS requires companies to publish an environmental statement, and provides for a certification system with independent environmental verifiers and registration bodies.

The most striking outcome of the EMAS implementation in Europe is that participation figures in the scheme greatly differ among EU Member States. This to a great extent can be attributed to the existence of other environmental management system standards. Right from the start, EMAS had to compete with national standards such as BS7750 (British Standard 7750 1994, Specification for Environmental Management Systems) and from October 1996 with the international standard ISO14001 (EN ISO14001 1996, Environmental Management Systems, Specification with guidance for use). Obviously, a company's choice between EMAS and another standardised EMS depends on the net benefits it gains by participating in the different standards. The varying net benefits of EMAS in the Member States and thus its position in the competition with other standards are decisively influenced by the different implementation processes of the EMAS Regulation in the various countries.

This chapter aims to describe how the EMAS Regulation was implemented in France, Germany, the Netherlands and the United Kingdom

(UK), and to explain the varying number of EMAS participants in the four countries as a result of the different implementation processes. Against the background of the low participation rates in some Member States, the chapter additionally addresses the question of whether EMAS has been a successful policy instrument, i.e. whether it brought about more benefits than costs.

The chapter is structured as follows. Section 2 provides some background information. This encompasses a short description of the political genesis of the EMAS Regulation at the European level, a portrayal of EMAS and ISO14001, an assessment of the participation rates in the four countries under review, and a discussion of EMAS as a policy instrument from an economic perspective. Section 3 contains a description of the main features of the implementation processes in Germany, France, the Netherlands and the UK. Section 4 explains the different participation rates in the four countries by analysing the varying advantages of a French, German, Dutch and UK company's participation in EMAS and ISO14001. Based on companies' and society's costs and benefits related to EMAS, section 5 discusses whether EMAS has been a successful policy instrument. The last section summarises the main results.

2.   BACKGROUND

2.1   The Political Evolution of EMAS

The first idea of a European Eco-Management and Audit Scheme emerged in the Commission in 1990.[2] It led to the publication of a consultation document in December 1990 which called for the mandatory participation of companies in the Scheme. Industry responded strongly and homogeneously. It targeted its main criticism at the mandatory approach as it felt it was an undue interference in business affairs if the government prescribed which management tool a company should use. Strong resistance by industry led the Commission to accept a voluntary approach and it published a new proposal in March 1992. Industry responded in two ways. Firstly, with the exception of German companies, industry was less interested in the political process. Secondly, while the German industry and government continued to oppose the Scheme, the attitude of industry and governments from other Member States was now mostly supportive.

German industry continued to oppose EMAS for several reasons. One important one was that the approach of German industry towards environmental problems was different from that adopted in EMAS. EMAS is management oriented. The idea is to improve the environmental performance of a company by implementing management tools. German industry was 'engineer-driven': to improve its environmental performance, a typical German company tried to develop or install a new technology. The EMAS culture was therefore alien to German companies. In addition, the Scheme does not take into account the different environmental standards of the Member States. It was perceived as unfair that a company which must comply with ambitious environmental legislation (German companies believed that German legislation was ambitious) could use the same statement of participation as a company in another country with lower standards. Furthermore, German companies expected that they would have to take part in the Scheme due to high public pressure in environmental matters in Germany.

By contrast, the UK government was an active supporter of EMAS. It hoped that UK industry would gain a competitive advantage. The UK was the first country to develop an environmental management system with BS7750 and there was already a high number of companies working to implement this standard. Apart from supporting UK industry, the UK's Conservative government was keen to promote voluntary environmental action by industry, as part of its wider deregulatory and market-driven philosophy. The promotion of EMSs, external certification and environmental reporting were seen as fostering informed competition in the marketplace. UK industry was more divided on EMAS. While a voluntary scheme was generally welcomed, some sections of industry continued to oppose the scheme on the grounds that it went beyond the requirements of BS7750. It was especially criticised that the environmental statement disclosed information to the public.

The Dutch government was very active in promoting EMAS, too, for reasons similar to those of the UK government. Dutch companies had gathered considerable experience with EMSs, many of them using BS7750. Moreover, EMSs were considered to play an important role in deregulation efforts of the Dutch government in the context of environmental policy.

France supported EMAS as well, but kept a low profile during the political process. Although a French environmental management standard had been developed in NF X 30-200 (Norme Française Expérimentale; X indicates that it is a preliminary standard), there was relatively little interest in and experience of EMS compared to the UK and the Netherlands. However, bearing in mind that participation in EMAS is voluntary and no pressure for companies to join EMAS was anticipated, industry saw no need to lobby for or against EMAS (Franke and Wätzold, 1996 and Schucht, 2000).

At the Environment Council Meeting in March 1993 it became obvious that all Member States except Germany were in favour of the regulation.

Germany knew that it could only delay but not pre-vent EMAS, as the final ratification of the Maastricht Treaty would enable EMAS to be rati-fied by majority voting. Therefore, it gave in to the pressure of the other Member States and EMAS was adopted at the Environmental Council Meeting in June.

2.2　What are EMAS and ISO14001?

2.2.1　The main features of EMAS

In simple terms, the EMAS Regulation is a site-related environmental management system standard which additionally requires companies to publish an environmental statement and provides for a certification system with independent environmental verifiers and registration bodies. All companies operating one or more industrial sites are invited to sign up with the standard.[3] Participation in EMAS is voluntary, but once a company has decided that it wants a site to become registered under EMAS, it has to meet the provisions of the Regulation, i.e. it must go through the procedure shown in Figure 6.1. At first, the company must adopt an environmental policy in which its overall environmental aims and principles of action are fixed. In its policy, the company commits itself to complying with all relevant environmental regulations and to continuously improving its environmental performance. Afterwards an environmental review is conducted. This is an initial comprehensive analysis of the environmental issues, impacts and performance which are related to the activities of the site to be registered.

On the basis of the general goals of the environmental policy and the results of the environmental review, an environmental programme is introduced. The programme describes specific goals, along with measures and deadlines for their realisation. Furthermore, an environmental management system has to be established which encompasses the organisational structure, responsibilities, procedures and resources of the site's environmental activities. Once the EMS has been implemented, an environmental audit is performed which evaluates whether the system is suited to secure compliance with all relevant regulations and the company's own environmental goals. In the light of the audit findings, appropriate corrective action is taken and new environmental objectives are set.

In order to inform the public[4] about the environmental activities of the company or the site, an environmental statement is prepared. The statement has to include a description of the environmental policy, programme and management system as well as an assessment of all significant environmental issues related to the activities of the site. If appropriate, the environmental issues are to be presented in the form of quantitative figures on pollutant emissions, waste generation, energy consumption, etc. Finally the company has to commission an independent environmental verifier with the examination of the environmental policy, programme, management system, review or audit procedure and the validation of the environmental statement. Afterwards the company can apply to be registered under EMAS.

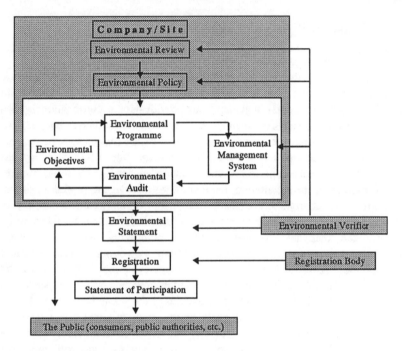

Figure 6.1 Procedure for participation in EMAS

When registration is granted, the company has the right to use a so-called statement of participation and employ it for advertising purposes. However, the statement may not be used for direct product marketing. Registration is granted for three years. If the company or site wants to remain registered, it has to repeat the environmental audit, to update the environmental statement, and to arrange for another examination and validation by an environmental verifier.

2.2.2 ISO14001 as EMAS's main competitor
Almost parallel to the formulation of the European EMAS Regulation, the ISO (International Standards Organisation)[5] prepared an international standard for an environmental management system. Preparations began against the background in which a number of national standardisation organisations had already started to launch their own national standards. The

most popular one was BS7750, which had been published in 1992. Standards in Ireland, France, South Africa and Canada followed.[6] In 1992, the Strategic Advisory Group on Environment (SAGE) of the ISO recommended developing a standard for an environmental management system. To this end a technical committee (TC 207, Environmental Management) was set up which presented first Committee Drafts in 1994. The 'Final Draft International Standard' was published in August 1995.[7] After an international process of reconciliation, ISO14001 was finally agreed in September 1996.

Although ISO14001 is a certifiable standard (a 'specification'), it does not include provisions for a certification system. The verification of environmental management systems was integrated in the already existing certification system for ISO standards. Compliance with ISO standards is secured by accredited certification organisations. Accreditation is carried out by special accreditation bodies which base their decisions on the requirements laid down in ISO norms 14010 and 14011.[8] In contrast to the EMAS Regulation, the ISO Standard is neither site-related nor restricted to industrial sectors. Every organisation (company, authority or institution, or part or combination thereof) which has its own functions and administration may implement an EMS consistent with the ISO14001 and have it certified. Figure 6.2 depicts the model of the EMS provided for in ISO14001.[9]

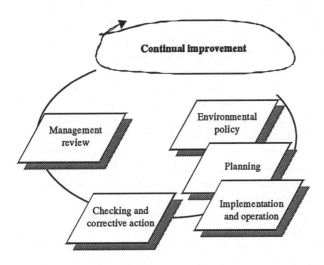

Source: EN ISO14001 (1996, p. 4).

Figure 6.2 Environmental management system model of ISO14001

The starting-point of the EMS described in the ISO14001 is the definition of an environmental policy. Similar to the EMAS Regulation, the ISO standard demands that the environmental policy includes commitments not only to comply with relevant environmental regulations, but also to continually improve and prevent pollution.[10] The second step, planning, requires the organisation to introduce procedures to identify the (significant) environmental impacts of its activities, products or services. Unlike the EMAS Regulation, ISO14001 does not provide for an obligatory environmental review. However, the ISO standard explicitly demands procedures to identify the legal requirements applicable to the organisation. At the end of the planning stage, the organisation must set environmental objectives and targets and establish an environmental management programme for their realisation. The programme encompasses the means and time-frames by which the objectives and targets are to be achieved.

During the next stage, implementation and operation, provisions are made to ensure that the programme is effectively put into action. To this end the organisation defines structures and responsibilities, trains its employees to support their environmental awareness and competence, and establishes procedures for internal communication. ISO14001 only requires the organisation to consider processes for external communication on its significant environmental aspects, but unlike the EMAS Regulation does not include any publication requirements. This is one of the major differences between the ISO standard and the EMAS Regulation. In the course of the implementation and operation stage, the organisation additionally documents its EMS and establishes procedures for document and operational control as well as for emergency preparedness.

Once the necessary structures and procedures have been implemented and put in operation, they are checked and corrected regularly. ISO14001 demands that the organisation monitors and measures the key characteristics of its ecologically relevant activities, tracks conformity with its environmental objectives and targets, and evaluates its legal compliance. If non-conformity is detected, corrective and preventive action is taken. Finally, the organisation must arrange for periodic EMS audits and top management reviews of the system.

As mentioned above, the organisation may have its EMS certified by an accredited certification organisation. If certification is granted, the organisation is entitled to use the logo of the certification organisation (not the ISO logo) in order to demonstrate that it has established an ISO certified EMS. Analogous to the statement of participation, the logo must not be used for product marketing. In contrast to the EMAS Regulation, the ISO certification system neither provides a registration of certified organisations nor any involvement of public authorities.

2.2.3 Participation rates in the four Member States

Participation rates in EMAS and ISO14001 significantly differ in the four countries under review. In order to be able to compare the number of participants in those countries, the figures need to be normalised. We have to take into account the fact that because the countries vary in size and industrial structure, the number of companies, i.e. the number of potential participants, is different. As an indicator of the number of potential participants, we use the number of companies from the manufacturing sector with more than 20 employees. The number of companies for which it is possible to become EMAS registered or ISO14001 certified is much higher,[11] as it includes smaller companies as well as companies and organisations from outside the manufacturing sector. However, there are no comparable data available that include all potential participants in the four countries. In addition, participation has been largely restricted to manufacturing companies with more than 20 employees.

Table 6.1 EMAS and ISO14001 registered sites in April 2000

| | EMAS | | | ISO14001 | |
	No. of potential participants*	No. of registered sites (industrial)**	In % of potential participants	No. of certified organisations**	In % of potential participants[12]
France	24 671	36	0.15	550	2.23
Germany	37 413	2432	6.50	1950	5.21
Netherlands	6 404	26	0.41	606	9.46
UK	29 608	73	0.25	1014	3.42
All Member States	-	3325	-	7140	-

Sources: * Eurostat – New Cronos Datenbank 12/98, ** http://www.ecology.or.jp/isoworld/english/analy14k.htm (16 June 2000, 10:29)

Table 6.1 shows that Germany has by far the most EMAS registrations, both in absolute and relative terms. Altogether, Germany accounted for approximately three quarters of the total number of EMAS registrations in Europe. In terms of absolute figures, ISO14001 is also most widespread in Germany. However, when participation in ISO14001 is regarded in relation to the size of the economy, it is highest in the Netherlands followed by Germany and the UK and France. Germany is the only country where more companies are registered under EMAS than are ISO14001 certified. In all the other countries ISO14001 is by far the dominant EMS standard.

2.3   EMAS as a Policy Instrument: Some Insights from an Economic Perspective

In order to explain the purpose of EMAS as a policy instrument from an economic angle,[13] we separately analyse its two central functions. The first function is to integrate environmental aspects into the organisation and management processes of a company with the help of the EMS (2.3.1). The second function is to improve the communication of a company with its external stakeholders by providing credible information through the validated environmental statement (2.3.2). On the basis of the analysis of these two functions we derive conclusions on the optimal number of EMAS participants from an economic point of view (2.3.3).

2.3.1   EMS to solve organisational failure

Until now there has been little analysis and understanding of EMS among environmental economists. The reason might be the environmental economists' view of firms which Gabel and Sinclair-Desgagné (1998, p. 89) describe as follows: 'It is a perfectly rational and efficient black box firm which maximises profits given whatever technological, market and regulatory policy constraints are imposed on it'. In such a perspective, environmental problems can only be caused by externalities, i.e. market failure which occurs if the decision-makers do not bear all the costs of their decisions. This failure can be remedied using various instruments such as tradable permits, environmental taxes or standards. In this context, the purpose of an EMS cannot be understood.

The underlying view of the firm is, however, not adequate, as firms are complex organisations and profit maximisation is far from being trivially easy. Gabel and Sinclair-Desgagné (1998) open the black box and suggest that a firm should be understood as an organisation that has a titular principal, its chief executive officer, but is actually run by vast numbers of agents, to many of whom may be delegated a great deal of autonomy to manage their day-to-day activities. In order to transform the principal's objectives (i.e. profit maximisation) into the agents' actions and to help work to proceed quickly and efficiently, a network of management systems and standard operating procedures is established. These systems are rigid and feature in-built inertia to change, so that once they are installed, 'they can act as a constraint on the firm's objective of profit maximisation' (Gabel and Sinclair-Desgagné, 1998, p. 98). They may prevent the firm from identifying and reacting to new threats or opportunities which would be evident to an unconstrained company. This is what Gabel and Sinclair-Desgagné call 'organisational failure'.

Transferred to the environmental arena, this means that firms find it difficult to avoid violations of environmental regulations or to realise cost-saving opportunities such as reductions in water or energy consumption if their management system is unable to adequately deal with the environmental repercussions of the firm's activities, i.e. if they do not have an EMS in place. If organisational failure leads to a waste of resources and a violation of environmental laws, it does not only impede profit maximisation, but also contributes to environmental problems.

To alleviate organisational failure, public policy can play an important role by setting (environmental) management performance standards and disseminating information on best practice. Management practices and standards are public goods from which exclusion might prove difficult. If a firm invests to develop industry best practice, other firms may observe and adopt these practices without paying the costs of developing them. This can undermine a firm's incentive to develop new systems and procedures. The development of such procedures by state organisations (as in the case of EMAS) or centralised non-governmental organisations (as in the case of ISO14001) might help to solve this problem (Gabel and Sinclair-Desgagné, 1998, p. 113).

2.3.2 External communication and asymmetric information

Besides improving the internal structure and organisation of a company EMAS also serves to improve the external communication with relevant stakeholders such as consumers, neighbours, authorities, banks and insurance companies. The core element of this aspect is the environmental statement which discloses information about the environmental performance of the company. The independent verifier who validates the environmental statement and verifies that a company complies with all relevant EMAS requirements adds credibility to the external communication.

In economic terms the need for (credible) external communication arises because 'asymmetric information' exists between the company and stakeholders. While the company is in general well informed about the environmental effects of its products and production, stakeholders are not – but it would influence their decisions if they were. In order to assess the contribution of EMAS to the reduction of asymmetric information, it seems useful to distinguish between 'markets' where the company sells its products and buys inputs for its production process, and the 'political arena' where the institutional framework under which the company acts is shaped.

With respect to the market, it is important to note that buyers with environmental preferences are interested in the environmental effects which arise along a product's life cycle, and this information may influence their decision to buy the product. If this information is not available (or only at prohibitively high costs), buyers cannot act according to their preferences. In contrast to a situation with symmetric information, the demand for (and hence also the market share of) environmentally superior products is too low. This indicates market failure (Karl and Orwat, 1999). However, the contribution of EMAS to mitigate this market failure is limited. This is mainly because EMAS is directed towards a specific site or company and not a specific product. To assess the environmental effects of products, other schemes such as the German 'Blue Angel' Environmental Labelling Scheme and the European Environmental Labelling Programme (Council Regulation 880/92/EEC) seem more suitable.[14]

However, there are cases where business partners are interested in the environmental performance of a specific site or a company in general. For example, some European car manufacturers are interested in the overall environmental performance of their suppliers, which can be documented by their participation in EMAS and by providing an environmental statement. Another example of business partners interested in the environmental performance of a site are insurance companies which have to assess the ecological risks and the potential for accidents. Here, EMAS can help to reduce asymmetric information.[15]

EMAS can also serve to deliver to stakeholders information that is relevant with respect to the shaping of the institutional framework in which the company acts. It enables those stakeholders to base their decisions on a higher level of information and, thus, increases the rationality of the political process. The relevance of these stakeholder decisions and resulting actions becomes evident from examples of the 1980s when several severely polluting chemical plants were closed down due to a combination of pressure from the neighbourhood and administrative action (Franke and Wätzold, 1996, p. 179).

2.3.3 How many companies should be EMAS registered and how many ISO certified?[16]

In order to answer this question from an economic point of view, we have to recall what ISO14001 and EMAS have in common, and what their crucial differences are. The similarity is the establishment of EMS-related company internal instruments (to simplify our argument we assume that the EMS requirements of the two standards are equal). The crucial differences are the improvements in the external communication EMAS provides for with the publication of a validated environmental statement (for simplicity's sake we assume that this is the only difference).[17] We start by analysing a company's choice between ISO14001, EMAS or no standardised EMS at all, and derive as a second step the socially desirable solution.

Following the above simplifications, a company participates in ISO14001 if the company's benefits of implementing the company internal instruments (b_I) are higher than (or equal to) the corresponding costs (c_I) for the company, i.e. $b_I \geq c_I$, but the benefits from improved external communication (b_C) are lower than the corresponding costs (c_C), i.e. $b_C < c_C$. However, a company chooses EMAS instead of ISO if $b_I \geq c_I$ and $b_C \geq c_C$. A company also participates in EMAS if the net benefit of implementing the company internal instrument is negative ($b_I < c_I$), but the company's net benefit of implementing the internal instrument plus the improvement of external communication is not ($b_I + b_C \geq c_I + c_C$). Figure 6.3 graphically illustrates the calculation of the company. However, a company's decision does not reflect the *socially desirable* solution, because a company's participation in ISO14001 and EMAS leads to environmental improvements from which others benefit. As the market often does not adequately reward the company for providing these benefits (for example through a higher demand for its products), they have the characteristics of positive externalities. Taking externalities into account, the conditions change under which the decision for EMAS, ISO14001 or no standardised EMS at all is optimal.

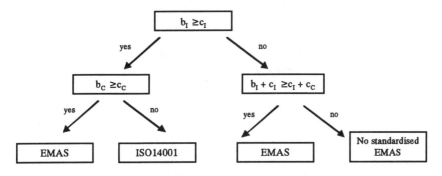

Figure 6.3 Variables determining a company's choice of standardised EMS

A company's participation in ISO14001 is socially desirable if the company's benefit of implementing company internal instruments (b_I) plus the positive externalities from this implementation (e_I) are higher than (or equal to) the corresponding costs (c_I) for the company ($b_I + e_I \geq c_I$), but the company's benefit from an improved external communication (b_C) plus the positive externalities from these activities (e_C) are lower than the costs (c_C), i.e. $b_C + e_C < c_C$). However, a company's choice of EMAS instead of ISO is socially optimal if $b_I + e_I \geq c_I$ and $b_C + e_C \geq c_C$. A company's participation in EMAS is also socially desirable if the total net benefit of implementing the company internal instrument is negative ($b_I+e_I < c_I$) but the total net benefit of implementing the internal instrument plus the improvement of external communication is not ($b_I+e_I+b_C+e_C \geq c_I+c_C$). The conditions for a socially optimal choice are illustrated in Figure 6.4.

In order to assess the desirable participation rate in reality, information about the benefits and costs for companies as well as the size of the positive externalities is needed with respect to both EMAS and ISO14001 participation. Obviously, this information does not exist or is (prohibitively) costly to collect. However, the analysis has revealed several important aspects. Firstly, it may be desirable from society's point of view for a company not to install a standardised EMS at all. Secondly, relying on a company's choice alone whether to implement a standardised EMS does not necessarily lead to the socially desirable solution. Generally, the inclusion of positive externalities increases the optimal participation numbers for ISO14001 and EMAS, because it makes the benefit side rise while the costs remain constant. Following Pigou's (1920) suggestion that subsidies should be used to internalise positive externalities, it is justified to subsidise companies' participation in a standardised EMS. However, the size of subsidies depends on the responsible government's assessment of the positive externalities generated by a company's participation in EMAS or ISO14001. And thirdly, whether EMAS is superior to ISO14001 from society's point of view depends on the additional costs and benefits (including positive externalities) of the improved external communication.

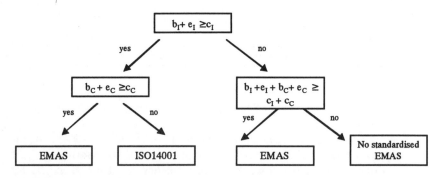

Figure 6.4 Criteria for the socially optimal choice of a standardised EMS

3.   IMPLEMENTATION PROCESSES IN THE MEMBER STATES

As a Regulation, EMAS is directly binding in all Member States. Consequently, translation into national law was not necessary. However, national authorities had to establish a system of institutions and organisations to make EMAS fully operational no later than April 1995. The main tasks of the Member States were to establish a system for the accreditation and supervision of independent environmental verifiers and to appoint a competent body for the registration of the sites participating in EMAS.[18] Moreover, the Regulation mentions a number of optional measures, e.g. Member States may promote companies' participation in EMAS, especially the participation of small and medium-size enterprises (SMEs).

The implementation processes in the Member States have been diverse due to different experiences with EMS, different backgrounds with respect to company culture and environmental policy as well as existing institutional and organisational frameworks. In the following we will describe the main features of the implementation processes in the four countries under review. The description and analysis of the national implementation processes follows the case studies by Schucht (2000) for France, Bültmann and Wätzold (2000) for Germany, Lulofs (2000) for the Netherlands, and Eames (2000) for the UK.[19]

3.1   France: Government Intervention in a Voluntary Scheme

The French implementation of EMAS is marked by the strong influence of government in the accreditation, registration and supervision system. However, this influence has not led the government to significantly grant regulatory relief in exchange or to actively promote EMAS. As there is also little or no market or other pressure for joining EMAS, participation rates are low and companies turn to ISO14001 instead or develop their own EMS without having it officially certified. Recently, the government has been trying to correct its policy by delegating more responsibilities to industrial organisations.

3.1.1 Establishment of the accreditation, supervision and registration system

The French Ministry of the Environment (currently called MATE) started preparations for the implementation of EMAS in spring 1992. It was decided that the Ministry would organise an experimental phase in co-operation with the Assembly of the French Chambers of Industry and Commerce (ACFCI) and other organisations that were either interested in the development of

EMAS or had experience relevant for the implementation of the scheme. The goal of this phase was to gain experience with respect to the implementation of EMAS at the level of industrial sites and the verification procedure. Moreover, it served to find the suitable organisations to carry out the accreditation, supervision and registration tasks.

The first pilot phase ran from May 1993 until February 1994 and involved 14 industrial sites. As there was considerable interest from industry to take part in the pilot phase, it was decided to conduct another pilot phase with the goal of investigating the application of EMAS to SMEs and to enlarge the test to companies from industrial sectors that had not participated in the first phase. Thirty-four sites took part in this second pilot phase, which lasted from March 1994 until March 1995.

A 'technical committee' was set up with the objectives of selecting the verifiers, specifying the verification process and examining the verifiers' reports. Furthermore, it answered the enterprises' questions related to the establishment of an environmental management system and was the forum for discussing problems. This committee consisted of the enterprises participating in the pilot phase, 'clients of environmental protection' (green associations, insurance companies, banks, municipalities, and so on), and both technical and legal experts. As of December 1993, the Environmental Agency (ADEME) was represented on this committee as well.

One of the main aims of the pilot phase was to find the organisations best suited to carry out the tasks of the accreditation and supervision body and the competent body. Basically, all institutions participating in the pilot phases wished to gain a place in the system. It seems that at least as far as the competent body is concerned, the MATE was determined right from the beginning to have a strong influence on it. However, this was not officially announced by the MATE, as it needed the experience (such as with management systems) of the other organisations during the pilot phase. Instead, the official decision was only taken at the end of the pilot phase. When the choice was to be made, there were three candidates for the competent body: the MATE, the ADEME together with the French association for standardisation (AFNOR), and the ACFCI. The final choice was based on a study by the law firm Maître London ordered by the Ministry itself. This study supported a decision in favour of the MATE. There has been no public discussion about the choice of the competent body. However, the ACFCI was clearly disappointed about the auto-designation of the MATE. To support the MATE by giving advice with respect to the registration of sites and the development of the EMAS system in general, the Comité d'Eco-Audit was established which largely consisted of members of the former technical committee.

In 1994, the French Accreditation Committee (COFRAC-Comité Français d'Accréditation) was set up following the decision of the Ministry of Industry to create one single organisation responsible for all accreditation tasks in France. When a decision on the accreditation and supervision body had to be taken in 1995, it was therefore clear that the COFRAC would be chosen as the accreditation body. Additionally, it took on the tasks of the supervision body as well.

3.1.2 EMAS's unsuccessful take-off

French industry had pointed out very early on that it would only get involved in EMAS on a large scale if its effort was rewarded by being granted regulatory relief. Soon, EPE (Entreprises pour l'Environnement, the lobby of huge firms with a pro-environmental approach) started a debate on the subject of regulatory relief for EMAS-registered firms. Without coming up with specific suggestions about how to facilitate general administrative requirements, it pointed out the necessity to lighten the regulatory burden on sites participating in EMAS.

The Ministry of the Environment heads the French environmental enforcement authorities, and is thus the organisation empowered to officially decide whether to grant regulatory relief. The MATE did not set up formal deregulation opportunities for EMAS-registered sites. It argued that it would be unfair to set up a formal framework for regulatory relief as all firms should be treated equally before the law. Furthermore, the MATE pointed out that not all registered sites achieved a comparable level of environmental protection and that regulatory controls covered not only the environmental performance of a plant but also other aspects such as measures directed towards the prevention of risks. In addition, the MATE has always regarded EMAS as an instrument allowing firms to advertise their environmental performance (i.e. a promotional instrument) and not as a regulatory instrument, and has avoided mixing these two approaches.

The current policy is that in a few regions, the local licensing and enforcement authorities take into account EMAS registration or ISO certification by reducing the frequency of the reporting requirements for those sites. Furthermore, as the authorities have insufficient personnel and have to set priorities concerning controls, they inspect EMAS-registered and ISO14001 certified companies less often.

In addition to a lack of regulatory relief there was little promotion of EMAS. Originally, the MATE had tried to promote EMAS via the DRIRE. However, promotion via the 'environmental police' was not well received by companies. Later on, there have been attempts to involve the Chambers of Industry and Commerce (CIC) into promotional activities. It seems that at the regional level, although some activities to promote EMS exist, their emphasis is more on ISO14001 than on EMAS. Overall, the level of promotional activities is low.

The position of industry towards EMAS was also influenced by the existence of ISO14001. French industry mostly preferred and still prefers ISO14001 to EMAS mainly because the former is a globally recognised standard, whereas the latter is only a European standard. Furthermore, companies complained that EMAS lacks clarity and is therefore difficult to apply. Additionally, companies already ISO9000 certified found it easier to establish ISO14001 as the systems have some similarities. Another reason for companies' preference of ISO14001 was the strong involvement of the MATE in the accreditation, supervision and registration system, which was regarded as an undue interference into companies' affairs.

The potential advantage of EMAS over ISO14001, the environmental statement as a means of external communication, seems of little relevance in the French context. Companies fear that communicating their environmental efforts damages their image. This is due to a perception which partly exists among the French public that the firms publicly emphasising their environmental improvements must be companies that are highly polluting or that have a 'bad conscience'. Thus, writing an environmental statement simply makes EMAS participation more costly, without any additional benefits.

The absence of public interest in a firm's participation in an 'official' management standard, relatively little other market pressure and no official regulatory relief for either EMAS or ISO14001 participants led many firms not to opt at all for an official standard. They established their EMS without having it certified at all, thus saving the costs associated with these procedures.

While ISO14001 clearly won the competition against EMAS, EMAS influenced the French interpretation of ISO14001. The French interpretation of ISO14001 is closer to EMAS than the original ISO standard. Normally, EMAS is more outcome-oriented than ISO, aiming at an improvement in the environmental performance, while ISO14001 instead aims at an amelioration of the system. By contrast, the French interpretation of ISO puts emphasis on environmental improvements as well.

3.1.3   Current developments: planned adaptation of the system

Currently a reform of the French EMAS system is envisaged, under which parts of the competent body and related tasks will be passed on to the ACFCI. Depending on the final degree of involvement of the CICs and the reduction of the MATE's influence, this may constitute a major reform, a switch from the centralised structure of the MATE to the decentralised structure of the CICs and from public to business organisations. However, discussions on the final model are still under way at the time of writing this chapter.

The main reason for this profound change is that the low participation of companies was partly due to the fact that industry did not have much confidence in an EMAS system strongly influenced by the MATE. The Ministry has acknowledged this and decided that it was worth testing a different model. Furthermore, the transfer of responsibilities to a business organisation is only consistent with its view that EMAS is a voluntary instrument by industry and not a regulatory instrument.

However, given the MATE's maintained involvement in the EMAS system, it is doubtful whether the firms' trust in the French EMAS system will significantly increase, and that, even if firms' confidence in EMAS rises, this will lead to a significantly higher participation rate. An analysis of costs and benefits of EMAS and ISO14001 participation may still make many firms decide in favour of ISO14001.

3.2   Germany: EMAS's Surprising Success

The establishment of the accreditation, supervision and registration system in Germany was marked by a strong conflict over business organisations' influence in the system. Finally a system was agreed in which business organisations hold a strong position. This is one important reason why Germany reached a relatively high level of EMAS participation. Recently, the rise in the number of EMAS participants has slowed down and ISO14001 has become more popular among companies.

3.2.1   The conflict about industry's influence in the accreditation, supervision and registration system

The implementation of the accreditation, supervision and registration system in Germany was marked by a conflict over the degree of influence business organisations should have in the system. The conflict was dominated by two opposing parties, i.e. the BMU 'Bundesministerium für Umwelt' (Federal Environment Ministry) and environmental groups on the one hand, and business associations and the BMWI 'Bundesministerium für Wirtschaft' (Federal Ministry of Trade and Industry) on the other.

The BMU wanted public authorities to have decisive influence on the whole system. It was convinced that the credibility and acceptance of the system would be reduced if it was organised by business associations. It believed that business associations were likely to come into role conflicts if they had to control their own members. The environmental groups pursued similar ideas to the BMU, but wanted to have even less business influence.

The BMU demanded that the relevant tasks be carried out centrally by one body, in order to ensure the nationwide uniform treatment of environmental verifiers and companies. It considered the UBA 'Umweltbundesamt' (Federal Environmental Agency) as the most appropriate candidate. The BMU knew that the success of EMAS was highly dependent on its acceptance by companies and the public. Therefore it was interested in developing a solution in agreement with all relevant groups. The first concept presented by the BMU already offered for the accreditation and supervision of environmental verifiers to be carried out jointly by the UBA and a business body. Additionally, the formation of an advisory council was proposed in which all relevant groups with an interest in EMAS were represented. The BMU planned to commission the German states to perform registration.[20]

The BMWI was very involved in the debate about the implementation of EMAS in Germany, not least due to the business associations' urging. It regarded itself as the advocate of business within the government and expressed itself in favour of a model with as little state influence as possible. The BMWI emphasised that against the background of voluntary participation in EMAS, it was necessary to develop a system which considered the companies' interests and set incentives to become registered under EMAS.

The business associations were of the opinion that if participation in EMAS was voluntary and if the system was to be promoted as a business initiative, business organisations had to be responsible. They argued that the idea of environmental audits was originally developed by industry and thus the responsibility for its implementation had to remain with industry. Many companies feared that EMAS would be turned into an instrument which enabled the state to (additionally) interfere in business affairs.

Several business organisations presented their own concepts of how to implement EMAS in Germany. All these concepts can be regarded as counterproposals to the BMU's concept, as they all exclusively proposed commissioning business bodies with the accreditation, supervision and registration. The business organisations sought to push through their concepts by arguing that in case the responsibility was placed on public authorities, EMAS would not be accepted by companies and participation rates remained low.

At the end of 1994, the concepts of the business associations and the BMU stood incompatibly against each other and neither side was willing to make concessions. This situation could not be overcome until the Federal Minister of the Environment changed in November 1994. The new Minister, Angela Merkel, quickly recognised that the success of EMAS was dependent on its acceptance by companies and that it was thus necessary to yield more to the business organisations. In December 1994, the dialogue between BMU and BMWI was resumed and was soon expanded to representatives of business organisations, the German States, environmental groups, trades unions, and (potential) environmental verifiers. A compromise on the accreditation, supervision and registration system was finally reached in early 1995. The concept which was developed is largely identical with the system currently existing in Germany. The main features of the system are as follows.

A new body was founded for the accreditation and supervision of environmental verifiers, because it was not possible to agree on one of the proposed organisations. The DAU 'Deutsche Akkreditierungs- und Zulassungsgesellschaft für Umweltgutachter mbH' (German Environmental Verifiers Accreditation Company) was conceived as a limited liability company in the hands of German business associations such as the DIHT 'Deutscher Industrie- und Handelstag' (umbrella organisation of the German chambers of Industry and Commerce). However, the BMU still has a supervisory function over the DAU. The Ministry monitors whether the DAU acts in accordance with relevant legal regulations, and checks whether certain decisions are correct in terms of content. The latter is mainly aimed at cases in which the DAU revokes or temporarily suspends accreditation. To support and control the DAU, a pluralistic Committee, the UGA 'Umweltgutachterausschuß' (Environmental Verifiers' Committee), was established.

Responsibility for the registration of sites was placed on the CICs (Chambers of Industry and Commerce) for industrial sites and the HwK (Chambers of Craft) for tradesmen's sites. The registration procedure demands the Chambers to inform the relevant enforcement agencies of the German States and to give them the opportunity to intervene should the site not comply with environmental legislation. The compromise came into force on 15 December 1995 as the 'Umweltauditgesetz' (Environmental Audit Act).

3.2.2   What factors made EMAS a success in Germany?
After the implementation of the accreditation, supervision and registration system, EMAS was quickly accepted by companies and many of them decided to participate in the Scheme. This is surprising considering that Germany was the only opponent of EMAS before 1993 (see section 2.1).

German companies greatly benefited from the advantages brought about by the implementation of an environmental management system because they had hitherto neglected the importance of EMSs. Ironically, the German 'technologically oriented approach' which had initially led German companies to reject EMAS was now one of the reasons for the success of EMAS in Germany.

By giving business organisations a strong position in the accreditation, supervision and registration system, the companies' fear that their participation in EMAS would lead to additional controls from enforcement authorities or unnecessary bureaucratic efforts has been overcome. In addition, business organisations are interested in the success of a system in which they play a key role. The IHK and HwK have a particular interest in high participation rates. They have invested in equipment and personnel to prepare for their registration activities; these costs can only be covered if many companies ask to be registered and pay the registration fee.

Promotional activities for EMAS have been widespread in Germany. Nearly all of the State Ministries of Trade and Industry and State Ministries of the Environment as well as nearly all of the IHK and HwK have contributed to the promotion of EMAS. While the IHK and HwK have concentrated on the provision of information and advice, the State Ministries have also financially supported participation in EMAS. It is estimated that between 30% and 60% of EMAS participants have received subsidies.[21] By contrast, financial support for companies certified with ISO14001 has been less frequently available and is lower than subsidies for EMAS participants.

German companies quickly called for deregulation in return for their participation in EMAS. As the German States are responsible for licensing, monitoring and enforcement, they were the ones who primarily responded to this call. Today, all the German States provide some form of a lighter regulatory touch for EMAS-registered companies. Bavaria has been the pioneer with the 'Umweltpakt Bayern' (Bavaria Environmental Pact) which was adopted in October 1995. We concentrate on the 'Umweltpakt Bayern' as the first and most comprehensive attempt to include EMAS in the implementation of environmental policy. In order to illustrate the diversity of the approaches adopted by the German States, we also briefly describe the situation in North Rhine-Westphalia (NRW). In NRW, EMAS participants were granted less regulatory relief than in Bavaria. Furthermore, the measures were not integrated into some kind of 'alliance'.

The 'Umweltpakt Bayern' is a comprehensive voluntary agreement between state government and Bavarian industry. The covenant means obligations for both parties. The companies involved guaranteed, for example, to increase the share of products they transport by rail and to intensify participation in EMAS. The agreement states that the number of 500 validated sites is to be reached in Bavaria by October 2000.[22] In return, the state authorities promised to financially support the application of environment-friendly technology as well as the installation of EMS, and to provide a lighter regulatory touch for EMAS-registered sites. The regulatory relief is based on the principle of 'funktionale Äquivalenz' (functional equivalence), which means the companies' measures to substitute the traditional reporting and monitoring duties need not be exactly identical to the traditional ones, but must be comparable in terms of scope and quality.

The basis for regulatory relief measures is the 'Substitutionskatalog' (substitution catalogue) developed in close co-operation between the Verband der Chemischen Industrie Bayern (the Association of the Bavarian Chemical Industry) and the Bavarian government. The substitution catalogue contains detailed proposals for deregulation measures, most of which have been integrated in existing administrative guidelines. Regulatory relief for EMAS-registered companies currently applies to reporting, documentation, and control duties, and covers the fields of waste, water and pollution control law.

NRW did not grant regulatory relief to the same extent as Bavaria, nor did it integrate it into a comprehensive voluntary agreement. It only enacted the 'Substitutionserlaß' in May 1998 which exclusively deals with pollution control law. It instructs the competent authorities to use their discretionary powers to substitute companies' self-control mechanisms for control duties and to substitute documentation and information provided for in the EMAS Regulation for those required by the pollution control law.

Both states offer regulatory relief exclusively to EMAS-registered companies and not to organisations certified with ISO14001. The reasons are that, unlike EMAS, ISO14001 does not make compliance with all relevant environmental legislation a necessary condition for becoming certified, nor does it provide for government involvement in the certification system. German policy-makers regarded both aspects as prerequisites for regulatory relief for legal reasons.[23]

Although it is hardly possible to ascertain the extent to which lightening the regulatory burden has influenced companies in their decision to participate in EMAS, comparison of the participation rates in Bavaria and NRW suggests that the Bavarian approach which provided for a higher level of regulatory relief and integrated deregulation into a comprehensive voluntary agreement was more successful in setting incentives for companies to become registered under EMAS.[24]

3.2.3 Recent developments: participation rates rise more slowly

Recently, the rise in the number of EMAS participants has slowed down. The main reason seems to be the increasing relevance of the competition of ISO14001. In September 1999, 1450 companies were already certified with ISO14001. This number surged to 1800 companies in December 1999 and 1950 companies in April 2000, whereas the number of EMAS registered sites nearly stagnated.

The central reason for the former dominance of EMAS is that it was the first well known EMS in Germany. When ISO14001 was introduced in October 1996, many companies had already registered under EMAS, were in the process of doing so or planned to participate. EMAS was initially actively discussed by industry and later on actively promoted by business organisations. Furthermore, at this time German companies had not been aware of the advantages of an environmental management system and EMAS was the first system that acquainted companies with it. For these reasons, EMAS became the dominant EMS standard in Germany.

However, recently ISO14001 has become more popular among German companies. Company surveys revealed a number of reasons explaining this development: ISO14001 is a global standard whereas EMAS is restricted to Europe, ISO14001 is closer to ISO9001, a system with which many companies are familiar, and the German interpretation of ISO14001 does not demand compliance with all relevant environmental legislation and the continuous improvement of the environmental performance. In addition, ISO14001 is less costly than EMAS as it does not include the publication of an environmental statement.[25] This factor is all the more important as many EMAS participants complained that the public showed only little interest in the environmental statement, and that the potential benefits had therefore not yet been realised.

3.3   The Netherlands: the Integration of EMAS into a Comprehensive Voluntary Approach

By contrast with France and Germany, EMSs were well known and accepted in the Netherlands long before EMAS was adopted. Since the end of the 1980s they have become an important part of the Dutch environmental policy that aimed at a more co-operative relationship between government and industry. This led to a smooth establishment of the accreditation, registration and supervision system of EMAS which was integrated into the institutional setting built to prepare and implement voluntary agreements. Nevertheless, ISO14001 has become the dominant standard with EMAS being nearly marginalised.

3.3.1   The tradition of environmental management systems in the Netherlands

In the Netherlands, the years 1980–85 were a period marked by the quest for deregulation. Economic growth was small, and the Dutch government believed that over-regulation was one of the reasons. The interest in deregulation also included environmental legislation. Industry perceived environmental regulation as fast-changing and too detailed. It needed legal stability in order to properly plan and carry out investments. Industry perceived self-regulation and environmental management systems as suitable strategies for deregulation. Although the government was interested in EMSs, it considered them inadequate for deregulation as such. It demanded uniform and trustworthy EMSs. Standardisation and certification were believed to be the preconditions for high quality EMSs. Industry accepted that a trustworthy EMS required a high quality and some government involvement in standardisation and certification.

In 1989, the government issued a memorandum on environmental management systems which was written in close co-operation between government and industry. The memorandum on environmental management was accompanied by a 'learning' oriented programme of about 60 million Dutch guilders financed by the government. It aimed at the stimulation of EMS in organisations, and included the development of checklists, handbooks and courses on how to implement EMS in companies. There were also some projects about standardisation and certification of environmental management systems.

Since the early 1990s, the Dutch government has integrated EMSs into its deregulation efforts. The general idea behind the approach by the government is that 'pro-active' companies that internalise environmental values into their organisations and perform well should be treated differently from 'laggards' as far as monitoring, enforcement and licensing are concerned. Pro-active companies are trusted to properly perform measuring duties, self-reporting and self-control. An EMS is considered to be the tool to implement self-regulation and to produce the documents and data needed to convince the authorities of one's environmental credibility. Having its EMS certified or verified helps a company to become a trustworthy partner.

3.3.2 The integration of EMAS in Dutch environmental policy

As there was a consensus on the role of EMSs in the context of the Dutch environmental policy, the establishment of an accreditation, supervision and registration system went smoothly. The foundation SCCM 'Stichting Coordinatie Certificatie Milieuzorgsystemen' (Co-ordination Certification EMS) was established with the aim of implementing EMAS in the Netherlands. Beyond this particular objective, the SCCM aims to (1) promote EMSs and (2) promote the incorporation of EMSs in permitting, monitoring and enforcement procedures by governments. The SCCM has also taken on the function of the Dutch registration body. It has to be interpreted as a joint action by government and industry. Its supervisory board consists of government and industry representatives. In the case of substantial policy-related issues, approval of the supervisory board is needed. Additionally, an advisory board was founded that consists of representatives from government, businesses and relevant 'third parties' such as environmentalists and labour unions.

The secretariat of the SCCM is accommodated at the 'Facilitaire Organisatie Industrie', which provides an institutional setting for industry and governments to communicate and prepare covenants. The SCCM was embedded in these structures, as they were perceived as the right institutional setting to discuss voluntary systems such as EMS standards. The embedding of EMAS in the context of the covenants is reflected in the fact that the requirements for EMAS registration include not only compliance with all relevant legislation but also compliance with voluntary environmental agreements between an industry sector and government.

In order to have uniform and credible environmental management systems, the SCCM has established a 'Scheme for Verifying EMAS' and a 'Scheme for Certifying ISO14001', and updates them regularly. These schemes provide blueprints for the verification and certification procedures and have to be used by the verifiers and certifiers.[26] The tasks of the accreditation and supervision of environmental verifiers were delegated to the Dutch Council for Accreditation, a non-profit foundation established in September 1995.

3.3.3 EMAS and ISO14001

As mentioned earlier, it was a necessary condition for deregulation that the companies' EMSs were standardised and of high quality. Therefore, the advisory board linked to SCCM decided to harmonise the requirements for certification with ISO14001 and registration under EMAS. This led to the rather unusual situation that government had some influence on the national interpretation of ISO14001. The harmonisation of the two standards led to a rather progressive interpretation of ISO14001. This means that the Dutch NEN ISO14001 is more demanding for companies than the original ISO14001. Due to the co-ordination efforts, the additional requirements of EMAS on top of ISO certification are restricted to the publication of a validated environmental statement and the registration of participants.

Although environmental management systems are popular in the Netherlands, the overwhelming majority of companies prefer ISO14001 to EMAS. The large majority of EMAS participants are also certified with ISO14001. In the opinion of Dutch companies, the decisive advantage of ISO14001 over EMAS is that it is a globally accepted standard. The potential advantage of EMAS over ISO14001, which in the Dutch context is only the validated environmental statement, is generally not much appreciated by relevant stakeholders. Thus, participation in EMAS only leads to additional costs without providing any significant benefits for most companies.

3.4   UK: EMAS as a Late Comer

The implementation of EMAS in the UK has been markedly influenced by the fact that BS7750 existed prior to EMAS, and that both government and industry considered EMAS as something which could be done in addition to ISO14001 but not as a superior alternative. Thus, not surprisingly, participation in EMAS lags clearly behind participation in ISO14001.

3.4.1 The creation of the accreditation, supervision and registration system

Overall, the implementation process in the UK was without major conflicts. To oversee the implementation of EMAS, the UK government established an interdepartmental co-ordinating committee, with representatives from the Department of the Environment (DoE), Her Majesty's Inspectorate of Pollution (HMIP) and the Department of Industry (DTI). One week after the EMAS Regulation was adopted by the Council in June 1993, the DTI and DoE jointly issued a public consultation paper which outlined the government's proposals for establishing accreditation systems for both BS7750 and EMAS.

The National Accreditation Council for Certification Bodies (NACCB) was to be asked to develop a system to accredit organisations to certify to BS7750, and in due course also to provide a mechanism for such organisations to become accredited as EMAS verifiers. The accreditation systems for BS7750 certifiers and EMAS verifiers were to be as compatible as possible, so that the audit teams could provide certification for both BS7750 and EMAS. Moreover, the EMAS Regulation requires that sites using a recognised national standard to meet the EMS requirements of EMAS must have their compliance with that standard verified by a body whose accreditation is recognised by the Member State in which the site is located. The UK government regarded this as a compelling reason for establishing an accreditation system that covered both BS7750 and EMAS. At the time, the government also regarded continued rapid progress in implementing BS7750 as an opportunity to establish a competitive advantage for UK environmental consultancy and auditing firms. Firms could be accredited as BS7750 certifiers first and subsequently apply for additional accreditation as EMAS verifiers, when EMAS came into force in May 1995.

In November 1993 the DTI announced as expected that NACCB had been awarded the role of accrediting organisations to both BS7750 certifiers and EMAS verifiers and also of supervising them. The NACCB subsequently changed its name to the United Kingdom Accreditation Service (UKAS) on 1 August 1995.

The DoE announced on 10 May 1994 that the Secretary of State for the Environment, assisted by a small secretariat within the Department, would fulfil the function of the competent body on an interim basis. In 1998 the competent body was finally handed over to the Institute of Environmental Assessment (IEA), a professional body to promote best practice in environmental assessment with the membership drawn from environmental consultancies, business, local authorities and academia.

3.4.2 EMAS as a late comer

Following its announcement as the responsible accreditation and supervision organisation, the NACCB rapidly developed the accreditation criteria required to bring BS7750 into operation, with the aim of quickly getting as many organisations accredited as possible. Development of the accreditation criteria for EMAS verifiers was treated as a secondary task. In March 1995, the NACCB's environmental accreditation scheme was officially launched, and the first eight accredited certification bodies for BS7750 were announced along with the first 20 companies to be certified to the standard. It was not until July 1995 that the NACCB's supplementary criteria 'The Accreditation of Environmental Verifiers for EMAS' were published and the first three organisations to be accredited by NACCB as EMAS verifiers were announced. All had previously been accredited as certifiers for BS7750.

At that time the British government had hoped that EMAS could profit from the rapid development of BS7750. It considered certification to BS7750 as a 'stepping stone' to EMAS registration. Therefore, it wanted to obtain swift recognition of the British national standard as equivalent to the EMS requirements of EMAS. However, recognition of BS7750 was reportedly blocked in March 1995 by Germany, who argued that the recognition of national standards should await agreement on an international standard. Indeed, it was not until February 1996 that BS7750 was finally recognised as corresponding to the equivalent requirements of EMAS by the European Commission. At that time, BS7750 was soon to become obsolete, due to the development of ISO14001. Due to the initial uncertainty over the relationship between EMAS and BS7750, the drive for a good start for EMAS hoped for by the government was lost.

In comparison to ISO14001, EMAS is lagging significantly behind in terms of the number of participants. Furthermore, nearly all of the EMAS participants are also certified with ISO14001. Besides the fact that UK firms had already gained experience with BS7750 and its subsequent internationalisation in the form of ISO14001, an important reason for the dominance of ISO14001 is that it is recognised world-wide, whereas EMAS is only accepted in Europe. Furthermore, ISO14001 is less demanding than EMAS, especially because it does not require the publication of an environmental statement. This is all the more important as in some branches of industry reservations towards the concept of public disclosure of environmental information existed and continue to do so.

3.4.3 Hardly any impulse for EMAS from promotion and deregulation

There was only little or even no impulse for an increase in EMAS participation from promotional activities, even though some activities existed. The UK had adopted a largely centralised approach to the promotion of EMAS, with responsibility for this task assigned to the Competent Body, although some limited collaborative activities were also undertaken with industry, environmental and professional bodies. With respect to industrial activities, the DoE's promotional strategy focused upon awareness-raising, the provision of practical information, and the Small Company Environmental and Energy Management Assistance Scheme (SCEEMAS). SCEEMAS was established in November 1995, with the principal objective of encouraging EMAS registration among SMEs. However, it was abolished in July 1997 due to the poor uptake. Official promotional activities in the UK portrayed EMAS and BS7750 (and later ISO14001) as complementary, with the latter being viewed as a 'stepping stone' to EMAS registration. The DoE has not sought to portray EMAS as markedly superior or preferable to BS7750/ISO14001, which might be another reason for the dominance of ISO14001 over EMAS in the UK.

The possibility of linking EMAS registration (or BS7750/ISO14001 certification) to some form of deregulation has generated considerable debate within policy circles in the UK, but almost no concrete action. Furthermore, the public discourse in the UK largely treats EMAS and ISO14001 as equivalent. To date, the only formal way in which EMAS registration (and ISO14001 certification) is taken into account by the EA is as just one of a number of factors used in the Agency's Operator and Pollution Risk Appraisal (OPRA) risk assessment system. The OPRA system is intended to provide an assessment of the operators' performance and the intrinsic risk of processes regulated under the UK's IPC regime. The OPRA system is supposed to be used to guide the frequency of inspection visits. EMAS registration is therefore one of a number of factors that may theoretically lead to a reduction in the number of such visits. However, the number of such visits is in many cases already minimal in the UK due to staff shortages amongst the inspectorate.

4.   EXPLAINING VARYING PARTICIPATION RATES

The purpose of this section is to explain the central outcome of the EMAS implementation processes: the varying participation rates in the four countries under review. Based on the information provided in section 3, we explain participation in EMAS as a result of the companies' choice between EMAS and ISO14001. Furthermore, we discuss the influence of the implementation process on some of the parameters that determine this choice.

4.1   Companies' Choice between EMAS and ISO14001

Being a voluntary scheme, participation in EMAS depends on the decision of companies to join it. This in turn depends on the net benefits companies expect from their EMAS participation and on the net benefits they expect from joining the alternative EMS standard, ISO14001. Companies will ultimately choose the standard with the highest expected net benefits, provided they are positive. As described in detail in section 3, these benefits differ in the four countries under review depending on the institutional structure, the importance of external communication, and the informational as well as financial promotion of EMAS and ISO14001. Table 6.2 shows where which EMS standard is preferred (or where standards are considered equal) in terms of participation costs and various benefits by companies from the four case-study countries.

With the help of Table 6.2, the differences in participation rates can be easily explained. In France, the Netherlands and the UK the only advantage of EMAS over ISO14001 is that EMAS is better suited for external communication than ISO14001. This statement has to be qualified with respect to the UK and especially France. As mentioned earlier, in France, public disclosure of environmental information is sometimes seen as a sign that a company has to justify itself, thus turning the advantage of external communication into a disadvantage. It is a similar case (albeit to a lesser extent) in some branches of UK industry, where revealing information to the public is still seen as problematic. However, even French, Dutch and UK companies that see a possible advantage of improving their external communication via EMAS consider it as rather limited. This is partly due to the high reputation of ISO14001 especially in the Netherlands and the UK, but also partly due to the low public response to EMAS. It is therefore not surprising that the additional benefits of EMAS only outweigh its additional costs for a few companies, and as a consequence participation in EMAS has remained low.

Table 6.2 Advantages of EMAS and ISO14001 from companies' perspective

	France	Germany	The Netherlands	UK
Participation costs	ISO14001	ISO14001	ISO14001	ISO14001
International recognition	ISO14001	ISO14001	ISO14001	ISO14001
Clarity of EMS	ISO14001	ISO14001	Equivalent	ISO14001
Similarity to ISO9000	ISO14001	ISO14001	Equivalent	ISO14001
Regulatory relief	Equivalent	EMAS	Equivalent	Equivalent
Involvement of business organisations	ISO14001	Equivalent	Equivalent	Equivalent
Promotion (information)	Equivalent	Earlier: EMAS Now: Equivalent	Equivalent[27]	Equivalent
Promotion (funding)	Equivalent	EMAS	Equivalent	Equivalent
External communication	EMASS ISO14001	EMAS	EMAS	EMAS $\lessgtr$ ISO14001

Notes:
ISO14001: Advantages from ISO14001 participation are higher than from EMAS participation.
EMAS: Advantages from EMAS participation are higher than from ISO14001 participation.
Equivalent: Advantages resulting from participation are the same for both standards.

EMAS $\lessgtr$ ISO14001: Whether the advantages from EMAS or ISO14001 participation are higher varies from one firm to the next.

Germany is the only country where EMAS provides other advantages besides external communications. For legal reasons, regulatory relief is only granted to EMAS-registered companies, and in the mid- to late 1990s there was more information and funding available for EMAS participants than for ISO14001-certified companies. This led to high participation rates in EMAS, not only in comparison with other countries but also to ISO14001. Recently, however, this situation has changed and ISO14001 has been quickly catching up. This is mainly due to the facts that the level of companies' information about ISO14001 has risen; companies have become more aware of ISO's advantages such as world-wide recognition, and are partly disappointed about the benefits of improved external communication brought about by EMAS.

4.2   Influence of the Implementation Process on Participation Rates

Among the factors that influenced the choice between EMAS and ISO14001 in Table 6.2, only 'international recognition' and 'participation costs'[28] are not linked to the implementation of EMAS in the four countries. All other factors have been or could have been influenced by the implementation process. Among these factors we can distinguish two groups.

The first group contains the factors where ISO14001 had an initial advantage over EMAS because it was closer to business, and not government-initiated. These factors are 'clarity of EMS', 'similarity to ISO9000' and 'involvement of business organisations'. Here, the implementation process could serve to eliminate the initial advantage of ISO14001 and to make both systems equally attractive to companies. For this to happen, the decisive requirement was close co-operation between government and business organisations.

In the Netherlands, for example, government and business organisations agreed to harmonise the EMS requirements of EMAS and ISO14001. Whereas this factor did not outweigh the other disadvantages of EMAS in the Netherlands, the integration of business organisations in the accreditation, supervision and registration system certainly contributed to the high participation rate in Germany. By contrast, in France, the strong influence of the government in the accreditation, supervision and registration system was one of the factors that led to the low number of EMAS-registered companies.

The second group entails factors where EMAS gained or could have gained an advantage over ISO14001, but this depended largely on the decision of government to treat EMAS as superior to ISO14001 in the implementation process. The factors 'regulatory relief', 'promotion of EMAS' and 'external communication' belong to this group. For instance, public authorities could have granted more regulatory relief to EMAS-registered than to ISO14001-certified companies.[29] This was only done in Germany and is clearly one of the factors that led German companies to prefer EMAS to ISO14001. Additionally, government could have provided more information and funding for EMAS than for ISO14001. Here again, Germany was the only country to follow this approach. Finally, the government could have helped the external communication factor to be a real competitive advantage for EMAS by providing the public with information about the scheme. Only a public which knows about EMAS's main contents and goals is able to appreciate a company's participation in the scheme.

Overall, the implementation process obviously had a decisive influence on the number of EMAS participants. However, given the 'natural' advantages of ISO14001 over EMAS of lower costs and of being an internationally recognised standard, high participation rates required both close co-operation between government and business organisations in the implementation process as well as government giving EMAS participants preferential treatment.

5.   A COMPARISON OF EMAS COSTS AND BENEFITS

Against the background of the low participation rates in some countries the question arises of whether EMAS has been a successful policy instrument. To address this question this section presents data that allow us to assess whether EMAS has brought about more benefits than costs. The data is taken from the individual case study reports. To gain the relevant data and information expert interviews were conducted, the relevant literature was reviewed and identical company surveys in all four countries were carried out.[30]

From the angle of a simple comparison of benefits and costs, EMAS can be considered successful if the overall benefits exceed the costs[31]

$$B_P + B_S > C_P + C_{SS} + C_{SR}$$

On the benefit side we distinguish between benefits for companies (B_P) and benefits for society (B_S) which result from environmental improvements brought about by companies' EMAS participation.[32] On the cost side we distinguish between participation costs that are partly borne by companies (C_P) and partly borne by governments via subsidies for EMAS participants (C_{SS})[33] and government costs incurred in running the accreditation, supervision and registration system (C_{SR}). In our assessment of the cost side, we concentrate on the costs for running the EMAS system for the following reasons: EMAS is a voluntary scheme, thus companies only participate when their benefits exceed their costs, i.e. $B_P > C_P$ must be true. This implies that companies participating in EMAS realise a positive net benefit ($B_{PN} = B_P - C_P$). We can therefore neglect the private costs by substituting B_P by B_{PN}. Similarly, the provision of subsidies by Member States is voluntary. This implies that once a government financially supports EMAS participants, it believes that the benefits from the environmental improvements they realise are higher than the subsidies. This means that $B_S > C_{SS}$ must be true,[34] which implies positive net benefits for society ($B_{SN} = B_S - C_{SS}$). Thus, EMAS can be considered successful if

$$B_{PN} + B_{SN} > C_{SR}$$

We will discuss each of these benefit and cost categories in detail (sections 5.1 and 5.2).

5.1   Benefits of EMAS

5.1.1   Companies' benefits

With respect to companies' benefits from EMAS, we distinguish between benefits from the introduction of an EMS and benefits from improvements in the communication with external stakeholders.

Benefits from EMS. The benefits brought about by the introduction of an EMS are virtually nil in France, the Netherlands and the UK. The reason is not that companies consider the internal instruments as useless, but that the establishment of these instruments mostly did not take place in the context of EMAS. Nearly all Dutch and most UK companies already had an EMS (either internal or ISO14001) in place prior to their EMAS registration, and the large majority of French EMAS-registered firms obtained ISO14001 certification together with their EMAS registration or were already ISO14001-certified beforehand.[35]

For Germany, it is estimated that only 31% of EMAS-registered sites are also ISO14001-certified (UBA, 1999, p. 57). Most German EMAS participants did not follow a systematic approach to environmental management or even had no environmental management at all before taking part in EMAS. Consequently, on average German companies rate all EMS-related elements the EMAS Regulation provides for as important and helpful (see Figure 6.5). Figure 6.5 presents the answers EMAS participants gave when they were asked to rank the importance of the different elements of EMAS on a scale from very useful (1) to not useful at all (6). The figure shows that the elements directed at companies' internal management and organisation were all regarded as rather important, while the external elements all come at the bottom of the list.

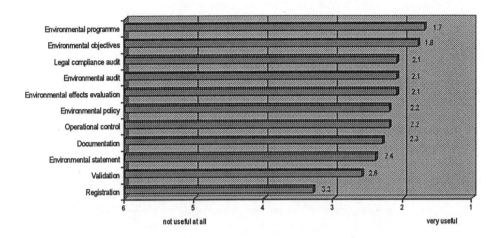

Source: Unternehmerinstitut e.V. (1997, annex Fig. A49).

Figure 6.5 Importance of different elements of EMAS for German companies

A company survey carried out by the Umweltbundesamt revealed that by systematically integrating environmental aspects into their management systems, German companies on average realised cost reductions of DM140,000, which exceeded the average participation costs of DM116,000 and thus led to net benefits of DM24,000 (UBA, 1999, pp. 39 and 35). While this figure represents only a part of companies' benefits, it already suggests that the magnitude of BPN is not insignificant. The fact that companies achieved such noteworthy cost reductions indicates that many of the activities they undertook in the context of their EMS implementation consisted of what is described in the literature as 'picking of low hanging fruits' (Gabel and Sinclair-Desgagné, 1998). Low-hanging fruits describe improvements that do not only reduce the environmental impact of companies but also lead to cost savings with a relatively short pay back period e.g. a reduction of energy consumption and waste production. In addition to the monetary benefits, the introduction of an EMS has led to benefits not directly measurable in monetary terms such as a better knowledge of environmental regulations applicable to a company and the motivation of employees (UBA, 1999, p. 37).

Benefits from improvements in the external communication. External communication can lead to benefits when it triggers positive reactions of the companies' stakeholders. In order to help companies to improve their external communication, the EMAS Regulation provides for the validated environmental statement. It enables EMAS participants to supply their stakeholders with credible information about their environmental performance.[36] The French, Dutch and UK companies explicitly registered under EMAS to improve their external relations. However, German companies hoped for positive communication effects as well.[37] As an indicator to what extent these expectations have been met, Figure 6.6 shows how important the companies value the environmental statement on a scale from very useful (1) to not useful at all (6).

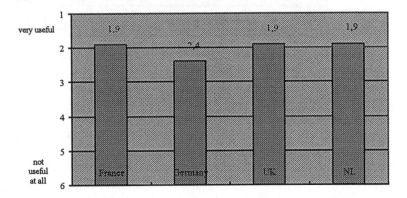

Source: Unternehmerinstitut e.V. 1997, annex Fig. A49 and individual country case studies.

Figure 6.6 Usefulness of the environmental statement for companies in the four countries

Figure 6.6 indicates that the environmental statement has largely satisfied companies' expectations in France, the Netherlands and the UK. Although German firms clearly regard the environmental statement as more than medium useful, they appear to be somewhat disappointed. This result is confirmed by the survey of the Umweltbundesamt, which has revealed that in Germany those stakeholders that EMAS participants wanted to address and that could have provided them with substantial benefits have shown relatively little interest in the environmental statements (UBA, 1999, p. 43).

Benefits for society. The benefits EMAS generated for society resulted from environmental improvements brought about by companies' EMAS participation. In order to assess ecological effects that have been reached, we again rely on the company surveys. EMAS participants were asked to indicate what ecologically oriented measures they have undertaken or intend to undertake in connection with their EMAS participation and whether these measures have brought about environmental improvements. The firms' answers with respect to the measures EMAS has triggered are depicted in Figure 6.7.

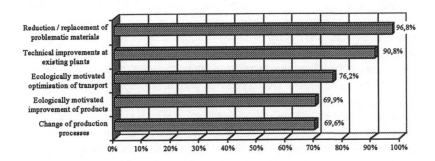

Source: Unternehmerinstitut e.V. (1997, annex Fig. A27) and individual country case studies.

Figure 6.7 Measures companies have undertaken or intend to undertake
within their EMAS participation (percentage of companies,
geometric mean of the four countries)

Figure 6.7 shows that a large majority of companies are planning or have already undertaken the reduction or replacement of problematic materials (96.8%) and technical improvements at existing plants (90.8%). EMAS has also been fairly effective in encouraging the ecologically motivated optimisation of transport (76.2%). Ecologically motivated improvements of products (69.9%) and production processes (69.6) have played the least important roles. A comparison of the country-specific results reveals that EMAS has triggered most measures in Germany and least in the Netherlands. The difference can be explained by the countries' different experience with EMSs. As nearly all the Dutch companies already had an EMS in place, it was difficult for EMAS to trigger additional measures.

The companies' answers to the question over what environmental improvements the measures have brought about have shown that they mainly resulted in the reduction of solid waste, energy consumption, water usage and effluent water. Companies from all four countries described the environmental effects that resulted from the introduction of the various measures on average as medium. When stating this, companies probably compared these effects with the effects of environmental legislation which – according to companies – is still the most important driver for environmental improvements.

While the companies' assessment of environmental improvements provides an overview of the benefits EMAS brought for society (B_S), for the evaluation of EMAS as a policy instrument we are interested in the net benefits for society (B_{SN}). Assessing B_{SN} on the basis of the equation $B_{SN}=B_S-C_{SS}$, we face the difficulty that B_S is a qualitative assessment of environmental improvements whereas C_{SS} is a monetary term. A proper comparison of these two terms requires the monetarisation of the environmental benefits. However, even without monetarisation we are able to determine more closely the size of B_{SN} with the available information. We know that in Germany[38] 40–70% of EMAS-registered companies did not receive any subsidies. This means that the benefits for society arising from the improvements in the environmental performance of the participation of these companies in EMAS equal the net benefits for society. This allows the conclusion to be drawn that a substantial part of the benefits EMAS generated for society are net benefits.

5.2   Costs of EMAS Borne by Governments

The costs of the EMAS regulation which are borne by government have arisen through administrative costs of establishing and running the accreditation, supervision and registration system. As it proved difficult to collect data on the costs of establishing the system, which happened some years ago, we restricted our assessment to the costs of running the system. As an indicator to assess these costs, we used the working time for running the system in the last five years, which we measured in man-months. As the period of our analysis stretches over several years, we faced some difficulties in collecting all the relevant data. Therefore, our assessment on the amount of administrative work in the four countries under review is to some extent based on estimates. Although this implies that our cost assessment cannot claim to be precise, it still indicates the scale of the actual administrative costs of EMAS. As the coverage of the costs of the accreditation, supervision and registration system includes contributions from government as well as accreditation and supervision fees from verifiers and registration fees from companies, we also assessed the percentage of the administrative costs that are borne by government. Table 6.3 summarises our results.

Table 6.3 clearly shows that the administrative costs of running the accreditation, supervision and registration system are low.[39] Furthermore, in all four countries most or all (in the UK) of the costs are borne by verifiers or

EMAS-registered companies via fees. The reason for the low overall costs as well as low costs per EMAS-registered company in the Netherlands and the UK is that the EMAS accreditation, supervision and registration system is largely integrated into the administrative system for ISO14001. In Germany, although overall administrative costs are significant, they are relatively low per EMAS-registered company because of the high number of EMAS registrations. Average administrative costs per EMAS-registered company are comparatively high in France, which is due to the low participation rate. A great part of the French administrative costs arises independently of the number of EMAS registrations. Thus, a higher participation rate would decrease the average French administrative costs per company.

Table 6.3 Administrative work to run the EMAS system in the last five years (measured in man-months/mm)

	France	Germany	Netherlands	UK
Total administrative costs	57.1 mm	1204 mm	11.9 mm	36.7 mm
Overall administrative costs divided by no. of EMAS participants (average administrative costs per company)	1.59 mm	0.49 mm	0.46 mm	0.50 mm
% of total administrative costs borne by governments	Approx. 30%	Approx. 15%	Approx. 25%	Recently 0% after a registration fee was introduced

Source: Incountry case studies, author's own calculations.

5.3   Comparison of costs and benefits

At the beginning of section 5 we stipulated that EMAS can be regarded a successful policy instrument if

$$B_{PN} + B_{SN} > C_{SR}$$

Although we were unable to precisely assess the size of each term, the information we collected indicates that the inequation above is true. Companies' participation in EMAS brought them substantial net benefits (B_{PN}) because the average monetary participation benefits exceed the average participation costs. Additionally, other important benefits exist which are not directly measurable in monetary terms, e.g. an improved knowledge of company-relevant environmental legislation. Our analysis further indicates that net benefits for society ($B_{SN} = B_S - C_{SS}$) exist. Participation in EMAS is able to increase a company's environmental performance and subsidies are only granted to some EMAS-registered companies. By contrast, the costs of running the EMAS accreditation, supervision and registration system which are borne by governments (C_{SR}) are low. This suggests that the overall net benefits of EMAS are higher than governments' expenditure used to run the EMAS system. In other words, EMAS can be considered a successful policy instrument.

6.   SUMMARY OF RESULTS

Environmental management system standards are now well established in Europe. However, whether companies choose EMAS or ISO14001 varies significantly between the four EU Member States we analysed. The central explanation for these differences is that the way the EMAS Regulation was implemented in the various countries generated greatly differing net benefits of EMAS registration and ISO14001 certification for companies.

In France, the Netherlands and the UK authorities did not provide preferential treatment to EMAS participants, and business organisations do not support EMAS more than ISO14001. Therefore, the only advantage EMAS has over ISO14001 is that it is better suited for external communication. However, not much weight is attached to this advantage by the vast majority of companies and it is even considered a disadvantage by some firms in France and the UK. By contrast, companies in all three countries appreciate that ISO14001 certification is less demanding than EMAS registration as it does not demand a validated environmental statement. Additionally, companies value the fact that ISO14001 is a world-wide standard, whereas EMAS is restricted to Europe. Against this background it is no surprise that in France, the Netherlands and the UK, participation in EMAS is low and well behind ISO14001.

In Germany, the relative attractiveness of EMAS compared to ISO14001 was increased by granting regulatory relief exclusively to EMAS-registered companies and by providing EMAS with more and higher subsidies than companies certified with ISO14001. Furthermore, the involvement of business organisations in the accreditation and supervision system for verifiers and registration system for companies led companies to trust the system and business organisations to promote EMAS. Consequently, Germany is the only country where more companies decided in favour of EMAS and not ISO14001. Recently, however, this situation has changed and ISO14001 has caught up quickly. This is mainly due to the facts that the level of companies' information about ISO14001 has risen, they are more aware of ISO's advantages such as world-wide recognition, and they are partly disappointed about the benefits from external communication generated by EMAS.

Despite low participation rates in France, the Netherlands and the UK, EMAS can be considered a successful policy instrument, because the benefits generated by EMAS outweigh its costs. Companies only participate in the voluntary scheme when their benefits exceed their costs, thus participation provides positive net benefits for them. In addition, there exist net benefits for society due to EMAS-registered companies' improved environmental performance. By contrast, costs borne by government (and thus society) for running the accreditation, supervision and registration system are low.

NOTES

1. This chapter has greatly benefited from comments by Frans Berkhout, Malcolm Eames, Matthieu Glachant, Olivier Godard, Kris Lulofs and Simone Schucht. We are particularly grateful to Francois Lévêque, who was the discussant of earlier versions of this chapter during several workshops and whose comments have been very valuable.
2. The description of the political evolution of EMAS follows Franke and Wätzold (1996), some additional points on the position of UK industry are taken from Eames (2000).
3. The current draft proposal for EMAS II (common position of the Council of February 2000) stipulates opening EMAS to non-industrial sectors. Furthermore, all kinds of organisations that have their own functions and administration shall be allowed to participate in EMAS. This means that not only sites but also entire companies as well as parts or combinations thereof can be registered. In anticipation of this development, we will often speak of companies instead of sites in the following.
4. The public includes consumers, neighbours, commercial clients, authorities, banks and insurance companies, i.e. the companies' stakeholders.
5. The ISO is a non-governmental institution which serves as an umbrella organisation of the national standardization organizations.
6. BS7750 can be regarded as a kind of precursor of the other standards (see Thimme, 1998, p. 266).
7. See Müller (2000, p. 111).
8. See Thimme (1998, p. 281).
9. In contrast to the EMAS Regulation, the EMS of ISO14001 includes the entire process from the environmental policy and programme to review and corrective action. This definition corresponds to the usual understanding of an EMS. In the following we use the term EMS in this broader sense.
10. In contrast to the registration under EMAS, the realisation of environmental improvements is not a necessary condition for becoming ISO14001 certified.

11. For example the German Ministry of Trade and Industry estimated that in 1998 there were 300,000 potential EMAS participants in Germany.
12. When assessing ISO14001 participation, it should be borne in mind that ISO is not limited to industrial sites.
13. The choice of the economic perspective allows the development of a general framework to analyse which companies should be EMAS-registered, which ISO14001-certified and which should have no standardised EMS at all. Furthermore, the economic analysis clarifies the purpose of the different elements of EMAS, i.e. the EMS and the environmental statement.
14. See Karl and Orwat (1999, pp. 144–150) for a short description of the schemes.
15. However, the two cases mentioned have so far not played an important role.
16. The arguments of the following section are taken from Bültmann and Wätzold (2000), where they are also presented in a formal model.
17. Other differences such as the varying emphasis on legal compliance do not seem to have played a similar significant role in practice.
18. In the following we will call this the accreditation, supervision and registration system.
19. Other comparative studies on the implementation of EMAS include, for example, Hillary (1998) and Gouldson and Murphy (1998).
20. See Waskow (1997, pp. 111–112).
21. Please see Bültmann and Wätzold (1999) for more details on the promotion of EMAS in Germany.
22. This number was already reached in October 1999.
23. Only in recent months have a few German states questioned this position and considered offering regulatory relief to ISO14001-certified organisations as well.
24. There were 548 sites registered under EMAS in Bavaria and 467 sites in NRW. This is 8.17% in Bavaria and 5.00% in NRW of all companies from the manufacturing sector with more than 20 employees in 1999.
25. See Forschungsgruppe FEU (1998, p. 6).
26. The 'Scheme for Verifying EMAS', for instance, comprises three substantial sections: interpretation of EMAS, internal organisation of the verifying organisation (including competence), and operating procedures for the verifying organisations.
27. In the Netherlands and the UK, ISO14001 profited from the fact that companies were well informed about BS7750 which was in many respects similar to the ISO standard.
28. One could argue that the costs for participating in EMAS are influenced by the implementation process, e.g. by charging no registration fees, but in our analysis this would be considered a subsidy and taken into account under this point.

29. A detailed analysis of the Member States' experience in granting regulatory relief to EMAS-registered and ISO14001-certified companies is given in Wätzold et al. (2001).

30. The survey was based on questionnaires, which were sent to all EMAS participants in France, Germany, the Netherlands and the UK. In France, the Netherlands and the UK the survey was conducted in early 1999. The German data are taken from a survey that the Unternehmerinstitut e.V. carried out in mid-1997 (see Unternehmerinstitut e.V., 1997). At the time the questionnaires were sent out there were 32 EMAS participants in France, 22 in the Netherlands, 70 in the UK, and almost 700 in Germany. The return quotas ranged from about 20% in Germany to 63% in France, 68% in the Netherlands and 74% in the UK.

31. The variables in section 2.3.3 are benefits and costs related to the individual company whereas the variables here represent aggregated benefits and costs. We use lower case and capital letters to mark this difference.

32. We are aware that there is some overlap between BP and BS once the company is rewarded by a third party which benefits from the environmental improvements brought about by EMAS. The analysis will show that this area of overlap can be neglected as it does not influence the general result on the success of EMAS as companies significantly profit from benefits independent of third party behaviour (e.g. cost savings).

33. Note that in our interpretation subsidies are not a pure transfer between agents but form part of the participation costs, i.e. the sum of C_P and C_{SS} reflects the total costs incurred in companies' participation in EMAS. This is important as in the standard welfare economics framework transfers between agents are not considered as costs.

34. With this position we assume that the state maximises social welfare. Obviously, this postulation can be questioned from several perspectives. Governments might pursue other interests than social welfare maximisation. Even if they did, they might not have all the necessary information to assess whether $B_S > C_{SS}$ is true. However, for the purpose of this section we can rely on this assumption.

35. The benefits of the EMS requirements of EMAS and ISO14001 are similar in France and the UK and identical in the Netherlands. In fact, under the revised EMAS Regulation the EMS requirements of EMAS and ISO14001 will be identical, because the requirements of the ISO standard will be integrated into the EMAS Regulation (cf. common position of the Council of February 2000 and see section 6 for details).

36. The credibility of the information provided in the environmental statements is based on the verification and registration system. The quality and strictness of the controls performed by the environmental verifiers mainly depend on two factors: the competence of the verifiers, and the supervision procedures to which the verifiers themselves are subjected. Although differences exist with respect to the accreditation and supervision of the verifiers, we found no indications that

the competence of the verifiers is low or the supervision system is not working in any of the four countries. However, it should be borne in mind that this does not imply that the misconduct of verifiers is always detected (see e.g. Müller, 1998) as a perfect supervision system would require eye-witness validation of all verifications. With respect to the registration systems of the four countries, we did not find any indications of systematic malfunctions either. For details of the national accreditation, supervision and registration systems, please refer to the country case studies.

37. See (besides the national case study reports for the UK) also Strachan et al. (1997).
38. The other countries can be neglected, as approximately 95% of all EMAS-registered companies in the four countries under review are located in Germany.
39. Compared to overall participation costs for companies the administrative costs are marginal (see 5.1.1. for an estimate of German participation costs).

REFERENCES

Ankele, K., K. Fichter, K. Heuvels, E. Rehbinder and L. Schebeck (1998), 'Fachwissenschaftliche Untersuchung der Wirksamkeit der EG-Öko-Audit-Verordnung', *UmweltWirtschaftsForum*, 6 (4), pp. 38–44.

Bültmann, A. and F. Wätzold (1999), 'Die Förderung des Öko-Audit-Systems in Deutschland: Ergebnisse einer Befragung der Umwelt- und Wirtschaftsministerien der Länder sowie der Industrie- und Handelskammern und Handwerkskammern', UFZ-Forschungsbericht 12/99, Leipzig.

Bültmann, A. and F. Wätzold (2000), 'The Implementation of National and European Environmental Legislation: Three Case studies', UFZ-research report 20/2000, Leipzig.

Eames, M. (2000), 'Implementation of the EMAS Regulation in the United Kingdom', SPRU research report prepared for the EU Commission, Brighton.

FEU (1998), Vorläufige Untersuchungsergebnisse und Handlungsempfehlungen zum Forschungsprojekt 'Evaluierung von Umweltmanagementsystemen zur Vorbereitung der 1998 vorgesehenen Überprüfung des gemeinschaftlichen Öko-Audit-Systems', Institut für Ökologie und Unternehmensführung an der European Business School, Oestrich-Winkel.

Franke, J. and F. Wätzold (1996), 'Voluntary Initiatives and Public Intervention – the Regulation of Eco-Auditing', in F. Lévêque (ed.), *Environmental Policy in Europe*, Aldershot, UK and Brookfield, US: Edward Elgar, pp. 175–200.

Gabel, H.L. and B. Sinclair-Desgagné (1998), 'The Firm, its Routines and the Environment', in T. Tietenberg and H. Folmer (eds), *The International Yearbook of Environmental and Resource Economics 1998–1999*, Cheltenham, UK and Lyme, US: Edward Elgar, pp. 89–118.

Gouldson, A. and J. Murphy (1998), *Regulatory Realities. The Implementation and Impact of Industrial Environmental Regulation*, London: Earthscan.

Hillary, R. (1998), 'Pan-European Assessment of EMAS Implementation', *European Environment*, **8**, pp. 184–192.

Karl, H. and C. Orwat (1999), 'Economic Aspects of Environmental Labelling', in H. Folmer and T. Tietenberg (eds), *The International Yearbook of Environmental and Resource Economics 1999–2000*, Cheltenham, UK and Lyme, US: Edward Elgar, pp. 107–171.

Lulofs, K. (2000), 'Implementation of EMAS in the Netherlands', CSTM research report prepared for the EU-Commission, Enschede.

Müller, M. (1998), 'Der Umweltgutachter im Öko-Audit-System – eine entscheidungstheoretische Analyse von Determinanten der Prüfungsqualität', *Zeitschrift für Umweltpolitik und Umweltrecht*, **98** (2), pp. 213–238.

Müller, M. (2000), Normierte Umweltmanagementsysteme und deren Weiterentwicklung im Rahmen einer nachhaltigen Entwicklung unter besonderer Berücksichtigung der Öko-Audit-Verordnung und der ISO14001. PhD-Dissertation, Universität Halle-Wittenberg.

Pigou, A. (1920), *The Economics of Welfare*, London: Macmillan.

Schucht, S. (2000), 'The Implementation of the Environmental Management and Eco-Audit Scheme (EMAS) Regulation in France', Cerna Research Paper 2000-B-2, Paris.

Strachan, P., M. Haque, A. McCulloch and J. Moxen (1997), 'The Eco-Management and Audit Scheme: Recent Experiences of UK Participating Organizations', *European Environment*, **7**, pp. 25–33.

Thimme, Peter M. (1998), 'Der Wettbewerb zwischen EG-Öko-Audit-Verordnung und DIN ISO 14001' in Doktoranden-Netzwer Öko-Audit e.V. (ed.), *Umweltmanagementsysteme zwischen Anspruch und Wirklichkeit*, Heidelberg et al.: Springer, pp. 265–285.

UBA-Umweltbundesamt (1999), 'EG-Umweltaudit in Deutschland. Erfahrungsbericht. Herausgeber: Umweltbundesamt', Fachgebiet I 2.2, *Wirtschafts- und sozialwissenschaftliche Umweltfragen*, Bearbeiter: W.F.Schulz, Berlin.

Unternehmerinstitut e.V. (1997), *Öko-Audit in der mittelständischen Praxis. Evaluierung und Ansätze für eine Effizienzsteigerung von Umweltmanagementsystemen in der Praxis*, Bonn: Unternehmerinstitut e.V.

Waskow, Siegfried (1997), *Betriebliches Umweltmanagement. Anforderungen nach der Audit-Verordnung der EG und dem Umweltauditgesetz*, 2nd Edition. Heidelberg: C.F. Müller.

Wätzold, F., A. Bültmann, M. Eames, K.R.D. Lulofs and S. Schucht (2001), 'EMAS and Regulatory Relief in Europe: Lessons from National Experience', *European Environment*, **11**, pp. 37–48.

7. The need for adaptive implementation

Matthieu Glachant

1. INTRODUCTION

In the preceding three chapters, a set of Directives and Regulation has been evaluated. Based on this available material, is it possible to draw normative or prescriptive lessons on how EU environmental policy can be implemented in a more environmentally effective way?

The goal of this chapter is to try to do so, but to restrict the analysis to only one aspect of the problem. Its starting point is an empirical finding arising from the cases studied in the preceding chapters: the pervasive impacts of other policies on environmental outcomes. In almost every case, the implementation processes were dramatically affected by the existence of parallel policy processes. These parallel processes have had different origins: other EU Directives, national policies or even international policy schemes (for instance, the impact of the ISO14001 standard on the implementation of EMAS). Their impacts, either negative or positive, on environmental outcomes were very significant.

Based on this statement, the general argument developed in the chapter can be summarised in the following way. An important question for EU policy is how implementation can efficiently cope with such interactions; in other words, to find ways to maximise potential synergies, or alternatively to reduce inconsistencies, with the other policy components. Given that policy interactions are difficult to predict at the policy formulation stage of the policy, adjustments necessarily occur at the implementation stage. In this context, implementing EU environmental policy requires policy systems able to adjust at low costs. In the following, we call this property *adaptability* and try to give a precise meaning to the notion of adaptive implementation.

The structure of this chapter is straightforward. The second section discusses the results of the case studies regarding environmental effectiveness. It explains why the challenge for environmental effectiveness is to be adaptive. The third section presents selected examples of failures and successes in adaptive implementation taken from the case studies in this volume. These examples are used to break up the general problem into sub-aspects. Based on the economic literature, the fourth section explores the different issues and gives an economic view on what adaptive implementation might mean in the European Union context. A final section concludes and postulates some policy recommendations related to the implementation of EU environmental policy.

2.   THE PERVASIVE IMPACT OF POLICY INTERACTIONS ON ENVIRONMENTAL OUTCOMES

2.1   The Empirical Statement

Table 7.1 gathers the results of the preceding chapters on the degree of attainment of the Directives or Council Regulation's goals. A first remarkable observation is that over-compliance is frequent in the sample. Excluding the case of EMAS for which the notion of over-compliance is a bit difficult to handle, it occurred in six cases out of eight. It should immediately be emphasised however that the sample is not representative of implementation in the European Union. In particular, it does not include any southern Member States where the implementation deficit is said to be more acute.[1]

In some cases, the reason for over-compliance is straightforward. In Germany and the Netherlands for both the Waste Incineration and the Large Combustion Plant Directives, more stringent domestic policies pre-existed when the Directives were adopted. Basically, these cases are examples of the well-established role of policy diffusion of certain EU policies. Environmental front-runners like Germany, the Netherlands or other Nordic countries initially tackle new policy problems through domestic policies. Due to pressures from these countries (concerned by trans-boundary pollution, seeking competitive advantages for their companies or alternatively trying to prevent companies from other countries exploiting this as an advantage), an EU policy-making process is then launched leading ultimately to the diffusion of the policy in less environmentally advanced countries.[2]

Other reasons for over-compliance are related to the impact of parallel policy processes leading to major, albeit indirect, impacts on the kinds of pollution regulated by the Directive. This is the case in the United Kingdom for the Large Combustion Plant Directive where the privatisation process launched at the end of the 1980s led for market reasons to a major shift in energy inputs from coal to gas. The fact that gas-fired turbines emit virtually no SO_2 has made the completion of the Directive target much easier than expected. Similarly in France, over-compliance with the requirements of the Large Combustion Plant Directive was due to a shift in energy sources during the 1980s away from coal and fuel oil towards nuclear energy. Hence, compliance is strongly related to the evolution of the French energy policy.

Table 7.1 Degree of goal attainment

Large Combustion Plant Directive 88/809/EEC/SO_2 targets				
	France	Germany	Netherlands	United Kingdom
Emission as percentage of EU target (1993)	37%	67%	50%	75%
Driving forces in the electricity supply industry	Nuclear programme	Pre-existing constraining domestic regulation ('Waldsterben')	Pre-existing constraining domestic regulation (acid rain + Germany's follower)	LCP Directive. Privatisation leading to massive switching from coal to gas
Municipal Waste Incineration Directive 89/429/EEC				
Average emission as percentage of EU limits*	> 150% estimated	3.2%	15.4%	100% estimated
Driving forces	Long lasting uncertainty regarding the general domestic waste policy. Weak enforcement (political factors) Many small incinerators	Pre-existing constraining domestic regulation	Pre-existing constraining domestic regulation	Massive plant closures. Directive (co-implemented with the Integrated Pollution Control regime established under the 1990 EPA). Public pressure
Council Regulation 93/1836/EEC on Eco-Management and Audit Scheme (EMAS)				
Participation rate (April 2000)*	0.15%	6.5%	0.4%	0.25%
Driving forces	Central role of the regulator	Implementation institutions. Public subsidies. Regulatory relief	Preference for ISO	Preference for ISO

Note: *Sources and underlying assumptions for the figures are in Chapters 4, 5 and 6 in this volume.

But parallel policy measures have also affected environmental performances negatively. During the implementation of the Directive 89/429 on waste incineration, France has deeply modified its domestic waste policy by promoting both recycling and incineration with energy recovery. As will be detailed in section 3, this policy change generated large and long-lasting uncertainties during the 1990s on the role of incineration in domestic waste management. It contributes very much to the considerable delay of compliance of the big incinerators that has been observed in this country.

Policy interactions have also been at the core of the implementation of the EMAS regulation. In that case, the implementation took place along with the emergence of the ISO14001 standard. Given that the firms voluntarily participate in both schemes, it de facto created a situation of competition between the two standards. The stake was to attract as many participants to the different schemes as possible. The co-existence of two standards led to some adjustments in the EMAS implementation process. In particular, the question of the compatibility between EMAS and ISO14001 was raised at the national and the EU level. Another issue discussed at the national level was whether the public authorities had to promote the sole diffusion of EMAS or the joint diffusion of certified environmental systems. Various options were implemented.

To sum up, the impact of policy interactions on policy environmental outcomes is pervasive and can be either positive or negative. Such interactions occur as a result of:

- Pre-existing domestic policies that regulate the same environmental problem but which are more ambitious than the Directive. This simply reflects the 'leader–laggard' dynamic of some EU policies and illustrates the role of some EU Directives as policy diffusion devices and the ability of some Member States to influence environmental policy-making at the EU level.
- Other environmental policies or regulations emerging at the national, EU or international level. This is the case in France with the implementation of the Directive 89/429 and in all the countries with respect to the interactions between the ISO14001 and the EMAS standards.
- Non-environmental policies like energy policy (for instance, the development of nuclear energy in France, the privatisation of the British electricity supply industry in the case of the Large Combustion Plant Directive).

2.2   A New Formulation of the Normative Question

The generalised impacts of parallel policy processes on outcome should lead to the recasting of the very nature of implementation. It is clearly not a top-down process initiated by a policy decision at the EU level, which progressively reaches the policy targets in a hierarchical mode. Instead implementation of a particular European text should rather be viewed as part of a complex patchwork of dynamic interactions across a multi-level and multi-centred policy system. In this way, the ubiquity of policy interactions is the inevitable by-product of complex policy systems highly differentiated both vertically (territorial differentiation) and horizontally (functional differentiation).

Once this view of implementation is adopted, the normative question about the effectiveness of implementation also needs to be modified. The right question is how implementation can cope efficiently with policy interactions in order to ensure the attainment of policy goals. The solution is trivial when impacts of parallel policies were anticipated at the formulation stage of the Directive. It was the case in some cases we have studied. The fact that more ambitious domestic policies pre-existed in Germany and the Netherlands on air emissions by waste incinerators or large combustion plants was perfectly known, and thus the Directives were not adopted in order to have any significant impacts in those countries. Also, the impact of the nuclear programme on French SO_2 emissions was anticipated even though the precise magnitude may have been partly strategically hidden by the French government at the formulation stage. This is why the SO_2 targets for France were set at a high level (40% of reduction required by 1993). But, in the cases where impacts of the policies are not anticipated, this requires an adjustment of the policy accordingly at the implementation stage. Implementation thus needs to be adaptive.

The general claim that the major obstacle for efficient policy-making and implementation lies in policy interactions has been strongly made elsewhere, especially in the public policy literature. In particular, it is the core of a major, albeit old, contribution by policy analysts on implementation in a collective book edited in the 1970s by Hanf and Scharpf (1978). To a certain extent, this diagnosis is also underlying the so-called 'policy networks' school which emphasises that policy-making and implementation involve a set of pluralistic actors, loosely co-ordinated, pursuing different agendas (see Boerzel, 1997 for a recent review). One basic problem with all these contributions is that they remain mainly descriptive and positive and become elliptical when it turns to suggested solutions to the problem. We try in the following to start to fill this gap, restricting the focus to the question of environmental policy in the European Union.

3. SELECTED EXERCISES IN ADAPTIVE IMPLEMENTATION

How then can EU environmental policies be designed to face pervasive policy interactions? The first step towards the characterisation of possible solutions will consist in this section of looking at how the implementation was adjusted in the cases we studied in this volume. The goal is not to comprehensively summarise the cases that were already presented in the preceding chapters, but to selectively present examples of successes and failures in adaptive implementation, in order to get a more precise view of the range of difficulties and solutions involved.

3.1 The British Implementation of the Large Combustion Plant Directive: How a Policy Can Minimise the Need for ex post Adjustments in the Face of Unanticipated Structural Change

The United Kingdom was probably the major opponent to the LCP Directive when it was devised in the 1980s (Ikwue and Skea, 1996). This opposition was based on the expectation that compliance with LCP requirements would be very costly because of the weight of coal-fired plants in electricity generation at that time. To achieve the UK national targets in SO_2 emission reduction of 20%, it was expected to retrofit using flue gas desulphurisation techniques some 12GW (approximately 17% of total UK electricity generation). Shortly after the adoption of the LCP Directive, the context changed dramatically with the decision at the end of 1989 to privatise the electricity supply industry. The subsequent liberalisation of the UK market saw a very rapid growth of gas-fired electricity generation with so-called combined cycle gas turbines and the closure of many existing coal-fired plants. The change was very fast: in 1989, the respective share of coal and gas in the total thermal input to electricity generation was 64.6% and 0.7%. In 1996, these figures were respectively 43% and 21.5%! As a result, expensive investment in flue gas desulphurisation became unnecessary. To date, retrofitting has been carried out in only 6GW and a massive over-compliance with the Directive's targets has been observed.

This radical and very fast change in the electricity supply industry could not be anticipated. How then did public authorities react to adapt implementation to this new context? In fact, due to the initial adoption of a very flexible implementation strategy, no adjustments were necessary (see Chapter 4 by Malcolm Eames in this volume). Transposition of the Directive was achieved through a National Plan. As far as the electricity supply industry was concerned, this plan was negotiated in 1989-1990 between the Department of the Environment, HMIP (Her Majesty's Inspectorate of Pollution) for the public side and the two then newly privatised companies PowerGen and National Power. In the National Plan, PowerGen and National Power were given very great flexibility to comply with the Directive via the allocation of 'company bubbles'. In other words, the two electricity companies were totally free to allocate pollution abatement among their plants. This flexibility was extremely useful in terms of adaption to the new context. Instead of the initially planned FGD retrofitting, the two companies relied extensively on the shifting from coal to gas input for electricity generation.

The initial motives for adopting this very flexible implementation strategy were economic: to minimise abatement costs by leaving companies free to choose the least cost options. The economic dimension was crucial at that time because these companies were going to face potentially harsh competition on the liberalised energy market. In fact, this choice proves ex post very efficient in terms of adaptive implementation. The directive could have been implemented in a less flexible way. For instance, the results to be achieved at the plant level (through emission standards) or the technological solution to be used could have been constrained. Then, it would have required major modifications of the regulations, subsidy schemes, etc. devised to comply with LCP targets. The major lesson here is that the nature of the policy instrument used is not neutral to the capability of the policy to adapt to unanticipated changes.

3.2   Implementation of the Municipal Waste Incineration Directive in France: the Management of Policy Uncertainty

Table 7.1 shows a delayed compliance of the big incinerators in France with respect to the Directive 89/429. One important cause for this delay is in fact related to the existence of large and sustaining uncertainties in French waste policy during the 1990s (see Chapter 5 by Kris Lulofs in this volume). The Directive was adopted and transposed into French law in 1991. Then the owners of waste incinerators were confronted with a difficult decision: whether to close down plants or whether to bring the plants into compliance and – if it was decided to bring them into compliance – whether to upgrade or replace ovens. Such decisions are typically irreversible: once the decision is taken and implemented, it is very costly to modify the initial choice. Economic theory has shown how such a coincidence of both irreversibility and uncertainty may be damaging: uncertainty means that you may be wrong and irreversibility makes very costly the consequences of being wrong. To overcome the problem, the decision-maker will prefer flexible choices. In the context of our study, the only flexible choice was to 'wait and see' and thus to delay compliance waiting for uncertainty to be reduced.

In France, debates on the municipal waste policy provoked great uncertainties during the implementation period. In the period 1990–1992, decisions were hampered by uncertainty related to discussions on regulatory requirements for the treatment of off-gas cleaning residues. Then the adoption of the new waste law of 1992 completely changed the hierarchy of waste treatment modes (drastic reduction of waste dumping and increase in recycling). New requirements for packaging waste recycling were also defined in a new Decree in 1992. To cope with this new context, municipalities and waste operators initiated a process of reflection on how to adjust the waste treatment capacity at the regional level. Investment decisions – and thus the start of projects to bring the plants into compliance with the Waste Incineration Directive – were slowed down. A new source of political uncertainty emerged when in 1993–1994 the discussions concerning the project for a new Directive on municipal waste incinerators started. This introduced uncertainty regarding the future requirements for air emissions and contributed to the postponement again of local communities' decisions since at that time it was expected that the Directive would be adopted rapidly. In fact, the adoption of the Directive has been considerably delayed but will now take place soon. Finally, the waste policy context changed again when, in April 1998, the French Environmental Minister criticised the high prominence given to waste incineration in the waste plans and required the plans elaborated at the regional level to be revised.

This case illustrates two points. Firstly, it suggests how policy interactions can delay compliance by increasing the uncertainty surrounding compliance decisions and their complexity. When the compliance decision entails irreversible costs (e.g. major investments in pollution abatement), uncertainties clearly provide the polluters with incentives to adopt a 'wait and see' strategy and thus to delay compliance. Secondly, the interaction took place here with another environmental policy. This makes it a policy designed and implemented by the same public body, or at least in close proximity to those involved in the implementation in the Directives. By contrast with policies from other areas, intuition suggests that co-ordination should have been much more feasible. The analysis of this intuition is pushed forward later.

3.3   The Competition between Environmental Management Standards: EMAS versus ISO14001

One key goal of EMAS was to promote the diffusion of this environmental management standard in the European industry. Looking at the participation rate seven years after the enactment of the Council regulation no. 1836/93 in Table 7.2, EMAS does not appear as a success except in Germany. From 1995 onwards, the EMAS standard had to compete with ISO14001 and the figures in Table 7.2 clearly suggest that EMAS was not the winner (again except in Germany).

To explain such results, it should be restated that the participation for an individual company in either EMAS or ISO14001 is voluntary. Hence, the participation rates shown in Table 7.2 indicate that most companies have considered that their net benefit to participate in ISO14001 was higher than in EMAS. In this context, what was the reaction of the implementers to cope with the emergence of a rival environmental management standard? Given the voluntary character of EMAS and ISO14001, their only incentive to promote EMAS diffusion was to increase the net participation benefit. Was it done and how?

Table 7.2 Participation rate in EMAS and ISO14001 (adapted from Chapter 6 in this volume)

	France	Germany	The Netherlands	United Kingdom
(1) EMAS	0.13%	5.98%	0.36%	0.24%
(2) ISO14001	1.48%	3.87%	7.42%	3.41%
Ratio (2) / (1)	11.4	0.65	20.6	14.2

Note: % of companies that participated in September 1999.

Initially, it is worth noting that ISO14001 a priori enjoys an advantage over EMAS in terms of costs and benefits for participating companies. As regards participation benefits, the international character of ISO14001 is considered a key advantage for participating companies (Wätzold and Bültmann, Chapter 6 in this volume). On the cost side, EMAS is in a less favourable position because it is more demanding in terms of administrative procedures. Moreover, in comparison with ISO14001, EMAS registration contains an additional component, the environmental statement. This statement includes all the significant environmental issues which are relevant to the site's activities and a presentation of the company's environmental policy to deal with the identified problems. Certain companies are wary about this statement because it is made public.

As compensation for the unfavourable general cost–benefit 'profile' of EMAS, the regulators tried to increase the compatibility between the two standards. After decisions first debated and implemented at the national levels, a decision was made at the European level in 1997 to consider that the EMAS certification was equivalent to the ISO certification plus the environmental statement. It reduces very significantly the cost of the EMAS certification for companies that are already ISO certified. It also reduces the cost of a joint EMAS and ISO14001 certification. As a result, except in Germany, almost all companies are both ISO14001 and EMAS certified. In fact, this reaction by the implementation bodies is in line with a classical story told by the theory of standard competition (David, 1995). Laggards in the diffusion race (i.e. EMAS in comparison with ISO) generally seek compatibility to avoid being de facto removed from the market place at the end of the diffusion process.

In every country, compatibility was rather rapidly achieved. The only case where this raised a problem was the UK. This country was a very active promoter of ISO. At the beginning of the 1990s, the UK government launched a domestic environmental management standard, namely BS7750, which subsequently served as a basis for defining the ISO14001 standard. At that time (1994), the UK government wanted the certification to BS7750 to be a stepping stone to EMAS registration. This country thus asked the Commission to recognise the BS7750 as a standard applicable to EMAS. But due to opposition by Germany, the decision was delayed until February 1996. This illustrates how centralised co-ordination (here the necessity for a decision at the EU level) de facto leads to delaying policy responses.

Another major tool used to sustain the diffusion of EMAS was regulatory relief. Regulatory relief consists of the relaxation of certain requirements imposed by conventional regulations (in particular, monitoring and reporting provisions) for certified companies. The use of regulatory relief has been very important in Germany where the EMAS participation rate is the highest. Regulatory relief has also been extensive in the Netherlands where the diffusion of environmental management systems has been linked to a major reform of the Dutch environmental policy promoting 'deregulation'. However, in this country, EMAS and ISO14001 has been jointly implemented and deregulation has been equally granted to ISO14001 participants. By contrast, although deregulation and regulatory relief was subjected to policy debates around 1995 in France and the United Kingdom, the outcome was very vague leaving very little room for genuine regulatory relief.

How can these substantial differences in countries' responses be explained? The answer is complex but the comparison between the Netherlands and France sheds some light on this issue. Firstly, national 'policy styles' cannot directly explain these differences. For instance, the French policy style is known for being very flexible and informal. It leaves a lot of discretionary power to street-level enforcers which use it in informal bargaining processes to lead polluters to comply with regulation (Knill, 1998). Hence, one could have expected that granting regulatory relief might be easy in France since it fits with their usual practices. It has not been the case. Why? In fact, the French view has always been to consider conventional regulation and EMAS as two discrete policy approaches. EMAS is seen as a purely 'promotional' scheme to be used by companies in the market place. According to this perspective, the role of public bodies in the scheme is mainly to ensure a sufficient credibility of the scheme in the eye of the public. By contrast, in the Netherlands, environmental management standards and regulation have been considered in an integrated way from the beginning. Explicitly stated in a memorandum negotiated with industry in 1989, certified environmental management systems along with so-called covenants are a key tool to push permitting towards more integrated and simpler operating permits (see Wätzold and Bültmann, Chapter 6 in this volume). In this perspective, regulatory relief consists of using EMAS or ISO14001 certification as a part of a broader regulatory reform. In other words, environmental management systems are components of a broad policy mix. As a result, the participation in certified environmental management systems is much higher in the Netherlands than in France.

3.4   Intermediate Conclusion

These stories are too limited to provide by themselves a basis for general answers on adaptive implementation. However, they pose a set of questions that constitutes a first step:

*   The content of the policy is not neutral on the scope of the adjustments necessary to adapt to the new situation as illustrated by the implementation of the Large Combustion Plant Directive in the UK. This raises the general question of what policy approaches and instruments are to be promoted in this respect.
*   Furthermore, the occurrence of policy interactions is very difficult to predict for the implementation policy bodies. In the event that predictions are not made or are false, this leads to ex post surprises. This possibility is even reinforced by the fact that the time span between the formulation and the implementation stage of a Directive is typically about 3–5 years. It is de facto a structural source of uncertainty. Ex post surprises precisely mean that the policy-makers/implementers can only

observe the impacts of policy interactions on policy outcomes (e.g. on EMAS participation rate, compliance rate with standard). It follows that such an observation necessarily occurs at the very decentralised level of the polluter. This has important consequences for the theoretical analysis that is carried out in the next section. Once policy-makers become aware of the existence of policy interactions, one question is at what level of decisions do these adjustments need to be made? At high levels by the policy formulation bodies? At the implementation level?

4. WHAT IS AN ADAPTIVE POLICY? A PRELIMINARY EXPLORATION BASED ON THE ECONOMIC LITERATURE

Considering that the elaboration of a general theory of policy implementation is out of reach at this stage of the analysis, this section presents a point of view based on two pre-existing and very influential pieces of work from the economic literature by Bohm and Russel (1985) and Aoki (1986). The former have developed a systematic analysis of the adaptability of the different environmental policy instruments, whereas the latter, in a context apparently far from our questions, the internal organisation of the firm, has designed an analysis of the ability of different organisational structures to adapt to unanticipated exogenous shocks.

4.1 The Adjustment Costs of Different Policy Instrument and Adjustment Costs (Bohm and Russel, 1985)

In the case of the Large Combustion Plant Directive, the policy approach used (the SO_2 company 'bubbles') allows for a spontaneous adaptation to the drastic change in market conditions without the necessity to modify the policy. Instead of the expected massive retrofitting of coal-fired power plants initially planned, the British privatisation process led regulated firms to prefer the substitution of coal by gas to comply with SO_2 targets. If the policy instruments used had previously fixed – or at least constrained – the technical solutions to achieve policy targets, difficult policy adjustments would have been necessary to keep firms on the tracks when privatisation occurred. The general lesson behind this example is that the more lenient the constraint placed by the policy on the abatement decision of the regulated agents, the lower the necessity to revise components of the policy package, thus the lower the adjustment costs.

Table 7.3 The different policy instruments and their adjustment costs (Bohm and Russel, 1985)

Policy instrument	Brief description	Types of adjustments
Technological standard	Regulatory measure requiring polluters to insert in their production process or in their product a specified technical device aiming at abating pollution (e.g. catalytic converter for cars).	No discretion left to polluters => Whenever an adjustment is necessary, it requires a political decision.
Emission standard	Regulatory measure requiring polluters not to exceed specified level of pollutant emission for each polluting source.	Some discretion left to the polluters as to the means to be used to meet the standard => In case of necessity, adjustments by the polluters are possible.
Emission charge	Economic incentives for polluters to abate through the imposition of a tax to be paid per unit of pollutant emitted.	Large discretion left to the polluter. He is free to both select the technical means to abate pollution and the intensity of pollution abatement. Basically he selects its abatement level comparing tax payments and abatement costs. But political adjustments remain necessary if the unanticipated requires changing tax rates. This decision is politically very sensitive and can entail major decision costs.
Tradable permits	System of permits fixing a maximal amount of pollutant emission to the permit's holder. The permits can be sold and bought on a market.	At the polluter level, the same degree of discretion as the tax. The only difference is that the choice of the abatement level is made through a comparison of abatement cost and permit price. At the political level, there is an additional flexibility: unlike taxes, the permit price is not fixed by political bodies but by the market. => Exogenous shocks are tackled through spontaneous price adjustments on the permits market.

Bohm and Russel (1985) provide a simple and clear-cut analysis of the general problem. In their view fundamental differences exist between policies which are redefined in a very decentralised way through decisions made by the regulated agents, and systems which require a revision and a recalculation of some policy components by the implementation bodies, with all the related disadvantages in terms of delays, information costs and political difficulties attached to changes in the rules during the policy game. Their central assumption is that the cost of adjustment decisions is much more important when they are made by a political body rather than by the regulated agents.

Based on this premise, their analysis focuses on the location of the adjustment decisions – regulated agent's decision versus political decision – when using different policy instruments. It is summarised in Table 7.3. They end up with a ranking of the different policy instruments. The least adaptable approach is the technological standard, which prescribes at the level of each polluting source what is to be done to comply. Emission standards are more adaptable since they leave polluters free to choose the most appropriate technical solution. However, they prescribe the maximum level of pollution at the level of each source. There is thus no possibility of sharing the effort among different polluting sources. Economic instruments such as emission fees or tradable permits bypass this constraint since they leave the decision-maker free to select the most appropriate abatement strategy in response to the price signal. However, a further distinction is possible between charge system and tradable permits. The latter are far more flexible since exogenous shocks require the modification of charge rates, whereas spontaneous changes in the permit price avoid any form of public intervention.

4.2 Decentralisation Patterns and Adjustment Costs (Aoki, 1986)

The goal of Aoki's paper is to compare the organisational structure of the Japanese industrial firm (which he refers to as the J firm) and the American hierarchy-based corporation (the A firm in his terminology). As will become clear his stylisation of the two organisational forms is sufficiently general to apply to very different organisations. We present his analysis before considering how it applies to administrative/political bodies implementing environmental policies.

His starting point is to stylise the two organisational structures (see Figure 7.1). In the two cases, a central unit enjoys a hierarchical control over two decentralised units involved in a production process. The tasks undertaken by the two units need to be co-ordinated. For instance, the first unit produces the soles for the shoes manufactured in the second unit. In this case some kind of co-ordination is necessary in order to produce an identical number of soles and shoes. The two organisational structures differ with respect to the way the co-ordination decisions are made. In the J firm, co-ordination results from a joint decision by the two decentralised units without any direct involvement from the centre. In the A firm, co-ordination is the responsibility of the centre. This entails upward communication for sending information on the co-ordination problem to the centre and downward communication for sending back co-ordination instructions to the producing units. The necessity for upward communication is justified by the fact that the co-ordination problem is first observed at the decentralised level by the producing units.

In Aoki's framework, the advantages/shortcomings of the two modes are the following. In the case of the A firm, a first problem is that upward information on the co-ordination failure is necessarily summarised, leading to loss of information. Also the downward communication conveying instructions to the lower level is conversely expanded as instructions are formulated in a general way to be progressively detailed by the different levels of management. Being subject to interpretation, it potentially leads to errors when implementing co-ordination instructions (loss of control). Moreover this two-way communication takes time and causes delays. These are drawbacks but the co-ordination plans of the centre are likely to be more consistent because it has a more general view on the whole problem in comparison with the decentralised units. The advantages and shortcomings of the J firm are just the opposite. Horizontal co-ordination locates decisions where co-ordination problems are observed, permitting faster co-ordination decisions by avoiding vertical communication with the central unit. But the quality of co-ordination may be reduced by the fact that producing units only have local knowledge.

Aoki's view can be summarised in the following way: hierarchical decisions entail higher decision costs but better decisions than horizontal co-ordination. Depending on the context, these two 'profiles' lead to very different performances. In stable contexts, co-ordination decisions are typically very rare. Co-ordination can be made through ex ante planning. The centre is best equipped for this task: it makes better decisions while the decision costs remain reasonably low since the co-ordination decision is unique. By contrast, Aoki strongly advocates for the efficiency of the J firm in fast moving contexts where continuous adjustments of the co-ordination plan are necessary. In this case the A firm leads to high decision costs and delays.

How can Aoki's analysis apply to policy co-ordination failures in implementation? The stylisation of the organisational forms and of the co-ordination problem is sufficiently general to consider that the two decentralised units can be political/administrative bodies in charge of two distinct policies. In this context, the co-ordination problem is that the bodies bring two simultaneous uncoordinated policy signals at the level of the regulated agent. Aoki's model thus supports the thesis of relying on decentralisation by leaving implementation bodies large discretion to adjust the policy when necessary.

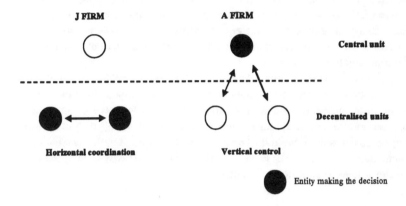

Figure 7.1 The A and the J firms by Aoki (1986)

There is a major restriction in the domain of validity of Aoki's analysis for our questions, however. In his analysis, the two decentralised units are assumed to pursue a common objective (i.e. firm's profit maximisation). It follows that horizontal co-ordination basically means information exchange where the two decentralised units explain to each other the difficulty encountered due to their counterpart. This discussion makes clear the causal mechanisms of the co-ordination failure for the two parties. Each body then adjusts its policy in order to restore the conditions for an effective attainment of the common policy objective.

This assumption is very strong in our case. The problem is that, by definition, functional differentiation (the principle that justifies the existence of two distinct policy bodies) consists of assigned specialised policy objectives. The two bodies pursuing possibly conflicting goals are thus differently affected by a given co-ordination plan.[3] Because there is no hierarchical relationship between the two entities, they must rely on consensus for making the decision. Horizontal co-ordination will necessarily mean conflict resolution, bargaining and costly negotiation. Centralised co-ordination avoids this problem since it transfers the decision to a level that is able to impose decisions on the lower levels.

It follows that a key variable guiding the choice between centralised or horizontal co-ordination is the degree of divergence between the policy objectives of the sectoral policy bodies involved. The situation is very different according to whether the co-ordination problems occur between two environmental policies or between an environmental policy and a non-environmental policy. In the first case, policy objectives are very close; decentralisation and horizontal co-ordination aiming at integrating the parallel policies in a broader policy mix seem to be the reasonable option. As far as EU policy implementation is concerned, the advantages of decentralisation are likely to be very strong given the delay of reactions at the EU level and the generally high heterogeneity in national conditions, requiring tailored adjustments.

In the cases where policy interactions occur with measures coming from other policy areas (e.g. energy policy, privatisation policy), integration is the privilege of the centre. As ex post adjustments are very costly, it requires very cautious ex ante planning. In this regard, the emphasis given in the fifth environmental action programme of the Commission on the need to pay much attention at the EU level on the integration between environmental policies and sectoral policies is rightly placed.

5.   WHAT POLICY LESSONS?

Our theoretical exploration remains exploratory, being based on a limited set of pre-existing economic analysis. Nevertheless it enables us to identify clear-cut policy lessons. Naturally, they concern both implementation procedures and the contents of the policy to be implemented. Indeed, both poor implementation procedures and inadequate policy design may cause implementation gaps. Due to the fact that implementation is just one ingredient in a dynamic mix of parallel policy processes which may interact with each other, individual environmental policies, and their implementation, need to be adaptive if they are to cope efficiently with largely unanticipated policy interactions. This means, both in policy design and implementation, promoting:

- Flexible policy solutions in the face of unanticipated exogenous changes, in particular those entailed by non-environmental policy measures, by avoiding over-specifying the means by which regulated agents shall attain policy goals. This is suggested by the analysis by Bohm and Russel. This militates for the use of economic instruments and 'bubble' approaches (e.g. voluntary agreements), where firms are given maximal freedom regarding abatement choices. At the EU level, this means that Directives should focus on specifying environmental objectives rather than the means through which these should be achieved.

- Integration in an environmental policy mix: here the message is to link together different environmental policy components in order to exploit synergies or avoid inconsistencies. At the EU level, this militates for broadening the scope of individual pieces of legislation.
- Decentralisation and subsidiarity: based on the Aoki framework, here the rationale is that decentralised political systems are more likely to adjust easily when unanticipated changes occur, especially because they do not occur in all Member States at the same time and in the same way. But the task of integrating environmental and non-environmental policies, or at least of avoiding inconsistencies between each other, needs to remain a central task for the EU level.

A final point is that the existence of ex post surprises leads us to stress the importance of policy learning and ex post evaluation. Practically, this involves 1) incorporating reporting requirements in Directives, 2) the necessity of developing ex post evaluation within the Commission and at the Member State level. The Commission has recently been very active in promoting ex ante cost benefit analysis of proposed Directives. Albeit undoubtedly very useful, the results of these studies need to be linked to ex post analyses in order to gain experience in this exercise and to verify whether the outcomes predicted by ex ante analysis are actually obtained.

NOTES

1. For an analysis of the veracity of this assertion, see Boerzel (2000).
2. This 'leader–laggard' dynamic in EU environmental policy enjoys considerable interest among political scientists or specialists in international relations (see for instance Andersen and Liefferink, 1997).
3. To a certain extent this is also true for two functional units within a firm. It thus constitutes a limit of Aoki's analysis, which by the way is acknowledged by the author.

REFERENCES

Andersen, Mikael S. and Duncan Liefferink (eds) (1997), *European Environmental Policy: The Pioneers*, Manchester: Manchester University Press.
Aoki, Masahiko S. (1986), 'Horizontal versus vertical information structure of the firm', *American Economic Review*, 76, pp. 971–83.
Boerzel, Tanja A. (1997), 'What's so special about policy networks? An exploration of the concept and its usefulness in studying European governance', European

integration online paper 1997-16, ECSA Austria, http://eiop.or.at/eiop/texte/1997-016a.htm.

Boerzel, Tanja A. (2000), 'Why there is no Southern Problem. On environmental Leaders and Laggards in the European Union', *Journal of European Public Policy*, 7(1), pp. 141–162.

Bohm, Peter and Clifford S. Russel (1985), 'Comparative Analysis of Alternative Policy Instruments', in A.V. Kneese and J.L. Sweeney (eds), *Handbook of Natural Resource and Energy Economics*, Amsterdam: North Holland, pp. 395–460.

David, Paul. A. (1995), 'Standardisation Policies for Network Technologies: the Flux between Freedom and Order Revisited', in R. Hawkins, R. Mansell and J. Skea (eds), *Standards, Innovation and Competitiveness*, Aldershot: Edward Elgar.

Hanf, Kenneth and Fritz W. Scharpf (eds) (1978), *Interorganizational Policy Making: Limits to Coordination and Central Control*, London and Beverly Hills: Sage Publications.

Ikwue, A. and J. Skea (1996), 'Energy Sector Responses to European Combustion Emission Regulations', in F. Lévêque (ed.), *Environmental Policy in Europe*, Cheltenham, UK, Edward Elgar, pp. 75–112.

Knill, Christoph (1998), 'Implementing European policies: the impact of national administrative traditions', *Journal of Public Policy*, 18(1).

Index

acid rain 61–2, 67–8
adaptability 7–8, 178
adaptive implementation 178–96
adaptive policy, economic literature on
    189–94
adjustment costs
    and decentralisation patterns 191–4
    of different policy instruments
        189–91
administrative compliance 89
Air Framework Directive 60, 64
Amacher, G.S. 39
Amsterdam Treaty 14
Andersen, M.S. 93
Aoki, M.S. 189, 191–4

Badrinath, S.G. 38
bargaining 47–8
Barrett, S. 45, 46, 47, 48
BATNEEC (Best Available
    Technologies Not Entailing
    Excessive Cost) concept 18, 39, 64,
    80, 118
Baumol, W.J. 31
Becker, G.S. 31, 33
Becker model 31–2
Bertossi, P. 102
Bertram, J. 70
Boehmer-Christiansen, S. 62, 78
Boerzel, T.A. 22, 23, 182
Bohm, P. 189–91
Bolster, P. 38
Bontems, P. 38
Brundtland Report 73
BS7750 134, 136, 139, 187
    and United Kingdom 159, 160
bubble approaches 91, 189, 194
Buchanan, J.M. 40
Buclet, N. 102
budget maximization 40
Bültmann, A. 69, 70, 71, 87, 100, 147

CEC 6, 15, 19
Chalmers, D. 22
co-ordination 44, 48, 192
    horizontal 192, 193–4
Cohen, M.A. 33, 34, 35, 36, 38, 40
Collins, K. 26
command and control directives 99–133
company bubbles 91, 189, 194
complaints procedure 20
compliance 2–3, 38–9, 40
    administrative 6, 89
    environmental 6
    formal 20, 22
    practical 20, 23
    subsidies for 39
    voluntary 38
Convention on Long Range
    Transboundary Air Pollution
    (CLRTAP) 62, 92
Corone, S. 20
cost effectiveness 3, 6
    of implementation of Large
        Combustion Plant Directive 90–92
Council of the European Union 26
Craig, P. 16
'Crime and Punishment: An Economic
    Approach' (Becker) 31–2

David, P.A. 187
de Burca, G. 16
decentralisation 8, 18, 195
decentralisation patterns, and adjustment
    costs 191–4
Deily, M.E. 40
Denmark 22
Desachy, C. 116
dioxins 106, 109, 110, 117
Direct Effect Doctrine 21–2
Directives 27
    legal weaknesses 25
discretion 46–7

197